GREETINGS from the PRESIDENT

Frank T. DeAngelo

BLUE NOTE BOOKS
FLORIDA

Copyright © 2003 Frank T. DeAngelo

All rights reserved. No part of this book may be reproduced or utilized in any form or by any means, electronic or mechanical, including photocopying, recording or by any information storage and retrieval system, without permission in writing from the author.

First Edition
Blue Note Publications

ISBN No. 1-878398-57-1 (Softcover)
ISBN No. 1-878398-56-3 (Hardcover)

Library of Congress Control Number: 2003106590

Cover Design by Carmen Abreu

Printed in the United States of America

DEDICATED TO THE FOLLOWING:

To my wonderful parents who were always there for me and taught me to do the very best I could do, no matter what was taking place.

My wife, Hazel R. DeAngelo, who understands that my time in the Army was important to me.

To my daughter, Lisa A. Fletcher, and her husband, Brad, who listened to me talk about this book which I felt needed to be written.

To our grandchildren, Garrette, Ashley, Carter, and Dawson.

To the two GI's who came into the minefield to get me out, their names forgotten, and sorry not to remember.

To my readers, so all may know what serving my country as a young man in WWII meant to me.

ACKNOWLEDGMENTS

The following people were helpful in putting this book together, and, yes, at times wondered if it would be done and completed for publication.

Liz Dennie
Jill Schaffner
Paul Maluccio

In World War II the infantry called each other by last names… never the first name. The reason was the casualty rate. So, DeAngelo it is!

Memories dim as years go by. Certain things do not.

DeAngelo had, and still has, an intense outstanding and incredible sense of humor. He could make any of us laugh in the midst of an artillery barrage or tank attack. No one ever figured out what platoon he was in… he was just all over the company.

Lt. HayDen W. Kane, March 14, 2001

I am pleased to learn that your manuscript has been completed and is now being reviewed for publication. Thinking of you and what you have accomplished brings to my mind our hours and days and months of World War II and some in nearness and parallel other in togetherness. Of course I refer to our time while assigned to the 30th Infantry and the 3rd Division. If memory serves me correctly, you were in "K" Company until transferred to "C" Company. After my assignment to "C" and while moving through our defensive positions to meet the men I could be expected to be fighting forward with, I met you and I believe that you were in the 3rd Platoon. I never saw you again for about 50 years until a reunion dinner, a great day.

DeAngelo I wish you continued good luck with your book.

Lt. David H. Oglesby, January 21, 2001

It was wonderful to hear from you, after all these years. I'm honored that you included me in your book. You were a good buddy those adverse conditions turned out to be facilitators of a great friendship.

Because you put down in black and white all those past events, a lot of my personal memories have resurfaced.

Good luck and much success with "Greetings, from the President."

Sgt. Joseph Polenchar, January 20, 2001

While reading DeAngelo's autobiography, "Greetings, from the President" I actually felt like I was catapulted back in time to World War II.

DeAngelo depicted his time spent serving in the war with dignity, truth, the seriousness of the times, and an amusing light hearted humor that keeps the reader's attention.

DeAngelo underwent many trials during World War II. But, always seemed to emerge with a sense and realization of a higher power, leading, guiding and protecting him.

There were several times that DeAngelo could have been mortally wounded that he knew God had intervened.

DeAngelo would not escape the war unscathed. He would eventually be wounded. But, the strength and dignity he would exhibit during this adverse time would prove to give DeAngelo a sense of his true self and a deeper sense of God. To this day… these experiences have contributed to shape DeAngelo's life. This true story is interesting, historical and intense this is a war story with a different flavor. I promise, the reader will not be disappointed.

Toni Bacaris, "Published Author." January 15, 2001

PROLOGUE

This book was written to give its readers a chapter-by-chapter chronology of what took place during my military service in WWII. I served a full 15 months of combat duty, which was a very long time to be in an Infantry Company. I served with a very outstanding Division for all those many months. We were always at the front lines, facing the enemy each time, trying to stay alive each day, each week, each month and each year. I would like to let the readers in some small way feel as I have felt when moving to meet the enemy and not knowing what the outcome would be. Each day could have been my last day on earth. I was always wondering how my family would have accepted my death if I was never to return and laid to sleep in a military cemetery somewhere.

It is my opinion, all contained within this book are accurately expressed both in the way they happened and the way I remember. It is not my intent to hurt anyone or lie about what took place day by day, not knowing what my next day would be like.

Table of Contents

Foreword - *xiii*

Preface - *xv*

Chapter One - *New York* - 19

Chapter Two - *Basic Training* - 37

Chapter Three - *Africa* - 66

Chapter Four - *Italy* - 79

Chapter Five - *Anzio* - 87

Chapter Six - *Rome* - 137

Chapter Seven - *Naples* - 154

Chapter Eight - *France* - 165

Chapter Nine - *Vosges Mountains* - 188

Chapter Ten - *Colmar* - 203

Chapter Eleven - *Paris* - 224

Chapter Twelve - *Strasbourg* - 230

Chapter Thirteen - *Army Hospital* - 240

Chapter Fourteen - *After Discharge* - 262

Chapter Fifteen - *Back Home* - 269

Chapter Sixteen - *Present* - 275

FOREWORD

The night after I joined Company C, 30th Infantry, as a replacement officer, I decided to move forward to an outpost to watch patrol actions in the valley below our hilltop defensive position. As I eased up to the outpost location in the pitch black night of Letholy France, I saw the shape of an almost invisible soldier, with a blanket thrown around his shoulders to ward off the chill and his helmet in place. As I knelt down near his position, the shadow stirred and a quiet voice asked, "Are you the new Lieutenant? I'm Pvt. Frank T. DeAngelo, 3rd Platoon." This began a long association between the two of us. The next morning as the new leader of the 3rd Platoon, Frank DeAngelo had been assigned, or perhaps asked, to be my personal radio operator since October 13, 1944. I discovered that he was a veteran of the fighting in Italy, and by the time I joined he was a battle-wise warrior, a hardened combat soldier not yet twenty years old, as I recall. As I advanced from Platoon Leader, to Company Executive Officer and to Company Commander, DeAngelo stayed with me. Except when one or the other of us was in hospital, he almost always was at my side or nearby. He served as my bodyguard, my advisor, and he cared for my personal needs to provide more time for me to devote to my troops and the business at hand. At times it appeared that he almost had an insight to the future, to the extent that I came to trust his intuition and to heed his warnings of danger or other possible difficulties.

DeAngelo was with me for five long, hard months until that fateful night in March 14, 1945, just short of the German border with France. The company was attempting to slip through a mine field to seize a critical hill position when DeAngelo hit an antipersonnel mine which the point guard and I had somehow stepped over in the dark. Frank T. DeAngelo's departure left a void in Company C. His departure left me short of one very loyal, very faithful friend.

Charles P. Murray, Colonel, US Army (Ret.) January 24, 2001
Congressional Medal of Honor Recipient

PREFACE

This first hand account of the military life of author, Frank T. DeAngelo, during World War II is an interesting and often riveting wartime story that provides not only a historical chronology of the events that took place but also presents a personal perspective of the intimate thoughts and feelings experienced by him on a daily basis as he faced the enemy in combat for 15 months.

Although this story is sure to catapult the reader back to the serious times of World War II, the author brings a different flavor to the book with an uplifting and underlying story of greater significance… that is, that despite hard times and adverse conditions, with perseverance, hard work and a belief in yourself, the seemingly impossible can be achieved. As the reader becomes engrossed in the detailed and sometimes nostalgic account of the daily life of DeAngelo and his colleagues on the front line, the introspective nature of DeAngelo's story subtly delivers the message that the difficult times strengthened his character, making him a better person and shaping him into the person he has become. This story is also peppered with seemingly coincidental and fortuitous situations which lead DeAngelo to the realization that there was a higher power leading, guiding and protecting him. This realization gave DeAngelo the strength to endure the tough times and would ultimately give DeAngelo a sense of his true self and a deeper sense of God. For example, DeAngelo once ignored his Lieutenant's order to dig a foxhole in a particular location and instead he dug it behind a tree avoiding a barrage of artillery which would have killed them if he had followed the Order. It is also interesting to note that DeAngelo's family crest and his Division patch are eerily similar in color and detail.

Although DeAngelo did not escape the war unscathed, the loss of his right foot did not stop him and he went on after his military service to become integrally involved in the early stages of the race to the moon. For his contribution to land a man on the moon, he was chosen Man of the Month and Man of the Year by Boeing Company which was one of the government contractors working with NASA to achieve this goal. NASA selected DeAngelo to be listed in their new project for 1968 called "Manned Flight Awareness". Names were placed on the moon, and also at the Library of Congress and the National Archives, Washington, DC. DeAngelo didn't stop at this success; he later invented the World's very first electronic magnetic digital compass. This was quite a feat for an individual who had no engineering degree nor any formal education past 10th grade. Naysayers didn't believe that he could build such a new product. They were truly amazed at this successful invention. Once again, his perseverance prevailed.

A personal face to face conversation with Frank T. DeAngelo, reveals a quiet, reserved and private man who was born to Italian immigrants and who grew up on the streets of the lower East side of New York City. His quiet reserve and private nature belies the story that he weaves… he holds little back in his open, honest and often gritty, serious account of the many adventures he experienced. His experiences begin with being drafted in the army months well before age 19 by the standard draft letter which began "**Greetings, From the President.**" DeAngelo's story continues with basic training, then as a replacement to the 3rd Infantry Division and his Divisions' movement throughout Europe as the war spurred on and his ultimate discharge at the young age of 21 due to the loss of his right foot.

The book is also filled with amusing, light hearted and humorous stories that will enchant and entertain the reader. One day, DeAngelo and a friend walked into a high quality shoe store to purchase a pair of shoes. DeAngelo describes the incident: "Walking in, the manager noticed I was having some problem walking. He asked what was the problem with the way I was walking. I said my right shoe must have a tack and I did not know where it was hurting. He then suggested to place both feet under the x-ray machine and he would find that problem tack. I did as he suggested and he turned on the machine. As I looked down he turned his head up to face me and said I had so many tacks in the right shoe, but lots of bones in the left shoe. He asked me to look down into the screen to see for myself. I looked down and saw what he had seen. I asked him which tack was the problem? He turned off the machine and went to the back and never came out to sell me a pair of shoes. My friend and I left with a big smile. At times I wonder what he thought. Did I play a joke on him? I just wanted to purchase a pair of shoes and nothing more".

Another amusing incident occurred while DeAngelo and his Division were in Anzio, Italy. During one particular cold and stormy night DeAngelo was maintaining his cover in a slit trench with running water while lightning crackled overhead when he noticed a barn in the distance. Tired, hungry, wet and sleep deprived he made his way to the barn, crawled underneath a big haystack and fell sound asleep. During the night the roof apparently had blown off wreaking havoc on the barn. When DeAngelo was awakened by daybreak, he was buried in the hay and his legs were seemingly paralyzed. What was wrong?? He pushed aside some of the hay and realized that a large cow had died and fallen on top of his legs. In spite of the turmoil surrounding him, this funny incident gave him pause to chuckle.

This detailed spellbinding story of the author's rollercoaster ride of personal triumphs and tragedies during World War II is a fascinating lesson in life and a true testament to the resilience of the human spirit.

Chapter One

New York

This is the story about a young boy, a street kid who lived on the Lower East Side, New York City. It's about his military life and the way things happened when he was drafted into the U.S. Army during WWII.

My parents, and their parents, were born in Italy in a very small town called Qualiano near Naples. Qualiano was a few miles from the town of Pozzuoli, a beach resort. I was born at two o'clock in the morning on July 8, 1924, at 179 Mott Street, NYC, in Little Italy. At the time Chinatown was nearby. The Chinese were not allowed to pass Bayard Street because of some unwritten law. I was the firstborn and my family became larger, by two sisters and a brother.

I was named Frank DeAngelo, after my father's father. I was the third male child named Frank, after him. My father's two older sisters both named their sons Frank, as was done by Italians.

In the winter of 1926, my father's older sister's husband was shot and killed. Why, I never knew. I recall seeing a very large photo of his funeral and there were five large Packards filled with flowers outside the church as his casket was being carried out. In the same photo there was a young man, who looked very cold, standing nearby. This young man was my mother's younger brother, Merrick. Some years later he was seen in the 1931 movie called *Little Caesar*, starring Edward G. Robinson. In this movie he was seen carrying the casket of the real slain man.

My uncle Merrick had paid us a visit some years back. We talked about the photo and he said that if my uncle who had been killed had lived, the man called Capone would not have been known. As was often the case, nothing more was said.

My Uncle Dominic was married to my mother's sister, Anna. One day we were talking and he told me he used to drive trucks full of beer for the notorious gangster, Dutch Schultz. When he found out who his boss was, he quit. They were hijacking trucks and he didn't want to be hijacked when driving. It was funny to hear him tell me he heard his boss was Dutch Schultz, the Beer Baron. Schultz was famous for trying to keep others from muscling in on his territory–beer and numbers.

I was the youngest of the three Franks. One Frank looked out for me and was kind to me when I was growing up. He was a ladies' man and good looking. I did not take to the other Frank as well. Now, both Franks were drafted before I was. They were never sent overseas, yet both were Sergeants, one in the Signal Corp. and the other a cook. These two Franks hated the Army. Both had the best the Army was able to give them. The one in the Signal Corp. was issued a Jeep, an aircraft, and a pass that could be used at any time on any train, plane or bus. If he needed to test fly his carrier pigeons miles away from his base, or if he wanted to travel to see someone, he would use his pass and report he had to train those pigeons.

In fact, there were two or three times when he was to be shipped overseas that those pigeons did not arrive on the dock. He was in total charge of those pigeons. He would not ship out without the pigeons, or allow the pigeons to be shipped out without him. If the two Franks were to have gone into combat, I feel Frank with the pigeons would have done better than the other Frank, who I think would have been unable to take combat.

My father worried about us walking to our public elementary school, PS 130. At 179 Mott we had to cross a big wide street called Canal Street that went from the Holland Tunnel to the Manhattan Bridge. It was called Canal Street because at one time it had a wide canal running through it. He didn't want to take the chance of us crossing Canal Street and possibly being killed. We had to get closer and ended up moving into another four-story tenement house at 182 Mulberry Street that was a block away from school. My teacher was Miss McGulf. She was not only a teacher, she was also a lawyer, and she was my first love. I built her a model airplane and gave it to her as a present just to let her know how I felt about her. Later we moved to the fourth floor of a tenement house again, on 187 Hester Street.

While living on 187 Hester Street in Little Italy (I think the year was 1939) I was looking out of my window one Saturday morning and I heard what sounded like firecrackers being fired to my left side and up the street. A man who was playing cards at a café came out bent over and holding his belly. He walked down to where I was looking, from the fourth floor, and fell down and died right there. We later heard that he was shot from under the table while playing cards.

One day something happened below in the bar on 187 Hester Street. We looked out and saw people running after a man up the street towards Mott Street. He turned to the right in an attempt to get to Canal Street when he fell down and died. His body was half on the sidewalk and half on the street, with blood running from his neck. The owner of the bar did the cutting and I don't remember the reason.

The bar owner lived in the same house, but on the first floor. They had a green parrot who was 75 years old and was kept in a cage out on the fire escape. Often he would turn the cage over and climb up on the ladders to the next flight, saying "Haw, haw, you cannot catch me", until he could no longer walk up. The parrot could also curse pretty good and I was told that during WWI, some sailor gave him to the bar owner.

When we were children we used to play stickball out in the street. We used a soft ball and a broomstick. I know this is funny now, but it was terrible then. Sometimes, believe it or not, we would play on the flat roof of our tenement houses. Since there were no walls around the roof, it was a wonder we didn't lose an outfielder playing ball. If our parents had known what we were doing they probably would have cracked us. We didn't do it for long.

My father had a fruit and vegetable business on the corner where we lived. One time, some Italian gentlemen came to see him and asked, "We'd like to know what time you close?" My father said, "About 7:00, no later than 7:30." One of the men said, "Please close your business no later than 6 o'clock and please tell your children to stay off the street."

My father did not say to him, "Who the hell are you?" He was very kind to have told my father to close his business and keep his kids off the streets. When I came home from school that day, my father said, "I want you to help me close the business and I want you off the street at 6:00." That's what we did. Around 8:00, I was looking out our fourth floor window, from which I could see my father's business on the corner, when I heard what sounded like firecrackers. Three guys, one from each corner, came out and shot a guy right at the other corner. I saw it. This was the reason they asked my father to keep us off the street. They just didn't want anybody to get hurt or killed. Apparently the guy they shot had taken $30,000 in cash and when he was asked to pay it back, he had told them no, so they took care of him. The funny part about this was that the New York City police headquarters was a block and a half away. It took them over three-quarters of an hour to get to the scene. The neighborhood was under Mafia control, but I remember some nice guys. There was one guy who went by the name of Joe the Wop. Joe used to get hold of kids who didn't have shoes, ask who they were, and then send them to the corner where there was a Jewish clothing store. He would tell them, "Go down there and get yourself some clothes or shoes. Just tell him Joe the Wop sent you." And he would take care of it. He just didn't like to see kids go barefoot, or be in need of shoes or clothes. He was from Italy, and perhaps he remembered a time when he had no shoes. These wise guys always wore the same style of shoes.

We had fun in school as the years went by, but my father was worried about me hanging around with some older tough guys so he sent me to live with his parents in Providence, Rhode Island.

That may not have been the main reason he sent me to them, I think he also knew that I could be a big help to them since they didn't speak or read English. They lived near Smith Street at 547 Chuckstone Avenue up behind the state capitol. I stayed there for about two years. I didn't speak Italian; they didn't speak English. We had a hell of a time trying to understand what each other was talking about. But eventually I understood some Italian and they understood some English. Later my grandmother said, "Well, your father wants you back home; he thinks you'll stay away from bad boys." So back to New York City I went.

Later, my parents again returned me to Rhode Island to keep me off of the streets. This time a bit longer. My grandmother was a short little Italian lady who carried a blackjack in her handbag all the time. She was actually a bootlegger. Some boys didn't want to play with me and I wondered if it was because their fathers used to come down to buy booze from my grandmother. What really bothered me was that I couldn't play with other children after school. I didn't know what was going on until I realized I was the only Italian in school. Soon I became friends with two brothers, Badger and Steven. Now these boys had the same problem I had, nobody would play with them either because they were Portuguese. So just the three of us got together to play and it was great fun.

My grandmother used to play tarot cards everyday. She would read the cards and say a blonde or a redheaded man was going to come to see us. Sure enough, someone with that color hair would come over to talk to her, or grandfather or me.

One night we had a great big snowstorm. The next morning when I woke up, I lifted my shade. There wasn't any sunlight and I found lots of snow banked up against my window. We were five feet off the ground, which meant the wind had blown the snow and it now covered all of my window. This snow stayed with us until May or June of that year, I think it was 1938.

My school in Providence was about two blocks away. Most of the children were of Scottish, Irish, and English descent. We got along pretty well in school, though. We enjoyed one another at recess and all that stuff. We started kidding around and one time we noticed that our principal would come down to talk to our Phys Ed teacher often. She was very attractive and he would lock her door and stay inside a long time. We knew what was going on for we found physical evidence on the street outside her window.

Walking home one day, I decided to climb a fence. I fell and broke my right arm. It was reset at the hospital and I had to go each week to Pawtucket, Rhode Island, to have my arm looked at and treated. Eventually it healed very well. I've never had a bit of trouble to this day.

Another day I had a toothache. My grandmother took me to a dentist. He didn't give me a shot of Novocain and when he started drilling the cavity, his drill slipped and went into my nerve. I jumped out of his chair and took off. I never went back. I don't know what the heck he was trying to do, but later I lost that tooth.

Downtown there was a sporting goods store that sold model airplane kits. They would build them to hang from the ceiling near the window. I would always stop to look at them. I enjoyed building the models. I remember one day when I went downtown with my grandmother and she bought a fully built model airplane for me. It was not meant to be played with, for it was very flimsily built. The store clerk wanted me to purchase another model he said was sturdier. Years later the company that manufactured the model he suggested became well known for building a quality product. It was called the Cleveland Model Airplane Company, out of Cleveland, Ohio.

My grandmother used to sneak me 25¢ every Sunday afternoon, saying "Don't tell your grandfather." I didn't know why not, but I took the money and walked downtown to the Fay Theatre to see a movie, a comedy or a serial. I saw Rose Marie singing on stage and in person a number of times. She later starred in the Dick VanDyke show on TV.

It was vaudeville. I paid 15¢ for the movie. Later I would buy a bar of candy for 5¢. Afterwards I would walk home, which took almost an hour. When I got home, I gave my grandmother the extra 5¢. She always asked me why I didn't take the trolley car home. I told her I didn't know and that I didn't mind walking, but to make her happy I jumped on a trolley car the next time. When I went to get off, I gave the conductor my nickel and he said it was 7¢. I didn't have the additional 2¢. I told him I was sorry but that all I had was a nickel. He looked at me kind of funny, and I guess he had to pay the balance himself. I never took the trolley car home again since I didn't want to ask for the additional 2¢. I never explained it to my grandmother for there was no reason to.

I became older and was returned to New York City to my parents. Each time I went back and forth I lost a complete year of education. I just couldn't catch up. I think the grade system was different, if an A grade was higher than a B grade in New York, it was the opposite at Providence.

I graduated from PS 130. Now I had to cross Canal Street to get to my next school, PS 23, a junior high school on Mott Street. In my classes we had male Chinese students who came from the mainland. They were much older and some were married. Their families must have owned a Chinese laundry since they were immaculately dressed and wore starched shirts. In the neighborhood there had to have been at least 50 Chinese restaurants on both sides of Mott Street. I don't know how they survived - there would be a restaurant down in the basement, one off the street and one the next flight up. This went on for about two or three blocks, on both sides of the street.

I met a Chinese student, Jimbo Jay, who was funny and always laughing. We all enjoyed him very much. There were very few Chinese girls in my class; we never saw them on the street and I don't know why since Chinese men were always seen. This was during the Chinese/Japanese War. There was an educational institute on Mott Street that had real airplane engines and lots of items for airplanes. All these male Chinese students were learning English so they could become mechanics or whatever. Eventually they probably learned how to fly, then went back to the mainland as lieutenants or pilots. Of course, our Gen. Claire Lee Chennault, who had led the Flying Tigers, an all-volunteer service, in China before WWII, took command of the Allied Forces in the far east when war was declared. He said the Chinese were the worst pilots because they crashed his airplanes and kept his mechanics working on the wreckages. Gen. Chennault informed Washington, DC around 1939 that the Japanese were flying a new fighter, but Washington paid no attention to him. It was the Zero Fighter, Mitsubishi Type O, Model 52 (AGM5c). This was well before Japan bombed Pearl Harbor. I recall reading an article which I believe was in the September 1941 issue of a magazine called *Popular Aviation*, where the writer had been in Japan. He stated that what he saw was old design aircraft with two wings and with around 500 to 600 HP engines. In other words, Japan was way behind in military aircraft. The article was written by a person in aviation, and I do not recall his name, but whoever he was, he lied.

My school had a woodworking shop. We started building sailboats that I guess were about 30" long, made of mahogany. We cut the planks and glued them together, then dug them out to put the deck on. One day we came to class and found that all 30 boats were gone. Our shop teacher had quit and taken all our boats with him. We went down to see the principal, Mr. Reader, who was 90 years old and wore a shoestring tie. We reported our stolen boats and he looked at us like, what the hell do you kids want from me? That was the end of the woodworking shop and I never went back. In fact, all of us lost interest.

My father was right about me getting mixed up with a bunch of bad guys. They were about four years older. I palled around with Johnny, who lived on my corner and whose father was a funeral director. One night we walked with the older guys. Johnny and I were about half a block away from them. They were in front of us and for some reason one of them broke a window in a candy shop, which was also a luncheonette, and then they started running. The next thing someone was yelling, "Halt! Stop!" Johnny and I looked at each other. We saw this guy running down toward us. Johnny asked, "What are we going to do?" I replied, "Run like hell!" This guy took out his gun and fired. I don't know if his bullet went up into the air or over our heads but it was the first time someone had taken a shot at me (early Army Infiltration Course?) I was running my little legs off and Johnny was doing the same. I noticed the older guys were running in one direction so I thought I'd be smart to run in the opposite direction. I ran right into a police officer who was in the doorway of the old Tombs of New York City. He asked, "Where are you going?" I answered, "Someone is shooting!" I thought he might let me go to find out who was shooting but instead he held me and the next thing I saw was Johnny running in a circle and a security guy chasing and nailing him. Soon a car came from juvenile hall and put us in the back seat. Then Johnny, believe it or not, had a bowel movement in the car. It was terrible; he was so scared. Our fathers came to get us and we went home. My father didn't say anything.

    We had to report to a judge in about three weeks. When our case came up, the owner of the store and the security guy were there. This judge was sitting behind his desk. He was about 300 years old and also had a shoestring tie. He looked at me and said, "Come over here, Frank DeAngelo." I went to him and he asked, "Do you go to church?" I said, "Yes." "Where?" I told him, "The Church of The Most Precious Blood." He said, "Do you know Our Father and Hail Mary?" I said "Yes, Sir." He ordered me, "Say it." I did Our Father and Hail Mary, all of it. He told me to go back to sit with my father. He asked Johnny to step up and asked him the same questions. Johnny said yes, he also went to church and catechism. He said, "Okay, then say it." Johnny was unable to say it. He didn't know it since he never went to church with me. So the judge got peeved with him, and said to Johnny, "You lied to me, go back and sit with your dad. I hope your dad takes care of you for lying." The man who owned the luncheonette didn't want to press charges and said,

"If the boys' fathers pay me $25 to replace the window I'll forget it." The security guy said, "Your Honor, these two boys were not involved. It was a bunch of older boys about a block away from them who broke the window." My father and John's father each paid half. We went home again. My father told me to stay away from those older guys. I agreed and stayed away from them for a long time.

Sometimes a group of us would walk down to the Hudson River around the old Aquarium at Battery Place, and if it was a hot summer day I would notice some young boys swimming in the water, just diving into the water with their clothes on. I also noticed prophylactics and human waste floating near where the boys were having a good time. I could not understand how someone could swim in this water and not become sick. I would have been crazy to do so. At this point, the Hudson and East Rivers met.

As I grew up, I saw much where I lived. I recall that each day something happened at any time of day or night. Some policemen were nice and some were not so nice. In fact, one named Jack was always looking after us, and when we were in trouble with Jack he went to see our dads. He was a good guy and we all respected him.

There were lots of strange stories about the Lower East Side. I will say one does not walk on the sidewalk or streets at 12 o'clock midnight on New Year's Eve. This is due to a very old Roman tradition to welcome in the New Year. For good luck, I was told, anything that was old was to be thrown out. I saw Christmas trees complete with lights and decorations thrown out of windows, followed by bottles and whatever. The streets were filled with trash and broken glass. The next day, no cars were ever parked from the night before.

There was a movie house called New Universal on the Bowery under the Third Avenue El tracks. The woman who owned the place was named Mazie; she had bleach blonde hair and always wore lots of jewelry and perfume. Her makeup was caked on and she had deep red lipstick. She seemed gruff and would wake bums in the theater and tell them to leave. Out they would go. She would use a flint gun to keep the odor down in the theater.

Mazie took your money and gave you a ticket. There were times when we had only a few pennies and knew we needed ten cents to get in. We would walk past her booth and look at the large movie posters on the walls. After walking back and forth many times, she would yell at us, "You little bastards! Go home and get a dime to see the movie!" Then, a few minutes later, she would call out, "Little bastards, come here!" We'd go to her booth and she would ask us how much money we had. When we told her, she insisted her boss would get mad at her if she let us in for a few pennies. This would go on for a few more minutes, then she would finally take our pennies and tell us to sneak by the ticket taker. My dad told me she always did this for the kids who didn't have enough money. He remembered her as a dancer or some type of performer on stage at the turn of the century. A new Cadillac was parked on the street in front of her booth every year. Years later when I read of her death, I recalled her kindness to us.

I was fascinated with flying and still can remember the first time I saw a large flying boat. It was the German Dornier DoX in pairs of six, with 12 engines on top of its wing flying overhead, low and slow, with a top speed of 130 mph. It couldn't go higher than 2,000 - 3,000 feet. What a sight for a young boy to see! Some time later, I saw our Navy and Army aircraft flying overhead, diving over New York City in a mock war, attacking buildings like the phone company and others. I also saw 23 large flying boats led by Gen. Balboa of Italy. These Savola Marchetti S-55's flew over the Atlantic Ocean from Italy. I saw three large Navy airships (the Los Angeles, the Macon and the Akron) fly together over New York City at about 2,000 feet. Sometimes one of these, or all three, would fly with the German's Hindenberg over the city. But late one dark, rainy afternoon I had a feeling something was wrong. A short time later, while landing at Lakehurst, NJ, it blew up and burned. Some months later, I visited Floyd Bennett field in Brooklyn, NY, and saw Howard Hughes'

Lockheed Lodestar, which had flown around the world. It was parked, looking tired, and no one was around. These sights were most interesting to a young boy who was happy to be part of it all growing up.

I graduated from PS-23 and was given a choice of going to Stewart High School, which offered a general business course, or to one of two aviation schools, both in New York City. The one I really wanted to attend was not available because so many students were taking aviation courses due to the war. So, the only one open to me was Harran High School, located on 103rd Street. I had to take the above ground train, the 3rd Ave. El, to attend.

When I enrolled in class, I told my instructor how much I loved airplanes. I had designed a model airplane powered by a rubber band, and he said he'd like to see it. I brought it in, he looked at it, then turned and walked away. He never told me it was bad, good, or mediocre. However, when I showed it to a couple of students, they said that for a first time design it was excellent. I might not have known the proper proportions of the wing, etc. but it was a try.

My teacher disappointed me. Soon I got a little tired of my classes since we were studying old stuff I already knew from having read model airplane books and magazines. Then I heard that they actually had airplanes with engines in school. Even though I really wanted to be in that class, they would not let me go, so I started cutting classes.

Soon enough, a truant officer found me and took me to see the principal. I told him how badly I wanted to work on those engines and he said I would be able to–during the last six months of my four years of schooling. I asked why I couldn't get in immediately, and he just said, "That's the way it's going to be." I thought this was a pretty sad situation. Here they had a student who wanted to learn and they refused to open a door for me. I know I could have been an excellent mechanic but when they told me I would have to wait three and a half years to take the class, I left school. (One instructor of that class had his students build an airplane for him. Well, they built it. They took it to a field where he climbed in, revved up its' engine, and took off. Up he went and then down he came. He was killed.)

Once in a while our Navy would sail their ships up the East River. They stayed at some piers near Wall Street and I would walk down there to see them. They also had a seaplane base. Planes would fly in from Long Island, land in the East River and then taxi up and onto a ramp on wheels that also retracted, after getting into the water.

One day I walked to one of the East River Piers to see our aircraft carriers. Along the way, I passed by Fraunces Tavern, where Washington bid farewell to his troops on Dec. 6, 1783, after the war with England. I happened to see something shiny in a trash can on the curb and went over and picked it up. It was a key with a tag. It said, "George Washington's desk key." I figured it didn't belong in the trash can; it belonged at his desk. I went inside and gave the key to someone in the restaurant but never found out if it was returned to its proper place.

That day, our fourth aircraft carrier USS Ranger CV4 had sailed in with the USS Langley CV1, our first carrier. I got permission to go aboard both ships. Both had Grumman F3F-1 and F3F-2 biplanes. These were stubby, beautiful and colorful tiny planes. The planes were roped off so visitors couldn't touch them. I asked one sailor about the aluminum skin of the plane. He said, "Aluminum is better than the canvas we used years ago. It won't tear and get holes in it like linen." I asked him if I could touch one, but he said, "I can't let you pass the rope."

Seeing these ships and planes made me want to join the Navy. I was then 17 years old. I went down to try to join up and they said, "Well, you're wearing glasses." "I've been wearing glasses since I was nine." "We can't take you." I went down to join the Marines and they also said they wouldn't take me because of my vision. The Coast Guard didn't even want to talk to me. They told me to join the Army. I didn't hate the Army, I just never thought of joining the Army.

My mother had worked ever since we were out of diapers. After having four children, she wanted to get out of the house. My aunts had been leaving their children with her so she figured the only way to get out of the house was to get a job, which she did. She made good money. In fact, at times she made more than my dad.

My mother worked as a pocket maker at a clothing manufacturer, and she was well liked. My father worked very hard at his fruit and vegetable business. I had to admire his getting up at 3 a.m. every morning, Monday through Friday, to go to market to buy produce. He would have about $500 cash on his person. No one ever robbed him on the subway or street. Some years later when we had a restaurant, my mother used to come home very late at night on the subway and, again, no one would ever bother her. At that time our streets were safe. If it hadn't been safe, I would have been with my mother all the time to make sure she got home safely. It was just before the war when she closed her restaurant, when supplies were getting hard to find and buy.

I remember one day when my Dad asked me to bring him an empty bushel basket. I did and he then opened a new bushel of string beans. He put half of them in the basket I had brought him. He then put a sign reading "10 cents per pound" on one basket. On the other, he put a sign that said, "15 cents per pound." When I asked him why the prices were different when they were the same beans, he explained that he always bought the best beans for the money, but knew that some people couldn't afford the 15 cent ones and would choose the less expensive ones. This way, he said, everyone was getting the best beans they could afford.

Most of the fruit we got was packed in soft tissue paper. Dad told me to be sure and save all of the paper, so I unwrapped all the fruit and put the paper in a shopping bag. One day he came to me and asked what fruits I had unwrapped. I told him apples, oranges, lemons, plums, pears, peaches and prickly pears. The prickly pears explained why he had nearly gotten killed that morning by a widow woman who had very little money and who had asked him to save the soft paper so she could use it as toilet paper. I don't know if she then switched back to real toilet paper!

There used to be a girl who lived next door to us who wasn't an orphan but her father couldn't take care of her and her mother didn't want her or something like that, so our older next door neighbors took her in. She was about 16 or 17 years old, not really pretty or ugly and a little on the heavy side. One afternoon, I came home from school and found her telling my mother about how she had gone to a candy store in the Jewish neighborhood the evening before. She said, "We had so much fun last night with these Jewish fellows. This one young man was very handsome. His name is Bugsy and he is so funny that all the girls like to be with him. He always has lots of money, and there are always lots of other young men around him."

The candy store was a local meeting place where they could sit around and drink Cokes, tell stories, and listen to the jukebox. She said this guy Bugsy lived in Brooklyn, a place called Brownsville. One day I was sitting around just thinking. I'm thinking: Bugsy, Bugsy, Brownsville in Brooklyn!! Candy store, Jewish neighborhood, candy store, Jewish guys. Then it dawned on me who this Bugsy was! He was Bugsy Siegel who had started the Flamingo Casino in Las Vegas. Bugsy Siegel, Murder Incorporated. The Mafia contracted Bugsy and his men to break a guy's arm or worse.

I guess it was funny he was so close to my neighborhood and even closer to her, but I don't know (or care) what went on between them. It was just strange for me to put it all together; my gut feeling works that way sometimes. It scares the hell out of me to be able to think of things that turn out later to be true. This was THE Bugsy Siegel. Even though she never mentioned his last name, I knew. How many Jewish guys do you meet in a lifetime named Bugsy who are from Brownsville, and meet in a candy shop located in New York City, in a Jewish neighborhood, with a bunch of Jewish guys around with lots of money? I remember going to the movies at the Strand or the Paramount on Broadway in New York City. In the morning I would pay .25 cents at either one and that afternoon pay

.35 cents at the other. Both would show first time movies, a stage show with the top bands, and the singers of the day. I saw Frank, Doris, Helen, Peggy, Bob, Tex, and even Red as he was drinking the Gin and falling all over the place. What great memories.

Soon I received a letter. I was assigned a number for Selective Service. I was ordered to report to Draft Board #4 located at Grand Central Palace near Bleeker Street, not far from my home. I was almost 18 when I went and registered. They told me I would be notified by mail if and when I needed to report back.

None of us *almost* 18-year-olds could get a job. Nobody wanted to hire us and then have us get drafted when we turned 18. My friend, Paul, who lived across the street and was about the same age, was crazy about my sister Theresa. He was a big fellow and one day my mother said, "Why don't you and Paul go look for jobs?" So we went to look for jobs. We went to Long Island City to the K&G Ship Building Welding Company, which had a Navy contract to build steel barges and steel ocean going tugs.

We were hired. Up river they were building PT boats. Every time one came by, I loved the sound of their purring engines. They put me and Paul down in the hold of a newly constructed barge where there was not much light except one drop cord light. Our job was to scrape rust off of the inside of the hull, after we applied a grease substance with a brush. We were spitting rust all day long and after eight hours would ride the subway to get home since we didn't have a car. We'd get into the shower or tub and leave rust rings around the tub. It was pathetic; I mean it looked like someone shoved us through a rusty, dirty pipe. This went on for weeks (I think we received $25 a week), until finally we went to our foreman. We asked him if there was some other job we could do, building, welding, anything. He said, "No, you are just young guys and you won't be here long so we want you down in those barges doing your job. We know it's dirty; nobody wants to do it. You young guys are going to do it or quit." We quit.

On Mulberry Street in Little Italy there was a restaurant called

Angelo's. The owner's son, Pat, was the manager. I know that Pat received a phone call from a well-known male singer who said he wanted to eat at the restaurant that night, but he didn't want everyone to know he was coming. Within just a few minutes of his arrival, a large group of people had crowded in to meet him. The singer ran into the men's restroom and climbed out the tiny window, leaving a couple of hundred people to wonder where he went. The names of two local restaurants, Angelo's and Maxie's, were both in one of the singer's classic songs called "Manhattan Melody."

Angelo had a granddaughter named MaryAnn who I took to the movies a few times. Years later, my friend Joe Kelly, who also worked at Angelo's, brought MaryAnn to visit me at the hospital in Atlantic City when I was recuperating. (Later, Mary Ann married a guy who always looked at me with hate in his eyes. I guess he heard that she had visited me in the hospital.)

Soon after, I received a second letter telling me to report to Grand Central Place. It was an all-day affair. We were put in this room, completely naked. They took some blood and told us to spread our cheeks. Now some of us knew what spread your cheeks meant, some others didn't. Some put their hands up to their faces to pull their cheeks apart. A doctor would say, "Spread your cheeks down there and bend over." They were looking for something. We sat all day on cold marble benches without a sheet or anything to wrap around us. There were hundreds of us. At the end of the day, we were told to get dressed, go home, and wait for further orders.

Someone told my parents they had taken a lot of blood out of us boys, so my father went to a butcher shop. He bought me the biggest steak. When I arrived home he said, "Eat your steak, it'll put some blood back in you." I said, "How much blood do you think they took–a gallon?" He said, "You eat it." Steak was expensive and hard to get, so I said, "I don't want the steak, I don't need it." He replied, "You eat it. I bought it for you." I felt kind of guilty about eating a steak for no reason.

One morning my mother asked me, "Why don't you look for

work where I work?" The clothing manufacturer she worked for made Army uniforms. As a pocket maker, she earned about 10¢ for every pocket she sewed. I was hired to bring a pile of uniforms to another worker who put the sleeves on, then take it to another who put on something else. We would then take the uniforms down to shipping and put them in cartons to be shipped to some military quartermaster location.

I stayed for two or three months until I received a letter on March 15, 1943 informing me I was to report to my draft board. When I reported I was asked, "Are you supporting your mother or father?" I said "No." "Are you going to school?" "No." "Do you know any reason for you not to be classified 1-A?" "I guess not." "OK, your classified 1-A. Go home to wait for further orders." My parents knew the military was going to draft me any day, but what could they do?

I received another letter on April 2, 1943. It started off with the words, "Greetings, from the President." The next word was *induction*. It said I was to report to Grand Central Place at 8 a.m. on April 9, 1943. I was to take only the clothes I would be wearing and should make sure all my affairs were in order. I kissed my mother goodbye and my father went with me that day. Mother had to go to work. After reporting in, I kissed my dad goodbye. We stayed in the building until our Army bus pulled up and our names were called to get on. We were taken to Grand Central Station and put on a train that took us to Ft. Dix, New Jersey, about 90 miles south of New York City.

Chapter Two

Basic Training

We were put in six-man tents, not in barracks, and the place was packed with soldiers. Our pyramid tents were located at the end of a runway. Every morning around 5 a.m., B-25s or B-26s would take off and fly right over our tents. You could not sleep; I don't care if you were dead, you would wake up.

It was very cold; we slept wrapped up in two blankets, overcoats, our uniforms, long johns, plus socks. We had a little potbelly stove in the center of our tent, and had wood to start a fire, but no one wanted to get out of a warm bunk to start a fire. So we decided to figure out a way to light the fire without getting out of bed. We took rolls of toilet paper and unrolled the paper into our stove. Whoever was to start the fire would light the toilet paper from his bunk. It would burn all the way into this stove. We wondered how we didn't burn our tents down using this system.

At our first meal, we saw three big galvanized garbage cans, 32 gallons each, full of water. They were sitting over hot fires to boil the water. The first can had Octagon soap, also called GI soap, in it. There were suds and some food particles in it. Whew. When we saw this, some GI's started upchucking.

Before our meals we would go to the third clear water can, and dunk the mess kit. After washing away any dust, we received our food. If we didn't eat all our food we found an extra garbage can to place it in. We were told to go to the first can with a brush. We put our dirty mess kit in, sloshed it around, and then brushed inside and out to make sure everything was washed out. We then dipped it in the second can that was filled with clear water to rinse off the soap. The third can also had clear water. We did this every day, after each meal.

Our meals were not eaten in a mess hall; we ate outdoors on 4 1/2 foot high 4' x 4' posts stuck in the ground with a big 12-inch wide plank placed on top of these posts. I stood on one side eating out of my mess kit. On the other side of this plank in front of me was a GI off to one side, and he too would be standing and eating. It was ridiculous–our food went straight down. Later in the day we had to get our shots and many big strong healthy-looking GI's were passing out when they were given tetanus shots.

We were measured for some other clothes then we went back to our tents. Soon, over the loud speaker, they started calling out names; they called everyone from our group. "All right, you GI's, meet us out at the training/exercise field." This was a big field and there were hundreds of us. The instructor would stand on a high platform and did some calisthenics. We would do the same, but he told us we were not there to do any calisthenics. He said, "Men, the lieutenant kinda wants to talk to you." The lieutenant said, "I know these GI shoes are tough on your feet. Get a bucket of water, soak your shoes and feet, then walk around. Eventually your shoes will be flexible for your feet. That's all I have to say. Dismissed!" The lieutenant jumped off and we never saw him again.

We went back to our tents and God help us tried to find buckets so we could soak our feet and shoes. We had hundreds of GI's looking for buckets. Where were they? We were to stay at Ft. Dix for two or three weeks. One day my name was called, "DeAngelo, you're going to work in the kitchen." So I worked in the kitchen for about 15-20 hours. Two days later, they called my name, "You're moving out." Before we left Ft. Dix, we wrapped up all our civilian clothing and an Army truck came around to pick them up. I had my parent's name and address on the package to be shipped back to our homes, free of postage. I had been given dog tags #32881054, which represented my military number, my religion (Catholic), and my blood type (negative). The first two numbers indicated I was from New York.

We were all packed up again. We had these great big bags called "A" and "B" bags marked with my army number 32881054 and name in which to put our new clothing and we carried these with us. We got on a bus that took us to our train. On the train we were told to leave the shades down until we stopped to get off.

The cars were not what you would call comfortable, they had wooden seats and no place to sleep so you slept sitting up. You couldn't lie down since there were two other GI's sharing your seat plus three other GI's facing you. Before the train moved, I said (jokingly) we would either go to California or Florida. We never knew where we were going, no one told us anything. Our train would often stop at a side track so other military trains could go that carried tanks, airplanes, etc. We were not essential; military equipment was.

Sometimes we stopped. The women of a town would come out and pass us sandwiches and doughnuts. We didn't get hot meals; all we had were sandwiches, milk and sometimes fruit. I don't remember much about our food. I guess a lot of us were excited about just being in the Army.

We used a latrine on our train and there was water for drinking. We were the first 18-year-olds to be drafted, so I guess they figured we could take anything.

After the third day we were told we would be getting off in about an hour. Everyone had to get their things together. Early in the morning, around 3 a.m., our train stopped. We couldn't see anything, we were out in the boondocks, but as I jumped off and my feet sank into soft sand, I said, "We're in Florida." A couple of GI's asked, "How do you know, DeAngelo?" "I just know we're in Florida." We were told to get on the road and had to march about a quarter of a mile where we saw a great big banner going across and above the road. It read, "Welcome to the 66th Infantry Division the Panther Division."

We had arrived at Camp Blanding, Florida, on April 18, 1943.

Now, I recall that when I took my aptitude test at Ft. Dix, I was asked what I wanted to do in the Army. I thought it was kind of ridiculous to ask me that but I said that I was crazy about airplanes. I had been an airplane buff since I was 9, and knew all types of airplanes. He said "You like airplanes?" "Yeah, I want to gas them, oil them, grease them, whatever you want me to do, fly them, gunner, whatever, you name it, I'll do it. No questions asked." The last thing he said was, "I wish you a lot of luck in the Air Corp." That was it. So when I saw the sign, "Welcome to the 66th Infantry Division, Panther Division" I thought, "Oh God, he lied to me." So when we were marched to our barracks, word got around that General H.F. Kramer, the 66th Division Commanding Officer, had shanghaied us troops to the Infantry.

Figure 1. General H. F. Kramer, Commander of the 66th Division, Camp Blanding, Florida. April 21, 1943.

Camp Blanding was located near Starke, Florida, where they have executions. The camp was 24 miles square. It cost $30 million to build for the Army. This camp could hold three full infantry divisions of 15,000 men each. Gen. Hart had shipped out with the 30th Division; I think they went to the Pacific. Another new division was needed for training at Camp Blanding. The 66th Division was the first batch of 18-year-olds drafted. I was told, not once, but a number of times, that we were on our way to Miami to the Air Corps when Gen. Kramer had shanghaied our troop train. I don't know how many of us were on this particular train, but he took all the troop trains he could get to put them in Camp Blanding. Once they processed your paperwork, you were in the infantry. That was it. You couldn't get out of it. No one bitched because the Army was

Basic Training

Figure 2. The 66th Division Patch called Panthers, Camp Blanding, Florida. Also called General Kramer's "Pussy Cats". April 21, 1943

the Army. The Air Corps was under the Army's control. We ended as infantrymen. My army code was 745 Infantry Riflemen, Queen of Battles and Light Blue was its color.

I was assigned to the 263rd Infantry Regiment, I believe K Company. Camp Blanding had pretty decent wooden barracks; it wasn't anything out of this world but at least it was better than Ft. Dix's tents. The first few days we were there, we marched out to our training field. A big rainstorm came up. It just poured on us; we didn't wait for anyone to say anything, and we all ran back to our barracks. When we got to our barracks, Lt. Young called out, "Attention! We are walking back to the training field as you are." He went on to say, "You are not supposed to do that again. You are soldiers and you are going to learn to be and act as a soldier." And that was it. This was our first problem with the Army and we never did it again. No one told us anything, they didn't tell us to stay or go, or what, we just broke rank.

When we first arrived at Camp Blanding you could tell who was who out in the field by their physical size. Some GI's were heavy, some were heavy on the bottoms only, etc. But after a couple of months of training, all the GI's started to look alike physically. Muscles appeared, fat disappeared. For Basic Training Infantry (521), *Figure 3* shows me standing in front of the barracks with a pipe in my hand on May 15, 1943.

Figure 3. The author standing in front of his barracks of K Company 263rd Regiment 66th Division at Camp Blanding, Florida.

Our first sergeant was Sgt. Kurt Jeck. For my platoon we had an old-timer named Sgt. Sizemore, and Sgt. Robinson was the Second

Basic Training

Platoon Sergeant. I don't remember the other two platoons' sergeants. Sgt. Sizemore had his own collection of shirts with the following ranks: Private, Private First Class, Corporal, Buck Sergeant, Staff Sergeant, Tech Sergeant. Whenever he was busted for drunkenness (or anything else), he would wear the shirt of the lesser grade than he had before he was broken. He was a strange one and had been in the service about 20 years.

Sgt. Sizemore was always asking a GI to give him 5 or 10 bucks, saying he would pay it back at the end of the month. Any GI who loaned this sergeant money never saw it again. Oh God! He was a typical old-time Sergeant. He wasn't bad, but just a con artist who would take your money, go have a beer, or go with his girlfriend, and forget your money. The other sergeant, Sgt. Robinson, was maybe in the CCC. He was transferred into the Army with a sergeant rank I think.

Figure 4 - shows my St. Christopher medal that was given to me by my cousin Tessie the night before I left for the Army. I always wore it around my neck and I was questioned about it when taking a shower one day. Why would I be wearing a St. Christopher medal? I explained it was the Patron of Safety medal. I wore it for so many years that eventually the little loop wore down and I had to drill a hole on the top and put the chain through it. It's made of sterling silver and I still have it mounted with my medals.

A fellow GI soon asked me if I came upon a member of the Italian Army would I fight him as well as the German. I took a long look at this GI and said, "It matters not to me if he is wearing the wrong

Figure 4. Author's Saint Christopher Medal, given to him the night before he left for the Army. April 8, 1943, from New York City.

uniform. As long as I am wearing my American uniform, I will and shall protect the American flag from all others."

One day my friend Andy picked up some boxing gloves and yelled, "Hey, DeAngelo, put the gloves on." "Naw, Andy, I don't want to." He said, "Put them on, come on, and we'll do some sparring." I told him I didn't want to, but he finally made me feel like, why not, so I said, "OK." I put on my gloves and we started sparring. In a minute I landed a hard right hook and knocked him down, driving the breath out of him for a good two or three minutes. When he finally came to, he looked at me and said, "My God, I didn't expect you to hit me that hard." I replied, "I told you I didn't want to spar with you." Then Sgt. Robinson, a lightweight boxer some years back, told me to leave my gloves on. I looked at him and said, "I heard you were a boxer, I'm not going to spar with you." He said, "I'm not gonna hurt you." I said, "I'm not gonna worry about that because I'm not sparring with you since you are a professional and I'm not." But maybe I should have. For when I was about 15 years old, I got into a fistfight with a guy in my neighborhood who had been picking on me. I had told him to leave me alone, but he started pushing me, so I hit him. With one punch, he hit the sidewalk. Then I hit him a second time and now he was in the middle of the street. I walked up to him, picked him up, hit him again, knocking him back again on the sidewalk. His uncle came from behind, grabbed me by my shoulder, turned me around and hit me in the mouth. My two front teeth were pushed in, I pushed them up into place. After that, I knew I didn't want to fight with anyone–not Andy, not anyone. I knew I was capable of taking a lot and giving more than I took, also, not being afraid to fight. No one asked me to put boxing gloves on again.

The guy I fought that night, whose name was Merrick, was drafted shortly before I was and was discharged within a few weeks. Why? Because he cut his pants cuffs off and they were called tapered peck pants.

At Camp Blanding we were assigned to K Company

Basic Training

Commander Capt. Palmer. Our Platoon Leader was Lt. Fransworth. Lt. Gee was another platoon leader and Lt. Young, second in command, was the one who ordered us back when we left the field during the storm. Our training was to last 15-16 weeks. Just walking to our training field and back, we averaged about 100 miles a week.

We were walking one hot day with Lt. Gee, who was only about 21 years old. It was raining and he needed to pee, but he didn't stop walking, he just peed. He said, "Boy, that feels good and warm going down my leg." We laughed, he was a good lieutenant and I have no idea what happened to him during the war but he sure gave us a funny experience to remember him by.

One morning I walked out of our barracks to go to the latrine and nearly fell in a hole in front of our barrack door. It was four feet square by four feet deep and down inside was a GI with a teaspoon, digging. His lieutenant came over and said the hole was big enough. The gum-chewing lieutenant took the gum out of his mouth and threw it in the very bottom of the hole, then told this GI to fill up the hole using his teaspoon. Lt. Hopkins was the one.

The GI was Pvt. Bryson from Bryson City, North Carolina. Every once in a while he would take off without a pass to go see his parents, The MP's always had to drag him back. Each time they brought him back, he'd have to dig another hole. He must have dug three or four holes, I guess, before they broke him from going AWOL. I was told his father was Judge Bryson.

I married Hazel R. Smiley in 1954, and her dad's file was turned over to me. I read a letter in which he had requested a Judge Bryson to look into some property in North Carolina. It all came to me, was this the same person who dug those holes? *Figure 5*.

One morning K Company was called out. We were ordered to wear shoes, no socks, with helmet liners and raincoats, that was all. It was a beautiful warm day, the sun was shining and all 200 of us were marching down Main Street. We saw some good-looking girls coming our way, probably paying a visit to their husbands or brothers, and I'm sure they were thinking, "Why are they wearing raincoats?"

T. D. BRYSON, JR.
ATTORNEY AT LAW
BRYSON CITY, N. C.

November 4, 1960

Mr. Garret D. Quick
Attorney at Law
334 Ninth Street
Eau Gallie, Florida

Dear Sir:

This will acknowledge receipt of your letter of October 27, regarding claim of Mr. W. G. Smiley to property in your area. I know nothing about this matter, and have no information that I could transmit to you. It may be possible that Mrs. DeAngelo has given you some confusing information as to the property's location being in the State of Florida.

If you will supply me with more data, I will endeavor to coordinate my information and thinking with you.

With kindest regards, I am

Very truly yours,

T. D. Bryson, Jr.

TB:c

Figure 5. This letter is possibly from the same GI with the teaspoon at Camp Blanding, Florida.

It wasn't raining. We were going to First Aid for a short arm examination to check to see if any of us had gonorrhea.

One morning they took us to see a movie, and sure enough they showed us the worst cases of venereal diseases they could find throughout the world. Oh, Boy! I heard some GI say, "I'm not gonna touch any woman–don't even talk about!" Some GI's got so upset they upchucked.

Another time they showed us movies about the 5th Column. Spies and things. As I looked up at the screen, I saw a familiar face. "By golly, that's my mother's cousin, Joe Spats!" I said. He had always wanted to be an actor. In fact, he knew two actors; George Raft and Jack La Rue. He even took the name of Joe La Rue, saying he was Jack La Rue's brother, which of course was not true. The town of Long Island City was where the Army movie industry was located and Joe didn't live far from Long Island City. They would ask him to make movies and act as a gangster, or whatever. It was strange to see him on the screen and, of course, some GI's didn't believe me. But it was true. Spats was short for Spatrozano and Joe had been trained as a master barber by his father. One day he visited us in Florida and told me about a lady who was starring in a TV series. She had come in to his shop to get him to trim the hair off her breasts. I shall not name this lady. As I will not name the young lady who dated his son Eddie, for both sang in the play *Oklahoma!* when it first opened in the early 1940's. Eddie had taken his mother's maiden name of Farrell and could play the accordion and sing. His father had pushed him into show business, which he didn't like, and even gotten him the job in *Oklahoma!*. He signed a contract to go to England with the play, but he only lasted a month or two before quitting and ending his career because his girlfriend wanted him to come home.

I remember one time after I was discharged I was at the Blue Haven Club in Woodside, on Long Island. Eddie was singing and his master of ceremonies was Jackie Gleason (this was before Gleason became well-known). Eddie finally got out of the music business but not before he made a few records. I don't have any of them, but I think they are still around and could be found if someone really wanted to search for them.

One day during lunch Sgt. Kurt Jeck told me to finish eating and then go over to the CP since he wanted to talk to me. I said I would, but I forgot all about it and went back to the barracks for a nap. The next afternoon he saw me in the mess hall. "Didn't I tell you to come and see me yesterday?" I said, "I'm sorry, Sergeant, I forgot all about it." He said, "Well, make sure you don't forget this time." I said "Yes Sir!" I went over to the CP and he asked me if I could type. I told him yes, I could, but only with two fingers. He said, "Well, like passes and things like that." I said, "Yes, if you think I can do it." He said, "I think you can do it, that's why I'm asking you." So I became the company clerk. My job was to be there from early morning until 8 or 9 p.m., taking messages, answering the telephone, making passes, and keeping the sergeant informed of what was going on each day.

I was in the CP office one morning when Capt. Palmer called in the First Sergeant. Through closed doors, I heard him say, "Sergeant, get rid of DeAngelo. I don't want him here." The First Sergeant said, "He's a good man, Captain." " I don't care, I want him out." When the Sergeant walked out I said, "You don't have to tell me, Sergeant. Thanks very much, you've been kind to me." I left. Capt. Palmer brought some GI's from New England to work at the CP. I wasn't jealous (or didn't care) but I thought as an officer he should never have acted the way he did. After all, the First Sergeant knew I could do the job and he should have trusted his judgment. But Capt. Palmer didn't trust anybody but Capt. Palmer. Many of our GI's didn't care for him. He didn't take any interest in us at all and never spoke to us. He was just one of those ROTC guys, a real nobody. The only ones we were close to were our lieutenants and sergeants.

I recall I was in K Company for only a week when Capt. Palmer, a graduate of Brown University, called me into his office. He wanted

Basic Training

to know why I lived in Providence, Rhode Island. I said, "Well, because my father's parents, my grandparents lived there." He was typically heavyset and looked as though he needed to exercise more than us GI's. He had a lot of weight on the bottom, if you know what I mean, and looked like a pear. He walked around with an attitude like, "Look at me, GI's, I'm your captain. You're nothing!"

One day I was on KP duty. We were supposed to read the bulletin board everyday, I mean four times a day, since we never knew what was going to be put on it. There I was on KP duty, and my name was also on for guard duty at 5 p.m. the same day. I wasn't getting off KP till 9 p.m. that night. I went to Sergeant Jeck and asked him what I was supposed to do. He was surprised that I had been given two duties in one day and knew the clerk who had replaced me had prepared the schedules. The sergeant said, "I'll tell you what, why don't you get off KP at noon, take it easy for an hour or two and then report here for guard duty." I think the sergeant was kind of embarrassed by the new clerk.

On Sunday mornings we ate a breakfast of eggs, ham, Spam, or pancakes. If we stayed in the company area for lunch or supper, we would eat cold cuts, cheese, ham and baloney we called Horse Cock. But if we didn't have any duty that day, we'd leave and walk to Kingsley Lake. The water was beautiful and clear and we'd stay all day for it was better to be away from K Company. If you were in the barracks sleeping and someone came to visit a GI who was on guard duty or KP, they would release him to visit with his guests. Then they would find someone to take his place and it usually would be the poor guy trying to sleep on Sunday. Later, on the way back from the lake, we'd often stop at the PX to drink 3.2 beer, or Cokes or eat junk food. The next day when we went out on the field, all that beer and junk food took effect and we would feel heavy and full.

Figure 6 - Taken 5/18/43, it shows me in the barracks with a helmet, a cartridge belt, and a bayonet, ready to meet the enemy. I didn't know how far away the enemy would be, but I was a tough-looking GI. Right?

Figure 6. Author in barracks, ready for action. Camp Blanding, Florida. May 18, 1943 in K Company, 263rd Regiment, 66th Division.

One day at Camp Blanding we were called out to be given assignments for the day. Standing in front of me was Daniels. He was fooling with his right ear lobe. He pressed it and out flew blood and pus all over the place. It was something to see.

Figure 7 - These three buddies were in my platoon. Roy is sitting down, and Corbett is on his left side. I don't remember the other's name. I don't know what happened to Roy or the other young GI, but I do remember Corbett was in the same 3rd Infantry Division overseas. Later, after being discharged, I ran across Corbett in my neighborhood. We talked for a moment. Corbett was not one to take showers, I don't know why, but we made him take one everyday. We GI's brushed him down one day. He took showers from then on.

Soon we were taken to the rifle range with our M-1's. We had to know its serial number, if we lost it and didn't know the serial number we were in big trouble and would have to pay around $90-$100 for the lost one. I was ready to fire my M-1. I took aim and fired. My first round fell short. The sergeant asked, "How come you're short, DeAngelo?" I said, "I don't know." When I looked at the rear sight I said, "This is not set right." So I reset some clicks for 300 yards, placed the M-1 on target and fired seven rounds. I hit

Basic Training

Figure 7. Friends with K Company 263rd Regiment 66th Division at Camp Blanding, Florida. June 8, 1943. Center: Roy Corbett, over Roy's left shoulder other names are lost. All three are around 18 years old.

the bull's eye each time. That one missed shot caused me to earn the title of "sharpshooter" rather than "expert." Someone had moved my rear sight down for 200 yards when it should have been set for 300 yards. I don't know who the hell did that and whether it was done accidentally or on purpose, but whoever pulled that on me really screwed me as an expert shooter. We were careful not to get what we called an "M-1 thumb," which was when your thumb got caught inside and the bolt would hit it hard.

On the rifle range, my ears started ringing. I thought, "Gee whiz, I better go and find out what's wrong with my ears." I went to First Aid and sat in a chair that looked like a barber chair. Another GI came in and sat in the chair next to me. The medic filled up a syringe with liquid and pumped it into this GI's ear. I didn't think an ear could take that much fluid. Then he told him to tilt his head to one side so the fluid wouldn't run out. About five minutes later the medic came back to tell the GI to tilt his head down over a pan, and, boy, what came out! I never saw anything like it; it looked about the size of an M-1 bullet. It was about 1/4" in diameter and dark brown. The doc said, "Well, you're next." He did the same thing to me, but nothing came out. There wasn't any wax in my ear, so I went back to the firing range. I'll never forget that wax coming out of that GI's ear.

During basic training I had a problem with my right trigger

finger. It became infected and blew up like a balloon. I had to get something done, so I went to First Aid. They looked at my finger and asked me what had happened. I said, "I don't know–it just got infected." They wiped it with some type of antiseptic and then got this long piece of wire, not quite 1/16" in diameter, stainless steel, and shoved it through my finger. I said, "Jeez!" Of course, the blood and pus came out. They told me to go back to my barracks, find an empty gallon can, wash it, add some hot water and salt, and stick my finger in it. I was off duty and spent the whole afternoon with my finger soaking. It's a wonder my finger didn't become useless. If I couldn't use it as a trigger finger, I might have been discharged. In fact, my Uncle Steve, who was to have been drafted in WWI, wasn't taken because his trigger finger was bent like a pretzel.

Jacksonville was 42 miles from Starke. After retreat on Friday, some of us would receive a pass. We would go to the ticket office to buy a ticket to get on a bus. Now this line had probably 300 or 400 GI's in it and by the time you bought your ticket, you had to get in another even longer line to get on the bus. We would arrive in Jacksonville at midnight when there was nothing for us to see or do. It was hard to find a room since the Navy and Coast Guard stations were nearby, and I believe some Marines were also stationed in town or nearby.

We had truck cabs with trailers called buses that we took to Jacksonville. When I say bus, please hear me out, these were cattle trailers with wooden seats and 2 x 4's across the outside. These were open to the elements and if it rained, we were wet. One weekend we left Jacksonville early on a Sunday afternoon to head back to camp when our bus engine just went dead. Our driver couldn't restart it. We got out to ask what was wrong, but all the driver said was that the engine had died. We had no radio, no telephone, nothin', and were out in the boondocks. He said, "I'm going to wait and see if another bus comes by, I'll tell him we're stalled." I went in to sit and wait, but it was hot with the sunshine beating down, and I fell asleep.

I woke up an hour or two later and we were still sitting there. No one had stopped by to help us.

I looked at the gas tanks. It had a gas tank on both sides behind the cab. There were a number of copper tubing gas lines, and I noticed that one copper tubing was broken in half, I guess from the vibration. I asked the driver, "Why don't you turn the pep cock to the other tank?" He did and soon we were on our way back to camp. Now, I don't know why this driver was not able to see this gas line dangling there, but somehow he should have seen it earlier.

One weekend when we were in Jacksonville we met a nice young couple who invited us to their home. We had a great time. Unfortunately, their phone number and address was lost and I was unable to contact them to thank them. It just disappeared.

On one weekend pass, we tried to hitchhike instead of taking the bus. This big Chrysler New Yorker was cruising down Highway 301. There was an old lady in the back seat and a young couple up front. I guess he was all of 15, she all of 12, and she was all over this kid while he was driving. They asked us where we were going and when we told them Jacksonville they said they were going down to the town of Maxville, I think, and would give us a ride. That young little female was all over this poor kid. We didn't know if they were brother and sister or what. The woman, their grandmother I guess, kept saying, "Now you keep an eye on the road." We couldn't wait to get the hell out of there; I didn't even know if he had a license to drive.

One weekend on a pass to Jacksonville, I stopped to get a photograph taken to send to my parents. I didn't know what was going to happen but at least if something did, then they would have a photograph of their son. I went to a studio called Bon Art Studio, and took the photograph which you see in *Figure 8*. I sent it to my mother.

Our main gate was at the town of Starke. I understand a GI was trying to get a pass to go home or some place. He was unable to get one so he pulled this trick. He went to the main gate at Starke. Both he and the MP's were inside the gate. He said, "I don't want to

Figure 8. Author photo taken at Jacksonville, Florida with K Company 263rd Regiment 66th Division. May 28, 1943.

go home, dammit, I want to stay to finish my training, I like it here." They threw him out of the gate without asking for his pass. Thinking he had a pass, he didn't want to go home.

One Friday afternoon Sgt. Jeck said "Men, I have 50 tickets for the USO tonight. I'm going to give out these tickets at 5:30 p.m. sharp." I went up to the sergeant and said, "I'm getting off KP soon, can I get a ticket?" He said, "Yes, I'll be giving them out at 5:30." Came 5:30 p.m. and I went to get a ticket, but noticed a bunch of GI's walking away with tickets in their hands. I walked up to Sgt. Jeck and asked, "Sergeant, I thought you were going to give out the tickets at 5:30?" He replied, "Well, a lot of GI's were milling around at 5:15 so I just gave the tickets out." I said, "Well, okay," and turned to walk away. He called out, "DeAngelo! Come back here." He put his fingers in his left shirt pocket to pull out a ticket, "I kept this for you." I never understood why he took a liking to me. Maybe he saw a street kid who needed a friend. I'll never forget him. I hope this book might reach him one day so he'll know how much I cared for him as a human being. He was a great sergeant and I'll tell more about him in the last chapter.

We had a GI named Newton, a crazy piano player, who tried real hard to get out of the infantry and into a band. I don't know if he was successful or not.

We GI's were never able to get a date, nothing. In Jacksonville we'd sometimes end up sleeping in a park, which was against the law, and get picked up. Then the MP's would come to get you. Then you were in trouble. Early one Saturday morning we arrived in Jacksonville and went to a hotel. The clerk said he had a room and all five of us shared it with three in the bed and two on the floor. Great sleeping quarters, right? In the closet we found a parachute, helmet and goggles–everything for a pilot. We later heard that this room was rented for months in advance by either a Navy or Army pilot, who I guess was on furlough. His room was unused for three full weeks. Whatever. The clerk rented this room everyday and, of course, pocketed the money.

In basic training we had to walk 100 miles a week and after 1500 or so miles, we were ready to be sent on our way, wherever. Every once in awhile, I ran across a friend, John DeFilippo, from my neighborhood who was also with the 66th Division, but in a sister regiment, either the 262nd or 264th. We always talked about being shanghaied. Years later I was reading a book and it mentioned Gen. Kramer as the one who shanghaied troop trains going to the Air Corps in Miami. The date was the same as when we were shanghaied for Camp Blanding.

One time, on bivouac, they marched us out in the field where we slept in pup tents to learn how to live in the field. One day we were to attack a position with live ammunition. Now, my friend

Larry was the smallest GI in my squad. They gave him a Browning Automatic Rifle (B.A.R.). This weapon weighed 21 lbs. complete. It was a sight to see him lug this weapon; they should've given it to a bigger GI. As we were moving forward, we were side by side in a line ready to fire. Some GI's were falling behind. I was in front with a couple of the other GI's when we noticed rounds flying over us. I turned around, and there was little Larry shooting the B.A.R. like mad. I said, "Jeez, we could have got killed. Larry, you're shooting at us!" He looked at me and said, "What are you GI's doing in front of me?" I said, "Don't ask me, there were a few of us in front." The line was not straight; it was zigzag. I don't know how the hell we didn't get shot or killed. In basic training we were told to hold our fire until we saw something to fire at, but when we went into combat that changed. We did a great deal of firing to keep the other guys' heads down. That way they did not know where we were and we could advance and not worry about them firing at us.

Then we had to run the Infiltration Course where we belly crawled through mud and water under barbed wire, while keeping our heads down so we wouldn't be hit by the live ammunition being fired 20 inches off the ground over our heads. One GI named DeFelice froze on the course, out of his mind with fear and too scared to go forward. Sgt. Robinson took a bayonet and crawled behind him to get him moving. Years later, I met DeFelice at the VA in New York City and I can tell you he did not want to talk about basic training at Camp Blanding Florida or the Infiltration Course.

When we were on bivouac at nights, we would hang our mess kits beside the pup tent poles. One night we heard our mess kits banging together. Wild pigs had come to our tent and were licking the mess kits! Of course, we shooed them away; we were trying to go to sleep.

During basic training, we were taught how to throw grenades and use a bayonet. I thought the bayonet lessons were pretty awful. Our bayonets were too long and heavy to be put at the end of the rifle, and I don't know why they were so long since all you needed to do was stick its cold steel of 10-12 inches into a guy. These bayonets were from World War I, and the Army later cut them down to about 10-12 inches, I believe a smart move.

It seemed as though I always ended up working in the KP for some reason. The Mess sergeant must have liked my work. I wonder if he always asked for me? Most of the GI's drew KP maybe once a month, but I think I was there every week. Our KP mess hall had unpainted pine tables and benches that weren't attached to the wooden pine floor. Our job after breakfast was to scrub them down with GI soap, rinse them down and let them dry. After lunch and dinner we'd do the same. It was a lot of work. Then we had to clean some great big pots and pans, and then the grease pit. It was a dirty job and I'd have to get up at 4 a.m. and work until 9 p.m.

I remember one time when I was at KP and I noticed two large glass jars, one was labeled peanut butter and the other was mayonnaise. I asked the Mess sergeant, "Peanut butter? What do you use it for?" He looked at me and said, "Are you kidding me?" I said, "No, I'm asking, what is it for?" So he got a slice of bread and spread peanut butter on it. "Here, eat it." I did, "Hey, that's not too bad, not bad at all." He said, "Are you kidding me, DeAngelo?" I said, "No, I grew up in an Italian neighborhood where we had no such thing as peanut butter, we used jelly or bananas." He couldn't understand it. Then I asked him what mayonnaise was for. He said, "Now don't tell me you never saw or tasted it?" I said, "That's right." So he gave me another slice of bread spread with mayonnaise. I tasted it. "Jeez, not too bad, what do you use this for?" He said, "Salad dressing." Again I said, "In my neighborhood all we have is olive oil and vinegar for salad dressing." He looked at me as though I was pulling his leg. I don't know what he thought. I had never tasted peanut butter or mayonnaise in my life until that afternoon.

A GI and I were shooting the breeze and I said, "My wife wants to divorce me since I'm not home anymore." Our Lt. Farnsworth overheard us but he didn't say anything. A couple of hours later he sent for me. He said, "DeAngelo, can I help you with your personal problem?" I said, "Well, what do you mean, Lieutenant?" He said, "Well, I heard your wife was going to divorce you because you're in the Army." I said, "Oh, Lieutenant, I'm sorry, I was just joking with that GI. I'm not married and I was just kidding with him. I understand what you're trying to do and I do appreciate it. I'm sorry." It was embarrassing to him, but I never forgot him. He was a nice Lieutenant.

When we received a pass to go outside the gate, we walked to the town of Starke. Now, the town of Starke had wooden sidewalks and every building or store had a jukebox outside. They would play "Lay That Pistol Down" or "Praise the Lord and Pass the Ammunition" or Spike Jones' "In the Fuhrer's Face." We'd go into a store to buy a bottle of beer, but I don't remember if it was 3.2 or anything higher. The people were not too friendly toward us. I guess they saw too many GI's and maybe the GI's were bothering their girlfriends or wives, so they didn't take too kindly to us.

The GI's made Starke prosperous with money coming from our GI pay. Don't forget, there were about 60,000 GI's in Camp Blanding and the money had to go someplace. I revisited Starke in 1955 and in one store I said to a girl, "I remember taking basic training here, the GI's helped Starke grow." She gave me a dirty look. It was true. Our money helped it to grow. I remember a bus driver with one arm, he drove the camp buses back and forth. I met him as a guard at Camp Blanding's main gate. I said, "I remember you driving a bus." He said, "Yeah, those were the good old days."

One nice thing for us was the mail call. When they called your name for your letters you'd look for a private place, a special place, to sit down and read your mail. It was interesting. I didn't receive much mail. My mother would write about once a week or every other week. Not much, just, "Dear Frank, everything's OK …" the same old thing, nothing much. I didn't leave a girlfriend behind to write me so it was just my mother and I corresponding. My father couldn't write, my sisters weren't letter writers, and my brother never wrote.

My mother never went into too much detail about things at home. I don't think she wanted to worry me about what was going on there. She just thought it best not to let me know too much because I had my own problems. I never told them what I was doing anyway. They knew I was not overseas, but wondered where Camp Blanding was and what I was doing. I just told them everything was OK. I didn't want to worry them either. We were training, seeing the sights, and going on weekend trips. When I did go overseas, I didn't think there was much sense in writing since the censor would cross out some words.

Our training was just about completed in thirteen weeks, and on July 10, 1943, we were told to pack up and walk to the trucks. They drove us down to our train, which took us to Camp Robinson in Little Rock, Arkansas. Our arrival was supposed to be part of a very secret move; no one was supposed to know–not even the people in Little Rock. When we arrived at Little Rock we saw a big banner that read "Welcome 66th Infantry Division." Somebody in town knew we were coming to Little Rock. We stayed in some beautiful little bungalows with six men bunks, practically right in town. They had natural gas heat. It was a nice setup, much different from Camp Blanding. I think Camp Robinson was a much older post than Camp Blanding.

Another GI and I visited Little Rock, which was just outside the main gate, one afternoon. His name was Duchon and he was from New England. We were walking, thinking about what to do, when I saw five or six girls in a group talking to one another. I went to one and tapped her on the shoulder. I asked, "May I speak to you?" She turned and said, "Yes." I asked, "Are you doing anything special today?" She replied, "No." I asked, "What movie would you like to see?" She said, "Well, I've seen the movie across the street, can we see a different one?" I replied yes. She said good-bye to her friends. Duchon, instead of asking one of the other girls for a date, started following us. I asked, "Where are you going?" He replied, "I'm going with you." I asked, "Well, why?" He replied, "Well, you got to know her while I was with you." I answered, "So what? Why don't you go back and ask one of her girlfriends? It'll make her feel better if you're with one of her girlfriends." He wouldn't go, but we went on to the movie. He drove us crazy. She told me, "Your friend is sitting on the other side of me." I looked over at him. "When are you going to leave us?" I asked. He wouldn't leave. Finally I said, "Wise up, Duchon, get out of here and get yourself a date!" He left.

After the movie we had something to eat. I said, "I'd like to see you again." She replied, "I work at the PX." I stopped by the PX a few days later; again I asked to see her. She said, "My sister and her husband want to go out for the evening. They want me to babysit so why don't you come over to help me?" I wouldn't mind doing that, after all the baby would go to sleep, her parents won't be home until midnight, and then I'd have some time alone with her. A few days later, I called her and she said, "My sister and her husband are not going out tonight, but why don't you rent a car and pick me up?" Well, renting a car in Little Rock at this time was impossible and it would cost five bucks, and that was all I had. But I did have a ruby ring my mother had given me for my 15th birthday and it was worth $15. I thought maybe I could leave the ring as a deposit and give him the $5 when I returned. But the big problem was that I didn't have a driver's license.

So, to make a long story short, I figured out what to do, phoned her and said, "I can't rent a car, they're all rented out." She replied, "Well, get a cab and come and pick me up." I called a cab and picked her up. She was about a year or year and a half older, very attractive, and she tells the cab driver, "Some friends of mine are having a party at the end of town near some motels. I don't know the motel name where they're staying, can you drive us near one?" He said, "But I don't know which motel." I said, "Who wants to go to a party? Wait a minute. Cab driver, we're getting out." It was a buck and a half, so I had $3.50 left. I asked, "Why do you want to go to a party? I want to be with you." She said, "Well, silly, I didn't want to tell the driver to take us straight to a motel. This way he would take us to a motel, thinking we were looking for a party, and then we'd get a room, just you and me." I said, "Well, why didn't you let me know what was going on?" I hailed another cab, we climbed in, and I called out, "Cabby, take us to the nearest motel." He told me, "It's gonna cost you $2.00." I said, "OK." He replied, "Also, it's gonna cost you $3.00 for me to pick you up." Now, I only had $3.50. I was wondering where I was gonna get more money. I said, "OK, take us." She didn't know how much money I had, but she pulled out a five-dollar bill out and gave it to me. She said, "Here." I said, "What's this?" She replied, "I know you GI's don't have much money; use this to pay for the motel or whatever." I said, "I'll pay you back." She said not to worry about it.

I paid the cab driver when he dropped us off at a motel. He said, "I'll pick you up in a couple of hours." I said, "Right." We got in our room and we made love twice … it was the first time for me, but I don't think it was the first time for her because she said she was married. I don't know where her husband was but I didn't know about him until we were leaving the motel. Our cab driver picked us up and took her home. He then drove me back to camp. A couple of days later I went over to the PX to see her. I tried to give her the five dollars back. She wouldn't take it. She said, "Well, I knew you might not have had enough money." I said, "I'd like to see you again." She said, "I'm married. I don't think I should." So I don't know if I satisfied her, or if she was disappointed, or if she met someone else. I have no idea. I never saw her again. But I do know that my friend Duchon was peeved at me for a long time. I didn't care, I mean he was kinda stupid. I don't know what was wrong with him. Gee whiz, guy, wake up.

One afternoon in Little Rock I met an older woman, Mrs. Lyons. She looked like she might have been a hooker but I wasn't too sure since I didn't have much female experience. We were walking down town and ran across a couple of GI's from my company who were wearing hats called Garrison hats. I said, "Hey, you're not supposed to be wearing those. You're supposed to wear the overseas ones–the ones that fold." They said, "Well, word got around that we can buy them since we've completed basic training." Every town had a military store, so I walked into the first one, found a Garrison hat for $2.75 or $3 and walked out wearing it.

While walking with Mrs. Lyons, I saw First Sgt. Jeck and his wife coming our way. He said, "Hi there, DeAngelo." I said, "Hi there, Sergeant." He said, "This is my wife, Wilma." I said, "This is Mrs. Lyons, a friend of mine." He said, "Well, have fun." Then they left.

A couple of days later Sgt. Jeck said, "DeAngelo, I want to talk to you. That was a nice lady you were with." I said, "Thank you, sir, and your wife is very attractive, Sergeant." He said, "Why were you wearing a garrison hat?" I said, "Well, I went to have a photograph taken for my mother. I picked up that hat. It belonged to the photographer, I put it on, he took the photo, I walked out with it." He said, "Goooood story, DeAngelo." My story was not true. I got rid of that hat that night after hearing later it was a no-no. Someone had told us a lie. I said, "I guess you're gonna give me some company punishment." He said, "That's right." I said, "No weekend passes." He said, "That's right." He said, "I've got something else for you." I said, "OK, I deserve it, I guess. I won't bitch about it." He said, "Good!" He said, "I'm going away on furlough for a month and Sgt. Robinson will give you your punishment with directions from me." The day he took his furlough, Sgt. Robinson said, "DeAngelo, here's your duty. You will take care of the officers' latrine and you won't have any passes for four weeks until First Sergeant comes back." The latrine was for four offices. It had a four man stall and sometimes four or six officers used the latrine.

My job was to get breakfast first, get there early in the morning and clean up, make sure there was paper, soap, razor blades picked up, and stock what was needed. Then I had to be back after lunch and clean up again. After supper I had to clean again and make sure it was ready for the next morning. Of course, I had breakfast, lunch and supper earlier than anyone else and I was going to town everyday.

Basic Training

I had asked Lt. Young, "I've finished with my duty, do you mind giving me a pass?" I received a pass every day for about a month. It was great duty, I'm telling you, no basic training, nothing. That was my punishment, that was it. Nobody could touch me, I came and went whenever I wanted. When First Sgt. Jeck returned, he asked, "Well, DeAngelo, did you learn your lesson?" I said, "Sergeant, it was the greatest company punishment I've ever had. Anytime you want to give me that kind of duty, please do." He was looking at me with a funny look on his face. I asked, "Is that all, Sergeant?" He said, "Yes, that's all DeAngelo." I don't know if he knew what I was talking about. I never did tell him I was in town every day.

There wasn't much training to do at Camp Robinson. I feel it was a place for us to lay over for a while until they told us where we were going. One day we were told, "Your names will be called to be transferred. You will be leaving the 66th Division and going to an eastern location." We were to take a furlough and when we returned we would be given the details. I had a fifteen-day furlough, but by the time I received my shots, I had fewer days and headed to New York.

I visited my parents. We lived in an Italian neighborhood known as Little Italy on the Lower East Side. My neighborhood had a lot of Italian restaurants. I was walking one night and I noticed one restaurant that was very crowded. When I looked in, I saw Tommy Dorsey drinking. He was having a good time with his lovely wife, Pat Dane, a model. I'll never forget her. She had her blonde hair in a bun and was a very attractive lady. As I was in uniform, the owner told the doorman to let the soldier come in. But before I went in, two girls I knew asked me if I could get Dorsey's autograph. "I will ask him," I said. I walked directly over to where he was sitting and asked, "Mr. Dorsey, would it be possible for you to give me your autograph?" He said, "No problem at all, young man." He was kind and nice, he had some drinks, and I can't say anything bad about him. I'll never forget him with his lovely wife standing close by.

I left New York City a day early. My father came with me to Grand Central Station. I kissed him, told him I loved him. I said, "I'm going overseas, I won't see you for a long time." He cried. I cried. That was my life in the Army.

On the way back to Little Rock, I met a nice lady named Mrs. Kintz with her daughter, Peggy. She and her dad worked for the Pennsylvania Railroad. Mrs. Kintz said if I ever found myself in Terre Haute, Indiana, I should look them up. I said I would and got their address. Then I left to change trains since I was heading south back to camp.

A few days after I returned from furlough, our names were called to be shipped to an eastern location. I was called with my buddies Andrew and Jimmy, but Larry was not. He went to our sergeant and asked, "Is my name on the list?" The sergeant said, "No." He asked, "Well, I want to go with these GI's, would you please put my name down so I can go with them?" The sergeant looked at him, "Are you sure?" He replied, "Yeah, they're my friends, I want to go overseas with them." In a later chapter you will understand why I have mentioned Larry's name. When I heard his request, I said, "Larry, you're crazy. Just play it, see what happens." I think I told him that you are not ever to volunteer in the Army. He was determined to go with us, wherever we were going, as friends. I appreciated it and I liked him for sticking with us.

We were told to be ready at any time to pack everything we had. We'd be picked up by our trucks in front of our company CP, and we were not to leave anything behind. We jumped on our trucks. Next we were on a train to Ft. Mead, Maryland. We arrived Sept. 24, 1943.

We moved into barracks again and we were getting more shots, etc. Later we were ordered to go to a huge Quartermaster building and leave everything that was not GI issue, which meant socks, t-shirts, shorts, sweaters, handkerchiefs, belts, you name it. There were big piles of clothing that had been purchased through the PX and now had to leave behind.

Basic Training

Before I went into the Army I met a girl on the New York subway who lived in Baltimore, Maryland. Her name was Janice Kling. I wrote to tell her I was in Camp Blanding. She wrote back with her photograph. I placed it in a frame in my barracks. We exchanged a few letters, not much. I didn't hear from her for a long time. I did see her once when we were sent to Ft. Mead, Maryland, before going to Newport News, Virginia, for overseas duty. We just talked on a Sunday, not much of anything went on.

They issued us everything we would need except rifles. They gave us our A and B barracks bags, which had a rope at the top so they could be tied together. These bags were filled and tremendously heavy. I saw a lot of GI's tie both ends together so they could swing them over their shoulders. They would go over backwards with them. Poor Larry, who was a little guy, had trouble carrying his bags. The GI barracks bags of today have a handle on the side to make them easier to pick up and carry. Everyone going overseas was issued a mattress cover; funny, we didn't have a bunk to sleep on, so why the mattress cover? We were told later in Africa that they were used to bury our GI's in. Some barracks bags were sold to the Arabs. They would cut two holes at the bottom and place their legs inside each and were used as their pants. The rope would hold them up. Thousands of both were stored at the Quartermaster in Africa.

I called Janice to say good-bye and asked her to write. I told her we were leaving and I would write her. We did for a while. We didn't stay long at Ft. Mead. We left for Newport News, Virginia, on October 4, 1943, to board the troop ship that would take us overseas.

Chapter Three

Africa

Figure 9. Our ship was named the *Empress of Scotland* but at one time it was named the *Empress of Japan*. She was built in 1930 in Scotland and was 666 feet long. Her beam was 83.8 feet. Her speed was 22 knots, her radius 14,000 miles. Propulsion was by turbine engines and she carried 530 passengers, with a cargo hold of 400,000 cu. ft.

This ship holds a record for crossing the Pacific in 8 days and 6 hours so she was very fast. It was one large WWII troop ship. The outcome of the ship is unknown. I believe this ship had a 5" naval gun and was crewed by English sailors. We had about 5,000 GI's

Figure 9. The ship the author sailed on, "The Empress of Scotland", to Casablanca, North Africa. On October 15, 1943 we docked.

aboard her. I didn't know if they were all from my regiment, I had no idea. It seems my friends were all over the ship because of our sleeping quarters. This ship sailed overseas without an escort of any kind. We had blimps flying out many miles offshore, later returning. We were told this ship was able to run from any submarine and it zigzagged all the way across the Atlantic Ocean.

Many GI's were issued bunks that pulled down from the wall. I ended up, believe it or not, sleeping in a hammock in the mess hall. I don't know how the heck I got this assignment. When they told us to get up to set up for breakfast, we couldn't go back to take a nap or anything. The other guys who had bunks would awake, have breakfast, then go back to their bunks and stay all day long. I had to find someplace to stay. I don't know where I stayed but I couldn't be in the mess hall sleeping or sitting around because they were always preparing or serving breakfast, lunch and supper.

Breakfast was fish and raisins and hot tea. We were told later that our government supplied the food for us GI's. I heard rumors that the ship's English sailors made use of our rations and that we were given theirs. If this is true, that was bad to hear. I don't remember eating anything but British rations. The deck of the mess hall was steel, and every morning we had to take our hammocks down, roll them up and put them in a corner. Our barracks bags were below the hold where we couldn't get to them. We had a PX where we could buy candy, oranges, apples and bananas until they disappeared. We had a pretty good assortment of things to purchase for a while. Like I said, British food was not what we GI's liked. It was frustrating to know they were eating our rations, while we were eating theirs. We were later told that our government paid England for our trip to Africa.

One night, while laying in my hammock, I heard a GI near me giggling with someone else. I turned around and saw this GI trying to cut my hammock rope with his very dull mess kit knife. I looked at him and yelled, "What are you doing?" His reply, "I thought I'd have some fun with you." I said, "Let me tell you something, if you cut my rope and let me fall and hit my head on the steel deck, I'm gonna kill you." He looked at me and said, "You won't kill me." I said, "No!?" I grabbed my mess kit knife and held it out saying, "You do that one more time ... " He was close by me in his own hammock and I could have shoved my knife right through his hammock's bottom into his back. "Do you understand what I'm saying?" He looked afraid. I don't know who the hell this GI was, but he was a complete idiot and quickly learned that I was very serious about killing him. That was the end of that particular incident.

We were given life preservers. Now this was a big joke because our life preservers were made from a material called Kopeck. The tag on the life preserver read: "24 hours only." That meant that it would only float for 24 hours and after that it would become waterlogged. I thought, "We're out on the ocean alone. Who's going to come and rescue us? It's going to take days to get to us, if there is any ship around." Meanwhile, British sailors were walking around with large cork life preservers. They could last for about 20 years in the water. Of course, they would just be bones by then but you could stay afloat with cork life preservers forever. Here we had Kopeck. Good for only 24 hours. It was kind of scary, especially since I couldn't swim, plus others I am sure.

We still had no idea where we were going. We knew we were sailing east, always zig zagging, and we heard gunfire on the aft deck a couple of times. They said it was a submarine but I think it was an exercise test to practice with the guns and to get the crew trained. I think it must have been S.O.P.

On October 15, 1943, we docked at Casablanca, Africa. It was strange being in another part of the world. We disembarked, and went to pick up our A & B bags. We had struggled with these two bags since Ft. Mead. They were so heavy and we had dragged them everywhere, including up and down the gangplank. Then we were trucked to our bivouac area at Camp Don B. Passage, where we were again put in six-men pyramid tents.

In Casablanca, we were told not to go to the Casbah. Some of us went into a bar. I guess I had been drinking a lot of beer and I asked the owner where the men's room was. He pointed it out to me. I walked into the bathroom; there was no commode, not even a stall where you could pee. I thought, I'm in the wrong place. I walked out and asked him again where the men's room was. He pointed to the door where I had just been and said, "There." So I went back inside, and finally noticed a water trough down on the front wall with water running from left to right. (I don't know where it ended up …) There were two sets of footpads made out of marble. With your back to the wall and your pants down, you had to put your right foot over one foot pad and the left foot over the other foot pad and squat. This method went back to the Romans. You squatted down to do number two and hoped it landed in the water to be carried off. I remember thinking that the Roman engineers who had designed this must have examined an awful lot of men to find out what their dimension was for number two to go straight down in the middle of this trough, rather than land elsewhere. My God! I couldn't believe I was this 19-year-old kid, straight from a big city with toilets, and now was standing or squatting down over a trough.

In North Africa we heard two names, one was "Dirty Gerty from Bizerte" and the other was "Moroccan Rot." I think Gerty was the name given to a women who went on the air for Germany and spouted propaganda to our GI's in between playing some great American band songs. The other, I assume, was for some kind of skin condition.

Many of the GI's chewed tobacco. We had a PX, and since I wanted to know what it tasted like, I purchased a package of Beechwood Chewing Tobacco. I put a big hunk in my mouth and started to chew. A friend told me to not to swallow the spit, it would make me sick. Here I was, chewing tobacco and spitting pretty good each time. A little later, I was on my way to the latrine which was about three or four hundred feet away from our bivouac area. I was walking pretty fast, chewing and spitting, when I realized that diarrhea was about to hit me. I decided I better pick up my pace and get to the latrine before I had an accident. In my hurry I stubbed my foot and tripped. I swallowed the whole wad of tobacco, spit and all. By that time I was sitting on the latrine and vomiting from one end and had diarrhea from the other end. A GI came in and said, "Boy, you have turned green!" I said, "Tell me about it." I stayed sitting until my upset stomach and diarrhea ceased. I got myself out of there. As I was walking back I handed the whole package of Beechwood Chewing tobacco to a passing GI. I never tried it again.

I had Janice's picture in a nice frame. I walked into my tent, her picture was there but my frame was gone. Some GI made off with it. I was upset about it, but what could I do? I didn't know if it was a GI in my tent or someone else who stole it.

There wasn't much to do. At night we went to outdoor movies, where we sat on a bench or in our helmets. There were officers and nurses. Of course, the nurses and officers always sat in front of us GI's. We were in the rear. When the movie was not on the screen some GI's would blow up condoms and flick them in the air, and some others would yell, "Ack, ack!" and the GI's would flip their cigarette butts and try to hit them. The nurses would get to giggling. The male officers never said anything to us, I guess they wanted us to enjoy ourselves. They figured that in a short time we would be in combat and in a great deal of trouble.

The next day I noticed an American half-track M5 running up and down the side of a small hill. I wondered what the heck the driver was trying to do. I saw him moving this way and that way. Then I noticed a little Arab kid about 6 years old being chased by this half-track. I don't know if this kid did something or not–he might have been caught stealing–or if the driver was drunk, but he was trying to truly run him down. He never did get the boy, who was better at dodging the half-track than the driver was at running him down.

At Camp Don B. Passage, I noticed our Jeeps and other vehicles had a steel V-shape approximately five feet high that was mounted

Africa

on the front bumper with a small "v" cut at the top, in front, to catch a thin music wire and cut it. This was done as a safety measure so as not to cut off the driver's head as the vehicles raced forward with the windshield down.

Not many people know this, but in Africa during the day the temperatures can get high, but at night it could get down to freezing. Many times we left water in our canteen cups and found it frozen by morning. This was strange to us. Some GI's knew how to ride horses. They rode Arabian horses and galloped like the dickens in front of us. Where they got these horses I have no idea. Either they paid some Arab, or maybe they stole them.

One day, a GI said, "Hey, some Arabs on the other side of the fence have some wine, figs and girls." I said, "Well, you know, I don't think we should go over there, the MP's will pick us up and put us in the stockade." He said, "Oh, don't worry about it, we can get outta there before the MP's know about it."

A bunch of us went with him. Jimmy was with me, but I don't remember where Larry and Andy were at the time. We seemed to be broken up for some reason. We climbed over the fence and sat on a wooden bench under a fig tree. The Arab would give us a half a canteen cup of wine for 25¢ or 50¢, I don't remember. After we drank the wine it would leave a mark inside the canteen cup. He would refill it to the mark left etched into the aluminum the first time wine was put in. Then another Arab came by and asked me if I would like a woman. I said, "No." He said he had two daughters. I looked at them and they had this black mark on their foreheads. I think when they're born they cut it open and rub some black stuff in it, I don't know what it was. They were kinda cute young girls; I think one was about 15, and the other about 16. Both of them were wearing a top section of our long johns, like a sweatshirt. That was it. It hung just below their privates, although we couldn't see anything we visualized what was there. I was not thinking about having sex with either one.

Then Jimmy walked over and said, "You know, I like that girl there. I want to have sex with her." I said, "Well, go ahead." "Well, I need you to help me," he replied. "What do you mean you need me to help you? Go over there and give her $2 and have her and do what you want to do." He said, "Do me a favor." I said, "What?" He said, "While she's down on the ground and I'm on top, will you sit next to me to make sure she doesn't pull a knife on me and stab me in the back?" I said, "She's not gonna do that; there are too many GI's around here." He said, "Well, I won't do it unless you sit there and watch me." I said, "Jimmy, I don't want to watch you do it." He said, "Please, DeAngelo." I said, "OK." So here I am, sitting next to them while Jimmy's going to town with this girl. He looked at me and asked, "Is she pulling a knife on me?" I replied, "No Jimmy, just finish and let's get outta here." Soon he finished what he was doing and we walked away.

While we were walking around, I ran across a GI I didn't know and he asked me, "Are you GI's having a good time." I replied, "Well, yeah." He said we shouldn't stay too long since the MP's were going to raid this place in about half an hour. I asked him how he knew and he said, "Because I'm an MP. You GI's better get outta here, I'm getting outta here myself." I got a hold of a couple of my friends and said, "Let's get outta here now. I've got a hold of some information, this place is gonna be raided by the MP's." Well, nobody wanted to go with me. Soon I noticed some headlights down in a little valley. They drove in fast, then turned the lights off. I felt sure it was the MP's and I quickly left, heading in another direction.

I went back to my tent and fell asleep. About 2 o'clock in the morning, I heard a commotion. Some GI's were caught by the MP's. The MP's took them to a first aid station where they were treated for sexually transmitted diseases. Those GI's were very upset about being caught. For disobeying orders, they were told to be up at 4 or 5 o'clock in the morning with full field pack to march 20 miles. A lieutenant on horseback led the 15-20 GI's as they marched 10 miles one way and 10 miles back. When they returned, they were exhausted since they hadn't been training for the last two months. Pfc. Daniels'

Africa

eyes were bloodshot as he came into our tent later that morning around 10 a.m.

From then on we kept our noses clean. We were told that Gen. Patton was very strict with GI's. He had been assigned to a very lax outfit and decided to make rules that would apply to all GI's overseas. He wanted all buttons to be buttoned, uniforms clean, ties to be worn properly, shoes polished, and no shoelaces left untied. If an MP found a shoelace untied and a button undone, you'd be fined $50 for each infraction. We made sure all were in order.

One day a GI walked by carrying a GI blanket over his shoulder, like an Indian in New Mexico. He found a spot, spread the blanket on the ground, got a pair of dice, and started throwing them. Soon there were about 20 GI's all around the blanket betting. Of course, I bet and lost $50. That was the end of my gambling experience. I imagine this GI was a professional, one of many who sent home thousands and thousands of dollars in winnings each month. We had a lot of money and no place to spend it. Later, these GI's were stopped from sending that kind of money home.

"DeAngelo! You'll be on guard duty tonight, see the sergeant of the guard at 5 p.m. to pick up your weapon." At 5 p.m. I reported to the sergeant, who handed me my weapon–a tent stick post about 20" long, 2" in diameter, and made out of oak. It was sharp on one end so it could be shoved into the ground and it had a slot at the other end so you could tie a tent's rope on it. I asked, "What is this, a joke?" He said, "It's your weapon." I said, "My weapon!" He said, "Yes, keep your eyes open; these Arabs have a tendency to climb over these three fences." Now the fences were no more than three feet high and were one behind the other. He said, "They'll climb over these fences to come in and cut your throat, just so they can steal your watch and money." I said, "You want me to stand out there tonight with this piece of wood to protect myself?" He said, "That's what we do all the time."

I don't know if this was a joke or if it was to teach us to stay alert when we were standing guard duty in the future. So all night long, Pfc. DeAngelo did not close his eyes. Every time I saw something moving out of the corner of my eye, I made sure it wasn't somebody climbing over one of the fences. It was kinda lonely being by myself; no one came by to check if I was standing or sleeping or what. When morning came I was relieved, went to my tent and slept all afternoon, getting up for supper.

One morning about 200 of us GI's were told to meet at a cross road. We were instructed to be dressed with field jackets, helmet liners, and ammo belts with no rounds – that was it. This was to be a speed march. The purpose of it was to train us for physical condition and stamina. It also was a test to determine a standard of capability. As a minimum standard each officer and GI must march five miles in one hour twice a week, and eight miles in two hours each week. Our results would be reported to a division commander. That morning we had to take 104 steps, each 30 inches long, per minute at three miles per hour. Then we went to 123 steps, each 34 inches long, per minute at four miles per hour. Then they increased it to 146 steps, 36 inches long, per minute at five miles per hour.

We had to walk three minutes at that pace, followed by one minute at a normal walking rate. After five miles, the ones who returned to the starting line had their names taken. I think out of the 200 about 75 or 105 names were taken. I was one whose name was taken. It didn't bother me, I enjoyed walking fast as a kid. We learned this march was called the "Truscott Trot." Now, Gen. Truscott was the commander of the 3rd Infantry Division. He was the one in the movie *Patton* who told Gen. Patton he was going to destroy the best division the Army had overseas–his division, the 3rd Infantry Division

I was told Gen. Truscott had been instrumental in training commandos and Rangers in England. He performed with the Canadians and British commandos. He had a bunch of GI's, called Darby's Rangers, training with those commandos. Col. Darby was in charge of that Ranger Regiment. He worked with Truscott and Truscott felt there was a big job ahead if we were going to have GI's who were capable of being on the move for long periods of time and who were able to do combat when the time came. His theory and practice are well known now. Our training really paid off when we were in combat. Sometimes we had to walk 40 miles, fight the enemy, and then, the next day, walk another 40 miles. His theory about us being able to do this was outstanding for us GI's and we proved it many times in combat. The training did a lot for us GI's.

We were always walking; all the time it was walk, walk, walk, and we seldom took a truck to get where we were going. We were in Casablanca for about two weeks. I always used to say I was looking for Rick's Place and friends would ask me – "who?" I'd say, "I'm looking for Humphrey Bogart's place." Two months later, "our" Humphrey Bogart and his wife, actress Mayo Methot, paid us a visit at the town of Caserta, Italy, in December 1943, and both were fighting. I understand they were called the "Battling Bogarts," but I was only kidding in seeing his place called "Rick's", if there was one in Casablanca. Again we were told to stay out of the Casbah because a lot of GI's were getting beat up there. We were informed that some Arabs would cut off a GI's penis and testicles and stick them in his mouth and sew it up. I don't know if this was true or not, but we were ordered to stay out. The Arabs didn't like the American GI's messing around with their women, I guess. I didn't go there period.

In one incident someone booby-trapped the spigot of a barrel of wine. I don't know if any GI's were killed, but that was a hell of a thing to do … booby-trap a barrel of wine. It didn't happen to us, but it got around that this did happen. I think it happened when the first GI's landed in North Africa.

One sergeant told us that if we saw a German weapon on the ground, we should not pick it up since it might be booby trapped. The Germans were known to do this. I don't know if this is true or not, but we were told that one day a sergeant was marching with his men when they came across a German weapon on the ground. He told a GI to find a string, which he tied to the gun. The sergeant jumped into a foxhole, to pull the string. It turned out that the weapon wasn't booby trapped, but the foxhole was. The Germans did a lot of crazy things our GI's didn't know about. Eventually these findings did wise up our GI's in Africa, Sicily and Italy. We passed all we learned to our GI's in England long before going into combat at Normandy.

We were now getting ready to move out. Remember those two big barracks bags, A and B? OK. We had struggled with these suckers from Ft. Mead to Newport News—dragging them on the ship, off the ship, down to the trucks, hoisting them on the trucks, and taking them to where we were staying. Well, now we were told we had to give up all our gear so the only thing we were left with was what we were wearing. Our A and B bags were now empty. I felt they used us as longshoremen to move this gear overseas for the quartermasters. The barracks bags had our names on them. Mine said Pfc. Frank T. DeAngelo and had my serial number on each, 32881054, so they had to go with us. Soon we boarded our trains. Our boxcars were called 38-40 and 8, which came from World War I and was supposed to mean something like 38-40 men and 8 horses. There was no place to sit so we all sat on the steel floor. There was a big Lyster bag hanging from the ceiling which was full of drinking water. Every time the train moved this bag would swing back and forth and if it was filled to the top it would overflow and we'd be sitting on a wet floor. It was a long train ride and, often, a wet one at that.

From Casablanca we were going to Bizerte. Our train took five days and nights to cross North Africa. We had to pass through some long tunnels along the way. The first time we went through one the smoke from the coal-burning engine was thick and black. We were covered with soot, and spitting coal dust so we wouldn't breathe in the cinders again. We put on our gas masks when we went into the next tunnel. It was a terrible situation. All day it was cold. When it rained we were totally open to the elements and would be cold and wet and completely miserable day and night. I can assure you, prisoners who were captured and shipped to the United States had luxury train rides, we did not.

Africa

Every once in a while we would stop for what was called a piss call. There were no facilities on the train and at the town of Sale we got off for the call. One day we came across a bunch of American Sherman tanks at Oujda. They had British insignias on them and were in a fenced area. We snuck over. I climbed in one and saw a compass. Well, I love instruments, so I pulled one out and carried it with me. I put it on the train's platform to see which way the train was going. Of course, the train was always going east, but it gave us something to talk about..

One afternoon we stopped at Mostaganem next to a creek that really wasn't much of a creek. We met some Arabs who had chickens for sale. One GI bought a live chicken and said he was going to kill it, cook it and eat it, but he didn't know how to wring its neck. Another GI came along, grabbed a hold of the chicken's neck and spun it around. The next thing you know, he held the head in his hand and the chicken went up in the air and fell into the creek. The GI who had bought the chicken went into the creek, picked it up and started taking its feathers off. He then started a fire, put some creek water in his helmet and placed it on the fire. I thought he was crazy. He didn't know if the water was bad or if the chicken was sick. I don't remember if he gutted the chicken, but he cooked it in his helmet for a long time. A couple of hours later, he tried to eat it but the train whistle blew and we had to get aboard. I believe his chicken was left there, but he took his burnt helmet.

We continued going east through North Africa to Algiers and on to the town of Bizerte, where we were ordered to jump off. We GI's hung around camp. We didn't do much of anything. I guess they were trying to figure out where we were going to go next. Then one day we were ordered to be down at the pier and ready to leave within the hour. But you've heard the old saying, "Hurry up and wait." Well, that's what we GI's did. We marched to the pier where the ships were docked. They were flat-bottomed (number 339) LCI's, "Landing Craft Infantry." We waited and waited. It started raining. For three or four hours, we were sitting on an open pier on our helmets, with rain coming down. The LCI was standing by. When we were finally ordered to load up, we were all soaked, drenched, and with no way of changing clothes. We wondered why we did not go aboard and get out of the rain sooner. My bunk was nearest to the floor, and there were three bunks above me. In the top bunk was a GI named Alex DeAngelico. The next bunk down was a GI named Ed Dannic. I don't remember the name of the guy who was right above me. The fumes of the diesel engine were strong, it was musty and uncomfortable, the weather was storming badly and the LCI's didn't ride very well in rough water.

DeAngelico became sick and called out to me. I stuck my head out to see what he wanted and that's when he upchucked. I pulled my head back just in time. I said, "What the hell is wrong with you, you're going to upchuck and you call me!" He said, "Umm, well, it came up unexpected, I'm really sick." I didn't get sick, but, boy, was he sick. I don't recall if Dannic became sick, but many GI's were. The LCI diesel fumes and heat were getting to us. We sailed across the rough Mediterranean Sea and disembarked at the town of Naples, Italy, on October 30, 1943.

Chapter Four

Italy

From Naples we were taken to Caserta. Caserta was where the Fifth Army Headquarters was located. We were told it was a King's palace. We stayed in pyramid tents inside a racetrack. In a day or two our names were called and we were ordered to be ready to leave. We weren't waiting long when the Fifth Army trucks came. We jumped on and I asked the driver where we were going. He answered, "You're going to the Third Infantry Division, 30th Regiment. From there I don't know where you'll be going, you'll be assigned to different companies." He said it was a good outfit and a short time later he dropped us off at the 30th Regiment. There we were given our battalion, company, platoon, and squad assignments.

I had been assigned to 30th Infantry Regiment, 3rd Battalion, K Company, 3rd Platoon, First Squad on November 2, 1943. When I joined K Company, Captain M.B. Edrich, Jr. was the Company Commander and Lieutenant Jack McClintock was the Executive Officer. About ten weeks later Lt. McClintock was riding a motorcycle when he hit a mine and was killed on Anzio.

Our six-men pyramid tents were near the road. Since we were replacements, many looked down on us. Soon I was told to pitch my pup tent up on the side of a hill about 50-60 feet from the road behind our large pyramid tents. Why were we not in the pyramid tents?

K Company had just came off the line where they had been in combat on Mount Rotundo and experienced a lot of hard fighting. They had mules to bring food and water up the slick and slimy mountain trails and bring the wounded back down on stretchers.

We were told that many GI's who were wounded in the butt died or some bled to death by the time they were brought down to the medics. That was bad news to hear and we thought about it.

The name of the town was Pietravairano, which we found very hard to pronounce. We were not in town; we were on the outskirts on the side of the hill. *Figure 10* shows a picture of our Jeep in mud on a road where we were bivouacked. *Figure 11* shows a dog named Chip, who was attached to our nearby sister company, I Company. He was one of two dogs (the other's name was Pal). Chip was awarded a Purple Heart for the wounds he suffered in combat. He was the only dog known to have captured the enemy by the throat in Sicily. When his original handler, Pfc. John P. Rowell, was wounded, Chip was assigned to another GI. I was trying to pet Chip one day and his handler said, "Don't pet him because he is a very vicious dog." He was a German Shepherd. I do not know if he was vicious. I therefore

Figure 10. With K Company at Pietravairano, Italy with 30th Regiment, 3rd Division with lots of mud. November 18, 1943.

Italy

didn't try to pet him. I don't know what happened to Chip or Pal, but I remember Chip was very obedient to his master. His Purple Heart was taken back.

Many times children would come around with empty gallon cans to collect our uneaten food. It did not matter what was placed in these cans, they would take it and eat it. Each GI would put something in because it was the thing to do to help these children. It did not matter what town we were in, hunger was all around us.

It had been raining for days and I was soaked and cold. I

Figure 11. The dog "Chip", assigned to L Company 30th Regiment of the 3rd Division at Pietravairano, Italy. November 19, 1943.

crawled into my pup tent to sleep and about five minutes later when a GI came up from the 3rd Platoon. He told me my squad sergeant wanted to see me down by the road. I walked down to his tent and found my sergeant and some other GI's sitting on a blanket writing or reading. They had some candles lit and a small fire going to try to keep the dampness out. Then my sergeant told me to go down to the side of the road to get some firewood and put it outside his tent. I went down, picked up the wood, and brought it up to his tent as ordered. I wondered why he had sent someone up the hill to get me specifically when he could have easily gotten the GI who came to my tent to fetch the wood. He was some nut, a buck sergeant from Eerie, Pennsylvania. I don't know why he had hard nuts for me. I didn't know him and he didn't know me, but he must have seen something in me that he didn't like and that was it. Pfc. Fox was reading a letter. "Hey, I want you GI's to hear this letter from my wife. I haven't seen her for well over a year and I want you to know that I'm the father of a baby boy born last month."

After he read her letter to us, we looked at each other, knowing he couldn't possibly be the father of the baby. But he just kept saying, "Imagine, I've got a little boy! He was so excited but obviously not thinking clearly. I guess war does things to people. More about Fox later in another chapter.

Figure 12 shows a bazooka that I was issued, called an M-1 of 2.36 diameter rocket. I became known as the "bazooka man." I fired it a few times for practice.

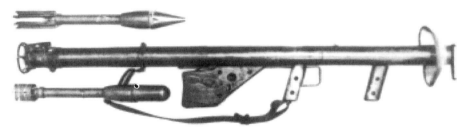

Figure 12. At Pietravairano, Italy with K Company, 30th Regiment, 3rd Division. I was given the above Bazooka, a new weapon, and fired it in the large field at Pietravairano.

Figure 13 shows us in a field, I don't know which side, but I am one of the GI's shown doing close order drill. This was a large field where we did our training exercises and where I learned to shoot a bazooka. Sometimes live ammunition was used to let the new

Figure 13. Our training field at Pietravairano, Italy on November 21, 1943. The author was marching when photo was taken.

Italy

replacements feel and hear what real combat was like. A live 60mm mortar round fell short and one of the GI's right in front of me was wounded when a piece of shrapnel hit his chest. I don't know how seriously he was injured, but do know that he didn't come back to our area or outfit.

As part of our training some GI's also fired German-captured weapons to give us an idea what these sounded like in combat. One night we were firing our weapons; some GI's were using live German and American ammunition and firing into the ground to keep the slugs from flying around, while others were shooting blanks. An Italian farmer, drunk, happy and singing a song, showed up and when the shooting started he fell to his knees, crying, shaking and praying. "Please help me," he begged, thinking he was caught between the German and American troops. We told him we were only training and he finally calmed down and ran off.

We were informed the Goumier (Arabs) from French Morocco would go on night patrol to seek Germans. If they found any they would kill them and cut off only their left ears. They would collect 50 cents per ear from the French government. We know of one night when these Goumier had found three Germans asleep side by side. One on each side had their necks cut; both had their left ear cut off. The one sleeping in the middle was left alone. I often wonder what happened when he tried to wake his friends to say good morning. He probably wasn't much use to his outfit.

These same Goumier would feel our leggings when we were on guard duty at night and once they felt our leggings they went on their way. They knew we were GI's. These Goumier travelled with their families and some goats. They had special goat food cooked for them. No matter how cold it was we saw some taking baths outdoors.

The infantry doesn't take many showers during combat. If we took a shower twice a year we were lucky. I don't know how we didn't smell. Our mothers always told us to wear clean underwear— if they only knew. On November 23 or 24, 1943, near the town of

Pietravairano we were ordered to take showers. Our outdoor showers were three or four miles down the road, always walking to the Trustcott Trot. There were long poles stuck in the ground with canvas barriers tied all around to keep the cold wind from blowing all over us. We took our clothes off, placed them in a big pile and then walked to the showers. We were allowed one minute to wash down, one minute to soap up, and only one minute to rinse. Of course the wind was cold on our wet, nude bodies. We received new socks, rebuilt boots (if needed), OD pants and OD shirts, long johns, field jackets, everything we needed. It may have been reissued clothing but it was all cleaned and pressed. Having showers and with clean clothes, we marched again at a Trustcott Trot pace back to our tents. It's amazing we didn't catch pneumonia.

We were told the Rapido River was for us to cross. Our training was done on the Volturno River. This was a fast running river, as I understand, about 16 miles per hour. We had to go across this river and move in from there. We took a few days of training. Some GI's swam across this river with a light rope. When they swam to the other side they would pull in this light rope that was attached to a heavier rope. However, in training one or two GI's had drowned. I guess they weren't strong swimmers. It was a shock to have GI's die in training. But these things did happen. Then two or three days later we received new orders for amphibious training. The river crossing was cancelled. Amphibious training was completely different. After dinner we marched down to Naples and boarded our LCI's (number 219). We stayed on them until midnight or one a.m., then our LCI would sail out, turn around and head toward shore. This was during mid-December 1943 and early January 1944. We were told the 36th Infantry Division took over our training for the crossing of the Rapido River.

Then we walked down a ramp, one on each side of our LCI. The ramps extended into the water, with two pontoons on each ramp. We walked into the water and onto the beach. The purpose of these flat bottomed LCI's was to get us as close as possible to the beach so we wouldn't drown while carrying all our gear, ammunition, mortars and guns. (We had life preservers which were pretty useless since they couldn't hold us up with all the equipment we had on us.) We usually walked down in water up to our knees, but occasionally as high as our chests. I don't know if the Navy or Coast Guard operated these LCI's. They never ran the LCI's up onto shore because they would have to pull themselves off if they got stuck. After we hit the beach, we walked 15 miles inland, wet. We heard water in our shoes going, squish, squish, squish. Plus it was cold at 3 or 4 a.m. in the morning. We walked through some farmlands and heard dogs barking. We came upon apple orchards with piles of apples on the ground and took some to eat along the way. At times a farmer, not knowing what was going on, fired his rifle into the air to scare us away, HA! Again, we wondered why we did not get pneumonia.

When we arrived at our destination, our trucks were waiting for us. The heat from our bodies had finally dried us, and we got onto the trucks and rode to our company area to have breakfast. Then we slept until that evening. Whoever was up had supper and then we repeated the same drill. This training went on for about 7-10 days. The Navy or Coast Guard on these LCI's had gasoline stoves on deck, on which they placed two big garbage cans filled with C-rations. They filled our canteen cups with Navy coffee and sometimes the GI's would buy a ham sandwich from them for about $1.50. Some of our GI's had captured pistols like P-38's, Germany's newest first line automatic, as well as some old Lugars. The P-38 sold for $75 and the Lugar for $100. We replacements did not have any to sell.

We had Thanksgiving, Christmas and New Year's Eve dinners near Pietravairano. Then on January 1, 1944, a big storm came up and blew our tents down. We were ordered to disassemble and pack everything up fast since we would be moving out as soon as possible. We dug a big hole and buried what we couldn't carry. I'm sure there was an awful lot of ammunition, grenades and other things we couldn't take with us. I'm sure it wasn't planned. We were going to another bivouacked area for additional training. There we received other new replacements to work with as a team. It was said it was the worst storm in Italy within the past 50 years. It was really bad–a terrible situation. We were wearing our raincoats over our overcoats, that's how cold and miserable that day was. Our trucks came for us. These trucks were always open, but in movies they are seen covered with a tarpaulin to protect the GI's from rain, etc. We jumped onto these open trucks, all standing up, and moved to a new location where we continued training for an additional few days at Mad di Quarto. Finally, some days later, we were ordered to be ready to board our LCI's (number 468) for a landing, but were not told where the landing was going to take place. After we boarded we were taken offshore to anchor for a day or two until D-Day.

We were told that the 509th Regiment paratroopers would jump inland behind the beach. They would fly over the area and drop, then wait for us to move off the beach. A paratrooper came aboard each LCI to show us what a paratrooper looked like. Unfortunately, the German paratroopers' (Fallschirmjager) uniforms looked very similar to ours. Now going back a few months, our Air Corps lost 24 transports with paratroopers when our Navy and Army personnel shot them down around Sicily. I heard that the hour our C-47's were supposed to fly over was changed and they arrived too early; everybody thought they were German planes and shot them down. These C-47's were fully loaded with paratroopers. It was very bad; we lost a lot of men for no reason at all. This paratrooper on our LCI told us a password, etc. to be used upon landing. Then, at the last minute, we were told our paratroopers would not be dropped. We didn't know why–maybe there was a change, maybe they didn't have enough paratroopers because of the last incident over Sicily. That was my thinking.

Chapter Five

Anzio

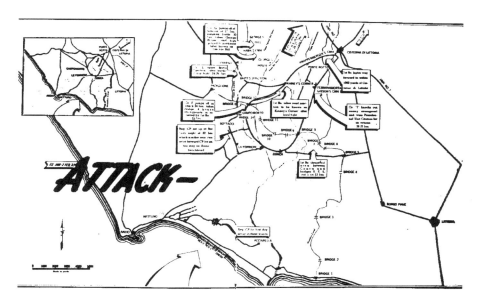

Figure 14. The 3rd Division makes the landing at Anzio on January 22, 1944.

January 22, 1944, *Figure 14*. At 2 a.m. that morning we were told to disembark. We walked off our LCI and the landing was at Anzio (the birthplace of Roman Emperor Nero) *Figure 15*, and Nettuno, *Figure 16*.

This was about 30 miles below Rome and 70 miles north of Naples. We were fortunate to be in water only up to our waists. We discarded our life preservers and walked in. By dawn it was very quiet, there had been no firing or anything, was something wrong? We didn't run into any enemy but at 7 a.m. we heard and saw Messerschmitt BF-109's flying north to south low over the beach.

Figure 15. Anzio and its harbor with ships.

Figure 16. The town of Nettuno next to Anzio, called Twin Cities.

Our antiaircraft guns started firing and we knew it wasn't a dry run. We all thought it was a dry run up to that time. A training exercise? No way!

Figure 17. On January 23, 1944, at the Mussolini Canal at Anzio. American paratroopers digging in their positions along the bank.

Figure 17. We walked onto Highway 7 up to the Mussolini Canal, a large canal dug to drain the land and turn it into farmland during the early days of Mussolini. Its' water came down from the mountains and flowed into the sea. Our landing at Anzio was called "Shingles." We walked to bridge #5. There were a number of bridges over this canal. We dug at the base of this canal to wait for orders. To do what? Now this Anzio landing was the brainchild of Winston Churchill, who while recuperating from pneumonia or a heavy cold at Casablanca, suggested to Roosevelt that if the Allies had a landing below Rome it would relieve Allied troops at Cassino. The thinking was that the Germans would pull back from Cassino and then the Allied troops below Cassino would move in, but that didn't happen as Churchill thought it would.

All the foxholes dug near the canal had spring water coming up in them. We had problems getting drinking water so we filled our canteens with the spring water and dropped some Halazone pills in the water so we could drink it about an hour later. At times paratroopers would come by to ask if we had water and when we offered them some, they would be horrified that we were drinking this water. Later some other GI's came from the other side of the canal and asked, "Are you GI's drinking water from the canal?" I said, "Yeah." They said, "Well, there are dead GI's, Germans, and cattle floating in that water." I said, "So, it hasn't hurt us." We didn't think anything of it, as long as we had Halazone pills to sterilize our water.

The night of our first day the Germans fired some 170 mm rounds into our area. I guess they must have known we were on our side of the canal. When these rounds came in it sounded like a freight train coming through the night air, hitting in K Company section.

At that time our Army didn't have a buddy system. In other words, we did not buddy up with another GI for protection, friendship, and comfort. We were by ourselves and it scared the hell out of all of us on our first night in combat. I was looking for a friend to bunk up with and couldn't find anybody, so I just stayed in my slit trench until the artillery barrage ceased, then went looking for someone to pair off with. The next night my sergeant put me on guard duty underneath bridge #5. I was to blow it if the enemy tried to cross. I was given the day's password and was told to stop anybody coming from the town of Cisterna. I was to give half of the password, they the other half. Then I was to ask who they were and what they were doing. Many times during that night I saw shadows that I thought were trying to get at me, my eyes were peeled for fast action, my M-1 was in my hands and not slung over my shoulder. The safety was off and my finger was on the trigger all the time. About 1 or 2 a.m., I heard some vehicles coming from Cisterna and said to myself, "Oh boy, I have company and something may come of it." I moved out from underneath the bridge where TNT boxes were placed and yelled, "Halt! Who goes there?" "Recon engineers," came the reply. I gave them half of the password and they gave me the other half. I don't recall that password at this time but some were crazy passwords like I would say pins and they would say needles, or the other way around.

A Lt. John T. Cummings was in the first Jeep with some others. I walked up to him and said, "I didn't see or hear you go over this bridge before." He said, "No, we went over another bridge. We were just outside of Rome, there is nobody there and we didn't see anything." Of course he was off to report what he had seen and that was the end of my experience meeting GI's from the other side of the bridge that night.

I learned while standing on guard duty to never look at anything straight on. I tried to catch a glimpse of whatever was moving by the action of my eyes as I looked from the corner of my eyes. If you put your eyesight to the extreme left or right I think you can catch a glimpse of something you wouldn't ordinarily see if you were looking straight at it. I found this to be true a number of times. Was it something I learned? I don't know if I was told or read about it. Using my eyes that way, I learned to spot something faster from the corner of my eyes.

Soon, at daybreak, I was relieved and walked to my slit trench. That afternoon my sergeant was picking some GI's for patrol. He looked at me and almost picked me but changed his mind. He picked Chambers instead. Chambers, a married man with two small children, was a small GI. About a half hour later we heard some rifle fire. Some of the patrol came back to report they had run into Italian and German soldiers. Our GI's fired and in the return fire, one of our men was hit. It was Chambers. He was killed instantly when he took a bullet in the face. His body was brought back. As he lay in front of me, I felt bad because it was my first time seeing someone killed in combat. I was sorry he was killed and he was possibly our first GI killed on Anzio.

One evening my Company Commander called me (now I was just a Pfc). "DeAngelo, I want you and two other GI's to go up on the same paved road the Recon vehicles came down and see if there is a paved road to the left side of that road. I want you to go as far as you can to find this paved road, I need to know." We moved out on patrol. We had walked about a quarter mile and still hadn't found this road or anything. I finally got on my hands and knees to see if I could find the paved road but all I could find were dirt roads. We returned, I reported to my Lieutenant that we had been unable to find that paved road. I don't know what his intentions were, but that was the end of the first patrol I was in charge of.

At night it was very quiet. From time to time we viewed flares, heard our machine gun fire and their tracers going in front or on the side of us. We knew something was going on, but didn't know if it was us or them shooting the flares. Later that night I heard an explosion and then an American voice cursed like the dickens. I was sure he was wounded. I didn't know if he stepped on a mine or what. I could hear him yelling and cursing at whoever did this to him. He was in pain, he yelled for a minute or two, then nothing. I didn't know if his wound was serious, did he bleed to death? Then it was quiet once again.

On Anzio the Germans would float leaflets down over our lines and our GI's got a kick out of them. They did this to the English troops as well. The English troops read these words, "American GI's are over in England, over sexed and over paid." I can tell you this did hurt the English troops. Some leaflets were called the Anzio Death Trap.

Soon, one evening our night fighter shot down a JU-88. We heard gunfire above. Of course both planes' lights were out. Soon I saw a fire in the sky above me. The fire got larger and larger. Then I saw a parachute or two floating down and the plane, on fire, started to spin down. From where I was on the ground, it looked like this JU-88 was coming down right over us. I thought, "Oh my God this plane is going to land on top of me." It crashed about a quarter of a mile on the other side of the #5 bridge. Of course, its German crew was not captured. They landed behind their line, but all night long we heard small arms rounds firing as it burned. The next day an M-10 tank destroyer showed up. Sherman tanks and M-10 tank destroyers were called "Bugs" and "Beetles," I don't remember which was called "bugs".

Figure 18 shows this particular M-10 tank destroyer being hit by a German 88 mm and destroyed a few minutes after it passed us. We saw it burn for a long time. I have no idea if anyone got out of it or if they perished, but what you see in this photograph is exactly what I saw. Its back was facing me when it was hit by the German tank, as I looked from bridge #5.

Figure 18. The author saw this M-10 Tank Destroyer hit by an 88mm and burn near Bridge 5 on January 27, 1944.

Sometimes GI's talked about an 88 mm gun the Germans had, a very flexible weapon. It actually started out as an antiaircraft weapon. It was also capable of firing in a horizontal position to knock out English tanks as well as ours. The 88 mm was a far superior gun with a velocity of 3,340 feet per second compared to our 75 mm which only had 2,680 feet per second,

I saw an incident where two Sherman tanks, one behind the other, were hit by the same 88 mm round. This round hit in front of the driver of the first tank. He never knew what hit him. It destroyed that tank, then it went out through its back to hit the second tank and destroyed it too. Both the Sherman tank and M-10 tank destroyer had armor in front of the driver, probably about 3-4 inches. You can

Figure 19. An M-10 Tank Destroyer, its gun in place at the rear.

understand how powerful this 88 mm gun was to go through those 3-4 inches like butter.

Figure 19 shows an M-10 tank destroyer. It was a very attractive vehicle with a 76 mm gun instead of a 75 mm. This gun had been a naval gun called a 3" M-32. It was a little more powerful than the 75mm.

The M-10 tank destroyer's one fault was its turret. Its top was wide open. Since there was no steel hatch, it was just an opening someone could throw a grenade into. A short time later, L Company and Capt. Britt's GI's waved as they passed us on their way attack

Cisterna. A firefight broke out and Capt. Britt lost his right arm at what became called Britt Junction. It just about destroyed his company. Capt. Britt had been an all-American football player before entering the service. They couldn't penetrate so they fell back. The Germans had moved more troops in to keep Cisterna from being captured. Within four days after our landing the Germans moved 10 or 11 divisions from Southern France and Northern Italy down to Anzio; they didn't move their troops out of Cassino, they just let them stay there. This was a big problem and we knew we were going to face these new and fresh Divisions very soon.

Some days later Col. Darby's 6615 Rangers Regiment also went through, also waving at us at bridge #5. They too were to capture the town of Cisterna. Things went wrong when they mistook German tanks as GI tanks. The Germans somehow knew beforehand that they were coming, so they set another trap. Out of 767 GI's less than a dozen came out of it; most of the rest were captured, wounded or killed. We could not do anything because we didn't have the manpower. My division landed about three-quarter strength or less. Most of the replacements, supplies and such were going to England. I don't know why we made the landing at Anzio. I think it was a big mistake to make this landing without 3-4 full divisions.

We heard the firing and fighting. Col. Darby's Rangers were counterattacked and it just about destroyed Col. Darby when he lost so many of his men. We were left to just sit and wonder how to get them out. We had no resources. Even the LCI's were used for the beachhead were gone. I guess without the LCI's they couldn't bring in more GI's from Naples to Anzio. Being we were at Bridge #5, we were told there were a number of homes on the right hand side of the road. There was a woman with a radio giving instructions to the Germans at Cisterna and that's why L Company and Col. Darby's Rangers were expected. There wasn't anything written about this and I'm not sure if it is true or not, but our MP's went in, arrested her and took her away. We did see the MP's at that house taking out a woman. Col. Darby's rangers were no more.

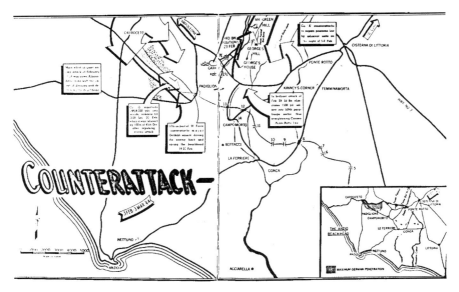

Figure 20. February 5, 1944. K Company counterattacks the Germans to regain F Company position.

Later, Col. William O. Darby was with the 10th Mountain Division as their Assistant Division Commander. In Northern Italy on April 30, 1945, at the town of Nago, he was killed by 88mm fire.

Our ex-Senator Robert Dole was wounded in Northern Italy with the 5th Army while serving in the 10th Mountain Division. This made three new Infantry Divisions (the 10th, 85th, and 88th) and I feel it would have been very different if these divisions had been with us when we landed on Anzio.

Figure 20 shows a counterattack by our K Company on February 5, 1944.

As a member of K Company, our sister F Company held the position. The Germans counterattacked and pushed F Company back. It was now K Company's job to push through F Company to counterattack and retake the lost position. Early in the evening, as we were walking forward, a machine gun opened up and of course when we heard firing we all hit the ground. Our names were called to move—where and in what direction? Then we moved and counterattacked, that was it. We retook the position once again, not ordered what to do by our sergeant. I don't know how far we pushed them back. At 4 a.m the next morning, our sergeant came to me and said, "Come with me." We walked to an unmanned machine gun position. "You stay here and man it." It was a light machine gun, 30 caliber Browning, with extra boxes of ammo. He said, "Now, you keep your eyes open and take care of this position."

When you see any war movies having a machine gun position, there are always 3 or 4 men around the machine gunner with rifles, ready to pick off anyone wanting to destroy the machine gunner. I was alone, no one was around. I thought, "I don't have some riflemen to protect me, to keep the enemy from firing at me or destroying my machine gun. The sergeant was wrong leaving me alone. I don't remember his name, but it wasn't the one who ordered me to pick up the firewood. This sergeant should never have been one. He told me to keep my eyes open, he said, pointing, "You see that dead GI laying there? That was F Company position. That GI went to sleep, and died. Every time the Germans attacked they took some GI on guard duty–again pointing where he lays–or killed him. So keep your eyes open." You talk about keeping your eyes open, both of them.

I was in a slit trench with a machine gun on a tripod in front of me on a slight mound. Alone I was getting sleepy and I dozed off for a moment. Then around 6-7 a.m. I heard "Piiing!" I noticed one of their rounds had penetrated my ammunition box and a tracer was on fire. I had extra ammunition boxes. The one in place had been damaged. I hit it with my right hand to knock it away from the machine gun, then opened up the breach, removing the damaged belt. I took another box of ammo, put its belt in place, locked it, cocked it, and was ready to fire. When the second round landed in the mound in front of me it threw dirt into my face. I put my hand to my face to feel if I was wounded. I noticed a lot of blood on my right hand. I thought he hit me in my face or forehead. Actually, when I had hit the damaged ammunition box, I had cut my hand on a ripped-open brass cartridge. He had a powerful telescope, if he aimed his rifle maybe 1/4" or less he would have hit me straight in my helmet or face and I wouldn't be writing this today.

I was ready for an attack. I was alone and in a very bad situation. Scared? Yes, but I was ready. How was I supposed to protect this position, without rifles, as it should be by the book? Then I heard a GI yell, "Medic!" a number of times. I called out, "What's going on?" He said, "I'm hit." I asked, "Can you come over?" He said, "No, I can't move, I'm shot in my right hip." I asked, "Well, what do you need?" He said, "I'm very thirsty, I've been lying out here for 2 days." I said, "I'll come with my canteen." Some GI heard what I said and called out, "DeAngelo, don't do it! That sniper will knock you down the next time he sees you in his scope." I said, "That GI has been out there for two days with a hole in his hip, he can't crawl and he can't get up." Another GI said, "I'll give you advice, DeAngelo. If you go, take your pistol belt off, leave your helmet, take no weapons, just carry your canteen, and hold your hands high. The sniper—he'll see it, he won't shoot, maybe." I took his advice but of course it all depended on the sniper with his rifle. Only a few minutes earlier he tried to kill me. With just my canteen up high, I walked up to this GI from F Company and said, "How are you doing?" He said, "I'm thirsty." I looked at him and said, "Here is some water. I'll get a medic for you, but I don't know when. It can't be daytime, I don't think it's safe besides they don't know where you are. I'll talk to my sergeant. Maybe I will get you out tonight." He thanked me and I left him. I'll never forget what he looked like. He was a long skinny GI with GI glasses, lying on his back, the sun beating down on him. I did get him out that night. I did not know him or see him again.

That dead GI near me had on a wristwatch. I looked at the watch and thought it might have been a recent present from his family, it looked new. I wanted to do something nice for this young GI and I thought about removing his watch, getting his name and address and mailing it to his family. But if someone saw me removing it, they might have thought I was trying to rob him, so I didn't do it.

Anzio

Some GI's who picked up our dead had a tendency to keep some items, I am sorry to say.

That evening the same sergeant came by and said, "DeAngelo, you are being transferred to C Company. You are going there as a sergeant. They lost all their sergeants in a counterattack a couple of days ago and now they have none. They lost a company commander, sergeants and corporals. You are going with your sergeant." (The same one who gave me the order to pick up firewood). The other sergeant said, "You two GI's are going there, he's going as a sergeant and you will be a sergeant in a short time; they need experienced men." Experienced men! I'd only been in combat a week or two. We were being transferred to C Company. We were told they couldn't get replacements. Like I said, replacements were going to England. They went to every company who had extra men and transferred them to C Company.

That night, I packed up to follow my sergeant. It was dark, it started raining cats and dogs, and I thought to myself, "I wonder if he knows where the hell he's going?" I was hateful of this sergeant. In fact he never liked me, I don't know why. Like going to get the wood, he could have gotten someone who was nice and warm and dry. So help me God, I thought about killing him right there. I'm not ashamed to say this, I thought about going up to him, turning him around and shooting him. To me he was not what the Army needed, not this sergeant. I guess it was wrong to think that way, but if he did anything else, I would have killed him. I wouldn't have been sorry. Later, in another chapter, there will be more about this GI who I was assigned with.

I believe that it was at Anzio that the first truce was made to help with the wounded and dead. GI's and German medics worked side by side to remove them. After this was completed both sides returned to their positions. Soon, again, the war went on.

A few days before we arrived at C Company, one of its GI's got the Congressional Medal of Honor for fighting off a counterattack. That same night Axis Sally had the names of captured GI's from C

Company on the train going to Berlin. It was funny how she got names right off the bat. She mentioned its Captain was going to see Hitler. It may have been Captain Miller, whom I never met but I had heard of him soon after joining C Company.

We were now attached to C Company. It was still raining very hard and long. I was lying in my slit trench with water running down my neck, down through my clothes and out of my shoes. I called it my slit trench with running water. It was early February and wet, cold, and dreary. I was all by myself again. I hadn't had anything to eat or drink; it was terrible. Lightning was striking all around the place. I noticed in the distance what looked like a barn and decided to go to the barn to sleep and get out of the rain.

I walked to the barn and inside was a big haystack. I crawled underneath, covered myself and went to sleep. The next morning I awoke and found that the roof had been blown off and I couldn't move my legs. Was I paralyzed? I just could not move from underneath the haystack. I moved some of the hay away from my face and saw that a cow had died and fallen on top of my legs. I pushed and pushed until I was out from underneath. Of course, I was covered with plaster (which I had read the Italians often mixed with arsenic) but at least I was dry. As I was walking back to my slit trench, the one with running water, the sun was shining. I turned around and saw a house 100 yards away and behind it was an M-10 tank destroyer. I walked over and saw that the crew had killed a pig and were frying it. These GI's with tanks and tank destroyers always carried cooking equipment, they always cooked things. I asked, "You GI's have any coffee?" They said, "Yeah, do you want some ham?" I said, "No." They said, "We've got plenty."

Up the street were a couple of Sherman tanks. Somehow the Germans knew there were a few Sherman tanks and M-10's in the area. They were lobbing armor piercing rounds onto the road behind the M-10. When the Sherman crew saw this they drove back on this road and drove off to the rear. This upset the GI's in the M-10. They said that Sherman crew was giving away our positions. They cussed at that Sherman crew and said, "That crew does it all the time." I think they would have shot them if they had the chance, maybe they did.

We heard some rounds coming over. These were not duds, all were hitting the ground, but it was very soggy and they were not exploding. The Germans knew there was another vehicle behind the house where we were. For some reason they couldn't get the correct elevation. The crew and I climbed in the M-10. I was sitting underneath the breech but, like I said, M-10's didn't have a turret steel hatch to close and there was only a canvas cover, period. All I could think of was a round hitting this breech. Soon it became quiet, I said, "You GI's can have this, I won't spend another minute in this turret." I took off and walked back to my slit trench to stay.

During Anzio, Gen. John Lucas was Commanding Officer of VI Corps. He was soon relieved by Gen. Clark. Gen. Truscott, our 3rd Infantry Division Commander, replaced Gen. Lucas. Lucas was sent home, Gen. Truscott became the VI Corps Commander. Gen. Clark was still in command of the 5th Army, Gen. Truscott turned his 3rd Infantry Division over to Gen. O'Daniels, a WWI veteran with a scar on the left side of his cheek. He was a tough little guy who was up there with his GI's like Gen. Truscott. The CO of the 30th Regiment was Col. Lionel C. McGarr. He seemed to know what was going on. Other commanders were Lt. Colonel H. Neddenson and Major MacKenzie E. Porter, 1st Battalion Commanders. I don't have much to say about those officers, they did their job like the rest of us.

On Anzio we received the Combat Infantry Badge which meant $10 more per month for each GI, which was nice. It made us feel good. Somebody wanted to show appreciation for the Infantry foot soldier. Congress issued it on October 27, 1943. I still have my original one in a frame.

We did not have extra GI's to do what we needed to do, so to keep the Germans confused, every other night C Company would move to another area, be in position, and later move to another

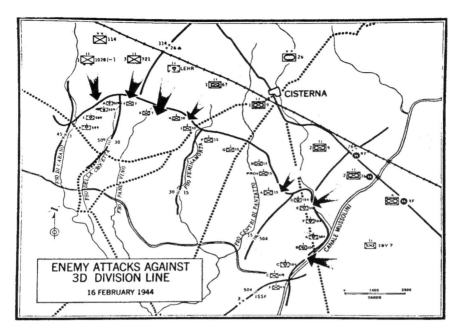

Figure 21. On February 16, 1944, Germans counterattack the 3rd Division and 504 and 509 paratroopers on Anzio.

area. We did this for about two or three weeks. We wanted the Germans to think we had more troops than we really had. Let's say the Germans sent a patrol in without meeting or seeing any GI's? Early the next morning their counterattack runs into a large group of GI's in that area. We hoped they would think that more GI's had been added to the Anzio beachhead in recent days. If they only knew.

There were times when we would pass a dead GI. It was very sad, but we couldn't let this get to us because it would break us down. It was a bad situation. I would remove a blanket I carried and cover his body. Later I would pick up a blanket. It was always easy to find one if mine was used. It was pitiful and I didn't like to see flies over his body where he was wounded. If he had a blanket I would cover him with it and go on. When we came upon a dead GI, (I don't want you to misunderstand me or think something was wrong), the thought that came into my mind was, "better him than me." Also, I never saw a rifle with a bayonet stuck in the ground with a

Anzio

Figure 22. GI's sitting by the Creek of Many at Anzio.

Figure 23. GI Foxholes dug by a creek on Anzio.

helmet on it for a dead GI. We were always moving forward, going to face the Germans.

Figure 21, February 16, 1944. The Germans counterattacked us as we were trying to capture Cisterna.

Figure 22 shows GI's sitting near foxholes with a small creek running

Figure 24. These are called "Fosso". A deep ditch with running water. One could walk in them. The author was on patrol in one.

in front of them, waiting. Sometimes we would drink this water when we dug a slit trench or foxhole. Since the water seeped upwards, we knew it was from a spring and okay to drink with halazone pills.

Figure 23 shows the type of bunkers or foxholes which were pretty decent looking. Sometimes we stayed in these all day long. We couldn't get out during the daytime, only at night.

Figure 24 shows deep ditches with some water called "Fossos." We could walk in them and not be seen. I remember going on patrol and walking in one when we were trying to get behind some Germans, but we couldn't go any further so we had to climb out of the Fosso. Walking on top exposed us, which was bad to do in the daytime. Being born and raised as a Catholic, each time we were to attack or were being counterattacked, I always made the sign of the cross and hoped for the best.

Figure 25. House number 6 on Anzio, blasted every night by M-10's and Sherman Tanks.

The Germans were up in the hills looking down on us all the time. In the daytime there was no movement at all, especially for our front line troops. We all stayed in our slit trenches. As nightfall came we would put our weapons in place to be ready for any counterattack. It was this way all those months. It was pretty hard during the day, especially if a GI had diarrhea or had to pee. He did it in his pants because if he exposed himself during the day we would be shelled by an 88 mm from some tanks up on the side of the hill some miles away.

Figure 25 was called house #6. Each house was given a number. Every once in a while at night, Bugs or Beetles (Sherman tanks and M-10 tank destroyers) would come up and blast the houses that were made out of three-foot thick stone and masonry. Sometimes the Germans with their machine guns would hide in big ovens in the yard and fire at us when we were moving up. When we heard Bugs and Beetles moving we knew they were going to fire on one of the houses.

We were up on the front one night and I was in a slit trench. We stayed put even though we were about 12-15 inches below the ground and I knew we were pretty safe. That night some GI's came up to relieve us. Behind me was a decent foxhole with sand bags around it that one would enter by sitting down inside and sliding in. One GI, who had just walked up, crawled inside, and then another GI got in and was sitting with his upper body exposed. The Germans fired a mortar round that hit right in front on top of the sandbags that were around the entrance. The mortar, either a 50 mm or 80 mm, landed right in front of him. I got out of my slit trench to get this GI to move but when I touched him my hand was covered with warm stuff. I realized it was his blood. I said to the others standing there, "This GI is dead. Move away! Find someplace safe so you won't get hit! Disperse! Get going!" I think they were our replacements. It was the only mortar round to come in that night. Was it just a fluke or a short round by the Germans or maybe our side? I was getting to be an experienced GI in a matter of 2-3 weeks.

Every once in a while, in the evening, we would hear something like a vehicle coming toward us; we couldn't see it, we could hear it, like tank tracks, it's motor grinding away. Soon we found out what they were. These were small remote German miniature tanks. I guess each weighed about 500 lbs. with about 100 lbs. of TNT. It was controlled either by radio or a long wire which unwound from a

Anzio

Figure 26. German remote control miniature tank called "Goliath", used on Anzio and was blown up at our positions.

spool of wire from its back. It had small little tracks, and was called "Goliath." *Figure 26* shows what I'm talking about. They moved these up to us and blew them up. By firing at these there was a pretty good chance of damaging its wire or controls, so every time we heard its movements we fired like hell to knock it out.

Each infantry company had two Jeeps with two small trailers and a 500-gallon water tank for cooking, washing, etc. We also had a Lyster bag. Taking water from this bag was much easier than going to the tank for water. The Lyster bag would be filled from the water tank. When they were out of water they would pull the water tank to a lake, canal or river. Our engineers would pump water out and use chemicals to treat the water. Then they would fill up the tank and haul it back to the company. It was great that we had good equipment to do what we needed it to do.

Since almost all men and equipment were going to England to build up for the Normandy Invasion, we had to beg to get LCI's, equipment, materials, and replacements. It was frustrating. Another thing that irritated us on Anzio was reading that our longshoremen at home were on strike. No one could ship anything overseas to us and that upset us very much. There was a lot of resentment and many GI's were peeved off. There we were being shot at and dying and we couldn't even get supplies. To me the military should have taken over to put some longshoremen under arrest or something. It left a pretty bad taste in our mouths. We were fighting and they were not worried about getting the ships loaded and shipped overseas so we could get our food or whatever we needed to fight the enemy. It was pretty hard to accept; we resented it and, yes, it hurt us.

From time to time, while in service in Italy, we read in our hometown newspapers, in Stars and Stripes or we would hear the news on BBC radio that the Italian Campaign at the front was very quiet, with little or no action. The 5th Army sent out small patrols to seek the front lines. These patrols were sent out at night and daytime. With each patrol, GI's were killed, wounded or missing. We, in Italy, felt we were forgotten and we became upset in knowing this was being told. It left a bad taste in our mouths. This information was from the 5th Army Headquarters and from Washington.

We read in Stars and Stripes that every GI on Anzio would receive a free bottle of Coca-Cola. We were looking forward to this. One day a GI showed up with two photographers and two bottles of Coke. He said, "I'd like you to pose for a photograph with a Coke." I said, "Sure, why not?" He explained, "We don't have Cokes for everybody; we only have these two. What I'd like to do is take as many photographs of different GI's drinking these two Cokes as possible." I looked at him and said, "We read there would be a Coke for each GI. How is it that all you have is two Cokes for 25 men?" He couldn't answer me. I said, "I know what happened, you GI's in the rear echelon have been drinking all these Cokes and now you come to us to take photographs of combat GI's drinking a Coke. If you want us to share one Coke with five or more GI's, you're crazy." I asked the GI's if they wanted to do it but they all agreed it was insulting and told him to take his two Cokes and shove them. They left, we didn't have any cokes to drink, plus no photos were taken.

When we met British Tommys, we would exchange C-rations we didn't like. We liked their rations of bully beef, also called corned beef. You can see it on the shelf today in grocery stores. (It used to be in a white, pyramid-type can, made by Libby from Argentina. Now it is made also by Hormel in Brazil and comes in a similar looking red can.) The British Tommys would always exchange their bully beef for our rations. This was great because we had been eating our rations for a long time, the British had been eating theirs even longer, and so we were all happy to exchange with one another. At times the British troops would stop for tea while moving up to the front lines to do battle. I never saw this happen, but that doesn't mean it never did happen.

In our C-rations we had biscuits that looked like what we have today (Nabisco lunch biscuits). They were round and came five to a can. Whenever you ate them and drank some water or coffee, they expanded in your stomach. One day we happened to throw one of these biscuits in a puddle of water and, my gosh, it expanded to three times its original size.

Our K-rations were a little larger than a Cracker Jack box. The outer box of cardboard was sort of wax protected to keep its contents from going stale. Inside was another box without wax. We used the wax outer box plus the inner box to light fires so we could heat our K-rations. They made a good fire. The K-ration cans were smaller than cans of tuna fish. Some were cheese with bits of bacon, which was very good, and others were ham and eggs. K-rations were liked

Figure 27. GI's playing ball wearing the new clothing called "Zoot Suits" on Anzio.

by our GI's. Each K-ration had toilet paper, five cigarettes in a small package, and some times a small can opener that could be put on our dog tag chains. Some GI's would put a K-ration can in a fire and forget to poke a hole in it so it would not explode. Without a hole, the one with the cheese and bacon would burst and it would make a mess. It was HOT!!!

On Anzio, the Germans would drop what looked like American-made candy chocolate bars thinking our GI's would pick them up and eat them. They were poison. These were reported when found.

Figure 27 shows what we called Zoot Suits. These were new, like a coverall, and we put them on over our OD pants. They had suspenders and a zipper front with slits to get to the OD pants pockets. There was also a jacket with knit collar, waist and wrists. The jackets zipped up and kept us warm. Both items had something like a GI blanket sewed inside them and were very warm and comfortable. These were made for tankers. After our tankers got theirs we started getting them. The foot GI's were always at the end of the line getting needed items. These were very good because we didn't have much to wear when it was raining and we were wet and cold. We needed new clothing because our old M-1941 field jackets were not really good; they were a joke. Many weeks before our break out on Anzio we turned in our zoot suits and then received new clothing that was very appreciated (shown in *Figure 28*).

Facing the photo's, the GI on the left side has on our new combat jacket, the M-43, and combat boots, which had an extra piece of leather sewed on top. The other GI shown on his left side is wearing what we had been wearing. You notice the difference between our old look and the new look which was very comfortable and welcomed. Soon after, I cut up a GI blanket and sewed it on the inside of my M-43 jacket, and hood, but not inside the sleeves. We were to get pants to go with this new jacket. Notice in

Figure 28. GI's of the 3rd Division, 30th Regiment wearing the old look, facing right side, and the new look, left side. Anzio.

the photo this new GI pants which went over your OD pants—I never saw those pants issued. Our new M-43 field jackets had four extra large pockets and a front zipper. It could be snugged around the waist by a cord. It covered our backsides better and of course the hood was very good. We could get the hood over our helmet without a problem. The combat boots were great and allowed us to get rid of our leggings that were a pain. These new boots had an extra piece of leather attached with two buckles. The quartermaster had taken the old design boot and sewed a piece of leather on its top. It was, however, a bad idea because as we marched we had problems with the back of our heels. They took away those boots and we received a new design boot shortly after that gave us more room behind the heel. Remember earlier I explained that the Goumiers used to feel the leggins of GI's. If he was not wearing leggins then he was a German and was killed. With the new combat boots, I do not recall what did happen, but I hope no GI was killed.

One thing that made us feel very secure was our M-1 rifles. We were far superior in firepower than our enemy. The enemy rifle had a five round clip, like our Springfield .03. They had to lift up the bolt, pull it back, and push it forward and down to fire. With the M-1 we just pulled the trigger eight times and eight rounds were fired. After firing, the clip jumped out and we reloaded with another eight round clip giving our GI foot soldiers a good edge over the Germans. Not many people know this, but near the end of the war, the Germans tried to design a weapon equal to our M-1, but it was never put into production for some reason. It would have been a bad situation if we had been fighting an enemy that had a rifle compared to our M-1 or maybe a little bit better.

One night I was on a very large patrol of 30 GI's. We were to capture some Germans and their new gas masks. As we were walking out toward the field our artillery and mortars were to adjust fire fifty yards in front of us each time we walked fifty yards further. They were to do the same, covering us on return. Then a short round exploded among us and killed 3 or 4 GI's. It blew a couple of arms

Anzio

Figure 29. German Canister Bomb flown over Anzio and dropped over the beach.

and legs off. It was a complete failure. Lt. Skeahan was in charge and he lost command. Lt. Skeahan was a nice guy and I felt sorry for him. Once Lt. Skeahan told me he had helped build Camp Blanding in Florida. More on Lt. Skeahan in a later chapter.

The photograph in *Figure 29* shows a large (Canister) bomb the Germans had dropped over our lines. This bomb carried many 1-2 pound small bomblets inside. At night a bomber released this monster and at a certain altitude it split open and these small bomblets fell out. When they hit the ground they would dig a big trench about 200-330 feet wide and 500 feet long, with a sound like brrm, brrm, brrm. It was scary. If it dropped in the right place it would have torn up a lot of GI's. We knew when the bomber engines slowed down they were going to drop one of those suckers on us.

Later, one evening, our Lt. Gayette said we were going out on a small six man patrol. Within 20 minutes we were on patrol, getting closer and closer. Now the Germans knew we were out in front of their lines. They were firing flares. We were all lying down and I peeked out from under my helmet to see barbed wire with tin cans hanging from it. I said to Lt. Gayette, "You know they know we're here." He said, "We have to go over the barbed wire." I asked, "What for?" He said, "That's my orders." I said, "We'll never get through that barbed wire, lieutenant. If we do get through, we won't get back and no one will know what happened to us." He looked the situation over, then he looked at me and said, "Do you think so, DeAngelo?" I said, "I know so, lieutenant. This is a bad situation, we'll never get in or out." We all crawled back to return to C Company. I don't know what he reported or have any idea why we

Figure 30. German Flying Remote Bomb used on shipping over Anzio. Henschel HS-293 Type.

went on that patrol. Later this nice officer was killed.

Figure 30 shows a remote control flying bomb, HS-293. It was also controlled by a spool of wire or remote like the miniature tank "Goliath." It was known to have been used 24 times around Anzio Harbor. It sank, I understand, one or two ships. I think one of them was the USS Savannah, a supply ship. We were told we wouldn't be getting any supplies because a supply ship had been sunk by a remote control bomb.

I don't know how many ships were sunk, but I know there were better than twenty HS-293 bombs used. They were pretty accurate and, of course, you had to have someone who knew what he was doing controlling this bomb. I think we had about five rounds of 105 mm for each gun at that time and I don't know if the USS Savannah had any other supplies beside ammunition or food when it was sunk.

Once, artillery fire from the Germans hit one of our ammunition dumps. We lost a great deal of ammunition. It was bad to hear of this loss. It left a big hole in the ground.

Another time our hospital was shelled by long-range artillery fire plus night bombing. We lost some nurses and a few GI's who had been wounded were injured again or killed. It was the only time this happened.

During the day we couldn't move about, we'd look up at the sky from where we lay in our slit trenches. It looked like waves were floating across the sky. We couldn't understand why these waves started at one end and went all the way up north. I think the sound of artillery barrage may have caused these waves. One particular day I was looking in the north direction at an Artillery observer cub used for spotting German artillery fire. I noticed something in the sky just go black. A 155 mm artillery round had hit this cub. The 155 mm were firing at the requested target and, unfortunately, he was in the line of fire. The 155 mm shell just blew him apart. Nothing came down, or was found. This cub was from the 45th Infantry Division.

There was an area called Padiglione Pines that was a large area of dense pine woods. It was also a great rest area. We GI's got off the line and went to this area to take it easy. I don't understand why it was never shelled or bombed, maybe the Germans didn't know its location. One day we heard a sound, something different, it looked

GREETINGS FROM THE PRESIDENT

Figure 31. US Army M-18 Hellcat Tank. Saw service first time in combat on Anzio.

like a German tank running around but was one of the new US Army M-18 Hellcat Tanks. It had different bogey wheels from our Sherman tanks and M-10's. *Figure 31* shows this particular tank. This tank was to mount a 90 mm gun. The photograph doesn't show a 90 mm gun but it may have been a 3" gun or a 76 mm gun, MI-A2. I don't know if they were diesel or gas. We really didn't know what was taking place. There were only six of them and they were going into combat for the first time. They told our bazooka GI's to be especially careful if they saw one since the new tanks could easily be mistaken for a German tank because of the bogey wheels. At the breakout, these new tanks were mistaken and destroyed. This M-18 tank may have had a M5-75 mm gun. It was designed from lightweight material used for aircraft installations on a B-25 Bomber for its nose gun. Also, a new, incredibly fast, twin engine aircraft by Beech Craft called the "Grizzly" XA-38 also had this M5-75 mm. This aircraft never went into production.

Figure 32 shows a church at the Pines. I'm in this photograph taking communion that day–and soon after, just sitting and talking and taking it easy. I don't remember if we had movies.

Once we came across a winery. We found an American

manufactured 5-gallon water can called a Jerry can. A German design, there were two kinds of Jerry cans: one for fuel, one for water. The one that held fuel had a screw cap with a chain. The water can had a cap that folded down over the opening and locked in place. This Jerry water can was filled with wine and we had a great time. For the first time in a while, we felt pretty good.

While we were in the Pines, my lieutenant ordered my sergeant to tell me I was to be in charge of digging a latrine for C Company. I was a private first class at the time. Dombrowski, another GI whose

Figure 32. GI's at Easter Sunday Services on Anzio.

name I don't remember, and I were to dig a four holer. We found a location and started to dig when I noticed that Dombrowski wasn't helping. I said, "Come on, let's dig." I always got myself involved in work even if I was in charge. He said, "You're not a sergeant, DeAngelo." I said, "Didn't you hear our sergeant say I was responsible and in charge? I don't have to have rank." He gave me a heck of a time so I told him if he didn't work, I was going to beat his brains in. He looked at me and said, "Go ahead." So I beat the hell out of him. He picked up the shovel and started digging. The other GI was a big guy, now years later I mistook him for Jim, an actor, because of his size. He was not in the 30th regiment. He was in the 7th, a sister regiment also with the 3rd Infantry Division. Jim, the actor, was also wounded. After lunch time he was the second GI I fought that day. He was trying to do the same as Dombrowski, he would not work. I was provoked by both of them. I wonder if he was that GI? Both started to work with me. We finished digging that latrine, set the wood frame over the hole and put lots of lime inside to kill the odor or whatever. Most GI's carried toilet paper in their helmets. We walked back to C Company and nothing was said about my two fistfights. I guess it was the way to get things done sometimes.

Some GI's just didn't like Italian-Americans, thinking we were wise guys or gangsters, and would give me a hard time. I got a little tired of it. I was a street kid who knew how to fight and how to take care of myself, and I didn't like anybody pushing me around. After supper I had another fist fight with Pfc. Vasion. He started picking on me calling me Dago. I had two fights, one that morning, the second after lunch, why not another one? I fought and beat him as well. Not many GI's got in my way. I think some GI's kept away from me, they knew I had a temper and would fight if messed with.

Every time we dug a latrine we had extra soil and we would pile it up over the top. As requested, when we closed one we would place a cross on top of the mound that read 3rd Infantry Division, 30th Regiment, B Company, 2nd Battalion, opened a certain date, closed a certain date. One day we saw some Italian girls placing flowers on the top of the mound. They thought some poor GI was buried and forgotten.

One morning when we were resting at the Pines listening to some bagpipers who were playing for our moral support, we heard the sound of ACK, ACK. We saw a flight of Spitfires flying low above us, and one was having engine problems. We saw some smoke, then fire coming from its cowl. The pilot bailed out from 500 feet and landed among us wearing shorts. Of course the bagpipers stopped playing to look up. He was a Canadian. His aircraft went gliding down next to where some GI's were digging a foxhole. A Jeep took the pilot to where ever he had to go, otherwise he would have been listed as missing in action.

Every day or so we would hear a great big explosion as a shell went off overhead. It sounded like it was put in second gear, as if it had an extra charge to get it going further. We'd hear overhead, BOOOOM, SSSSH, BOOOOM. We were told it was either Anzio Annie with an extra charge enabling it to reach targets on the beach or Anzio Express, a second gun?

Once I received a letter from a girl who wrote of a GI with the same name, Frank DeAngelo, from the 39th Field Artillery of our division. He received her letter written to me by mistake. He read it, he wrote to her, and she was upset. I never read her letter. I didn't know what she had written in it. I happened to visit his battalion and asked him what was going on. We got along OK, there wasn't any argument. I told him, "From here on if you get a letter with my serial number on it, just return it to sender and I'll do the same for you." Years later, I was in Orlando, FL, looking in the phone book and there was a Frank DeAngelo listed. I called him and we talked– it was that same GI. Not long ago I read he passed away. I understand there were 1,500 DeAngelo's in the United States. There were ten DeAngelo's in the 3rd Infantry Division, some with the same spelling and others with an apostrophe.

GI combat uniforms in the Mediterranean and in Europe were of Olive Drab (O.D.) wool. During the summer the O.D.'s were very hot. We asked why we couldn't wear denim like the GI's in the Pacific. We were told the wool O.D. cloth was best when someone was wounded because it helped stop the flow of blood and keep the wound clean. We questioned this.

All this time I was at the front I was without my glasses, since I had broken them in Africa. I asked one of the medics to help me get new ones and he sent me to Nettuno. I received GI glasses which were the wrong prescription. I tried to wear them for a while but couldn't, so I was in combat without glasses all those many months.

While walking in Nettuno, I came across a large pipe that I thought was a sewer pipe until I saw it had a rifling band around its outside. This means a big cannon round, either it was Anzio Annie or Anzio Express. There wasn't much to do in town so I became acquainted with a driver of a DUKW-353 vehicle. *Figure 33.* It was manufactured by General Motors' Yellow and Truck Division. This vehicle would go in the water, come out of the water, then go back on the road. I asked him, "How does she run?" He said, "Come aboard, I'm going out to a ship, I'll take you."

Figure 33. German long range 88mm hitting the water off Anzio as the DUKW-353 came to shore with supplies.

Before moving off the road to go into the water, the driver had to get off and deflate all four tires for riding on the sandy beach. When it came out of the water they had to start the DUKW's onboard compressor and get down again to refill its tires to drive back on the road. The later DUKW models, I understand, had a button or switch to deflate or inflate the tires. This was a good idea so the driver didn't have to get off and take a chance of getting caught in a barrage. They can have them, I tell you. They bounced all over, on land and on water. Boy was I glad to get off the DUKW.

Soon I came by a fighters' landing strip. There was a Spitfire on the strip with its 21-year old Canadian pilot. Radar was placed in a nearby field and if it picked up an enemy plane, the pilot would have to take off. I told him I always loved airplanes and he showed me how to start the Merlin engine. He didn't actually start it, but he did show me how it was done. There was a big piece of cast iron in the back near the tail to balance this aircraft and I was surprised to see how large it was for balancing this aircraft.

As I was walking later that afternoon, I came across a 90 mm anti aircraft GI crew. They had a radio and were listening to Axis Sally report on who had been captured the night before. She also

Anzio

played American music. Suddenly these GI's received firing orders. Boy, did they jump up and out! They brought their 90 mm gun into the position you see in *Figure 34*. Each gun fired about fifteen rounds, there must have been about six 90 mm's. They were using the new proximity fuse which exploded about 50-60 feet off the ground. It blew downward and caught a bunch of Germans on the ground or in foxholes or where ever. Counterattack was destroyed using the new proximity fuses.

Our radar set was installed in a field where there were a lot of

Figure 34. 90 mm anti-aircraft on Anzio in action. German counterattack was destroyed by this action as the author was standing by.

88mm duds lying around it. Smoke was generated to provide cover for us as we practiced close order drills in this field. Some idiot GI's kicked some duds and we were very lucky none exploded. We asked these GI's not to kick any duds. Some GI's were plain dumb.

At this field with our radar system in the center we noticed the ground was littered with 18" strips of dull black paper with aluminum foil material on the other side about 1 1/4" wide. These were called "Windows." We asked what they were for and were told they were sent floating down by German aircraft to confuse our radar operator into thinking their aircraft was flying to our direction. Our Air Corps used the same idea.

Every time a German artillery round exploded the smell of the gunpowder made us wonder what material they mixed with their gunpowder. We learned they were mixing urine.

Soon we were introduced to a new way of writing letters called V-Mail forms. When the 8 x 11 forms were completed a censor would review each one and block out some words. Then they would take a photo of the letters to reduce them and the originals were destroyed. They called this V-mail and they were much smaller and easier to send back home. The Division had one showing the 3rd Infantry Division Helmet Patch drawing which was interesting. It was to let others see how the helmet and patch looked over the head of a GI who wrote the V-Mail. *Figure 35* shows three V-Mails I had sent to my parents while I was serving overseas. Note the printed designs for the 3rd Infantry Division, 30th Regiment.

At the beachhead there wasn't any hand-to-hand fighting. Anzio was wait and see, find out what we were going to do, what they were going to do. We GI's were always fighting the Herman Goering Division, a division specially formed for him. They were tough fighters, they would fight us all the time and we beat them. They didn't like us and we didn't like them. They said our GI's yelled and screamed and fought them all day. They called us the Blue and White Devils. One day, as I was lying in my slit trench, I saw a Focke-Wulf 190A fly a couple hundred feet above me. These FW-190A's were called Yellow Jackets, also known as the Abbeville Boys from France. They were called Yellow Jackets because of the yellow paint around their aircraft cowl. They were supposed to be the top fighter pilots of the Herman Goering Luftwaffe. The FW-190A was called the "WURGER," the Butcher Bird. Another time I saw a Spitfire firing

Anzio

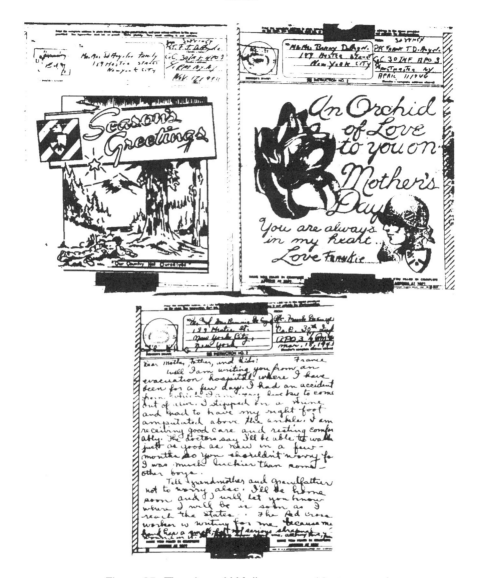

Figure 35. The above V-Mails were sent to my parents.

at a Messerschmitt BF-109-F, to shoot it down. They were weaving in and out, dodging, until finally, the BF-109-F started smoking. This Spitfire followed him close to the ground. The Spitfire pilot thought the BF-109-F was going to crash. The Spitfire went off in one direction, the BF-109-F poured the coal on. He flew off in another direction. He faked having been hit. When the Spitfire pilot saw his trick he turned and went after him. I don't know if he ever got him but many years later I was talking to a friend about this and he said, "Did you know that was me flying that Spitfire?" I said, "Larry, are you sure?" He said, "I thought I had that sucker that day but he sure fooled me. I chased him but I couldn't catch him." Was this not strange?

For months the Germans were looking down on us all the time. This is why we couldn't get out of our fox hole or slit trench until nightfall. Thus at dusk we set up our weapons. Then at daybreak we removed them to go to sleep. That was the way we fought for five months.

A German Division had 10,000 men, where our divisions had 15,000. The Germans brought 10 or 11 divisions from Southern France and Northern Italy down to fight the 5th Army. At Anzio, they had 100,000 to 110,000 men fighting against us. At the time we had three divisions (the 3rd Infantry Division, the British 1st Division and our 1st Armored Division) made up of approximately 85,000 men. I don't think any of the three were full strength. The Army 45th Infantry Division arrived later in the same condition. In fact, this also applied to the 34th and 36th Infantry Divisions.

One night, at a listening post with a sound power phone, we were about 100 yards in front of our line. I picked the phone up to call my CP when I heard a German voice speaking on our wire. I quickly followed our wire by hand back to our CP. I cut it and strung a new wire to our phone. I picked up the phone and again heard a German voice speaking. I couldn't believe it, I don't know if they were between us and my company or what. I don't understand how this happened. Soon we were pulled back. Was there some German between us?

Figure 36 shows some buildings called "La Ferriere." This was a place where the townspeople would grind wheat or grain. We were bivouacked on one side of the factory and you may be able to see a lot of straw on the left hand side of the building where we stayed.

Anzio

Figure 36. This was called Le Ferriere. The GI's called it the Factory and would grind wheat. Anzio.

One day I noticed from a long distance some B-17's and B-24's with fighters who were bombing some targets. The next thing I knew there was a great ball of black smoke and I saw that one of our bombers had been hit. With a load of bombs and fuel, it just disintegrated. He just disappeared. The others dropped their bombs to destroy the target. It was something I will never forget. Those GI's never knew what hit them, like the 45th Infantry Division Cub.

Concerning our Air Corps bombing, I had read that the Browning Plant in Belgium was never bombed, yet it manufactured weapons like the Browning high-powered automatic pistol that most of the Luftwaffe pilots carried. I wonder why?

One night a GI and I started to speak what we thought sounded like German, even though neither of us knew the language. Almost immediately, we heard some GI pulling the bolt of a Tommy gun. We started to yell, "No, no, no! GI's, GI's!" I don't remember if we had been drinking or not. Sometimes GI's do crazy things. It's fun today to think of it, but it was a crazy thing to do that night, for if that GI had blasted through from the inside of his tent, he would have killed us for sure.

While at the factory I noticed a ravine and in the ravine was a

Half-Track M-15A1 with a 37 mm gun and 50 caliber twin machine guns facing to the right. The GI who was sitting in the seat was being relieved by another GI. The job was to sit and have its guns ready to fire at any enemy aircraft. A Messerschmitt BF-109, believe it or not, flew low and fast in the same direction over the Half Track was facing west. The replacement GI accidentally hit the trigger of this 37 mm cannon. The cannon fired one round that knocked the aircraft's tail off. The aircraft hit the ground hard at full speed. They claim the pilot was in a one piece leather flying suit. His body was like jelly. I talked to a GI who took a very expensive Chronograph watch off the pilot's wrist. It wouldn't run because its back was pushed in from the crash. He took the back off and pushed it out, put it on his wrist and it was running again. I said, "That's something to keep." He said, "Yeah, that's a story I can tell my grandchildren." It was funny, a GI accidentally hit the trigger of this 37 mm cannon and shot down a BF-109 aircraft. *Figure 37*.

At the factory we were told to watch out for German

Figure 37. The Half-Track M-15A1.

paratroopers (Fallschirmjager) who might land in our area. They never did. One day a GI said, "I'm tired of being hungry for some meat. I'm going to go out and get some meat." Soon I heard a rifle shot. He came back with the hind leg of a cow, I asked him what he was going to do with it and he told me he was going to cook it so he could have a steak. He cut off a hunk of meat, found a frying pan and started a fire. There was a dog hanging around, the poor thing was skin and bones and looked like he had shrapnel in his hip. He was walking OK but he was dragging. I said, "Why don't you give that dog some? He looks like he's starving." So the GI gave the dog a piece of meat, but the dog just sniffed it and walked away. We didn't realize what happened until we checked. The dog didn't have any teeth.

At the factory we started to build a small crystal radio called "Foxhole Radio." This was done with a piece of wood, a razor blade, two nails, lead from a pencil, some wire and a set of earphones. The blade was set between the nails. A piece of wire went through both ends of the blade, each wire to each nail. Then, from the nail, a piece of wire went to some iron pipes driven into the ground to act as a ground plus having an antenna. When the lead was taken out of the pencil, attached between the nails, then to the antenna. By running the lead across the edge of the razor blade it was possible to bring in a station. I made one and got a faint signal, while others I know heard more.

Another time, in the same area, I had a deep foxhole. At nights I would find a lot of dirt coming down from the inside walls and I was wondering why. The next morning I noticed a mole digging nearby. I picked up my shovel and put it in front of him. He hit the shovel, backed up and started going in the other direction. I again put the shovel in front of him and he hit it again. Then he backed up again and went in another direction. I put the shovel in front of him, he hit it again. Finally after the third time he came up to the surface to see what was going on. I scooped him up. I put some dirt in an empty 10-1 rations box, put him in and played with him for a while. He was small and soft with black fur.

We had a Tech Sergeant named Collins. We didn't know what to do about this so-called sergeant; we all disliked him. He would give us hell, tell us to do this and do that, yet whenever we moved to the front he would disappear. When we returned to a rest area, he popped up again and started giving us orders. Finally we looked at him and said, "Hey! Don't screw with us." We ignored him completely and would only take orders from the other sergeants. Our other sergeants were with us, supported us, and they didn't like him either. He had a big yellow streak on his back, right Sgt. Collins?

Figure 38 shows my military missal, I would read two chapters everyday. I still have it, complete with perspiration stains and all. It gave me peace of mind. One day, I was ordered to stand guard with a GI named Tilghman (who ate sugar all the time, saying he wanted to get diabetes) by a crossroads at the town of Crocetto. We were just ordered to stay there, with no further instructions. Unbelievable. I was sitting outside in the warm February sunshine with my feet in the slit trench. I was getting sleepy and thought I'd read one chapter and then take a little nap. Tilghman was in his slit trench and had his hand outside so he could warm up some coffee on a Coleman stove. All of a sudden we heard five 105mm artillery rounds coming in. I guess they were trying to hit the crossroad and they exploded all around us. One landed next to where I was lying and when it hit below in the side of

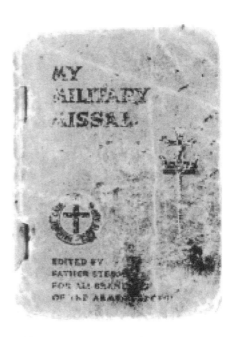

Figure 38. Author's Military Missal, written by Father Stedman, it was carried throughout combat.

the ditch, knocking out a great big piece of wet clay weighing 10 or 15 lbs., which then flew up. I was in the GI's normal position with my hands folded across my chest and my eyes open looking at the sky when, so help me God, the clay landed right on my chest. As soon as it hit me, I threw it off thinking it was a dud. Then I looked up and out at Tilghman. I asked, "Did you see that?" He was still holding the cup of coffee. I repeated, "Did you see that?" He said, "Yeah, I saw it." I said, "Boy you should see your face–you're as white as a sheet." "You think I'm bad, you should see yours, DeAngelo." I said, "I thought it was a round." He said, "If that had been a round, DeAngelo, you would have been long gone, even if it was a dud." Soon we were ordered to come back to C Company, but why we were put there, no one told us.

  The next day my sergeant ordered me to follow him to relieve a GI. The sergeant said he would return in two hours to bring another GI to relieve me on guard duty at our minefield. I had a good view in all directions and it was my job to keep anyone from going toward the minefield, which was on the other side of the road. At that time German Gen. Kissering was ordered by Hitler to push us back to the Mediterranean Sea. His orders, "Cut the abscess and push them back into the sea." We were prepared to hold back all counterattacks. Most of the higher officers were evacuated to Naples and we were left on the beach to take care of the coming counterattacks. Of course, I didn't have a foxhole or slit trench or anything dug. We were told to fortify our positions for the anticipated counterattacks. My sergeant said I would be on guard duty for two hours, then I was to dig in my position. That's the reason we were posted for a short time. I waited and waited–one hour passed, two hours passed, three hours passed–and my sergeant never returned. I was a little concerned about getting caught and not having a defense position. Some sergeants either forgot, or worse, they did not care. I made sure if I ever became a sergeant, I would do the best for my men. After many hours passed I had to go look for him. I would not desert my post and recruited a GI to stand in for me. I explained to him that if he saw anyone headed toward the minefield he was to holler and tell them it was a minefield. I told him I'd be gone no more than five or ten minutes. I had only walked about 25 yards when I heard the GI yell, "Get away! Get away! Get outta there! Get outta there–it's a minefield!" I turned around and saw a GI walking into our minefield. I also yelled. He paid no attention to us and kept on walking until he stepped on a Bouncing Betty, which jumped out of the ground and exploded. It killed him instantly.

Of course we were both upset, and mad. We don't know why he didn't pay attention to us, why he just kept going. I knew I would have a lot of explaining to do since I was the one on duty and the one who would be held responsible.

A short time later the same sergeant said our company commander wanted to see me. I didn't ask him why he never showed up with my replacement. I figured I'd say my piece at the right time. I walked to my company quarters, where the officers were sitting around looking upset but I can tell you that I was even more upset. They asked me what happened and I said, "Well, we were told the Germans were going to counterattack. We were to make our defense strong so we could fight and save the beachhead. I wasn't even given permission to dig one. All I know is that my sergeant came over and ordered me to relieve a GI who had been on duty for two hours, and he said I would be relieved by another GI in two hours so I would have time to dig my position. Over three hours went by. My sergeant never showed up with a GI to relieve me. I was concerned. I didn't know when their counterattacks would be coming. I asked a GI to help me and told him to watch for anyone going in the direction of our minefield while I went to look for my sergeant and ask why I wasn't relieved. The GI took my duty.

"As I walked away to find my sergeant I heard the GI yelling to someone to get out of there. But the other GI kept on walking into the minefield. In fact, he raised his hand as if to say don't bother me. Then he hit a mine and was killed. I'm sorry it happened but I don't think we could have prevented him from going into the minefield.

He looked like he was going to go in regardless; he was warned and yelled at so many times by both of us."

The officers didn't know what to say or do. They knew I hadn't deserted my post and realized that I had also found a replacement while I went to look for the sergeant. The blame fell on my sergeant. Nothing was said to me after the meeting and it seemed as though it was viewed as just one of those fluke accidents that was unavoidable. From that day on I knew that if I ever became a sergeant I wouldn't be like him. I would be a sergeant my men could be proud of and trust.

The Coleman stove was a good stove but it wasn't practical for GI's in the infantry. Each platoon was issued one. The Germans had a stove about the size of a metal cigarette box. They had cubes that looked like sugar. You would open up and stand both ends up, sit your canteen cup over it, and light the cube. It would give off a lot of heat for about two minutes. We were happy to find or capture these from the Germans. If we couldn't, we went over to artillery to ask for ammunition pellets. We used these to heat our water or food. We just used our own imagination to keep warm or warm up our food. With the Coleman stove, we had to put unleaded gasoline in it, otherwise it would screw up the valves. It was a three piece affair—a galvanized steel carrying case, a top cover, with the stove inside the other bottom case. We could use the carrying case or cover to heat water. Both always smelled of gasoline. These two cases were used only for heating water for us to wash or shave. We used our canteen cups to heat water or coffee. We placed it on top of our stove. It did a good job. A lot of GI's didn't like to carry these Coleman stoves. It was just another piece of equipment. If a GI was driving a vehicle then it wasn't a problem. To carry it was just another item that got in the way.

On Anzio late at night they would bring cold hamburgers and cold coffee up to us. This would be twelve or one in the morning, in big pots. These were called Mermite pots. They would keep food cold or hot. By the time we got them they were both cold. We ate and drank what was brought to us. We didn't complain. At least it was food and something to drink.

Figure 39 shows remembrance of mass and holy communion somewhere in Italy 1944 .

One day I was called in to our CP and told I was going on a 48-hour pass. Thinking I was going to go to Naples, I got pretty excited. But, no, I was told that I would stay on the beach. I received clean clothes, food, movies, the works; but no showers and slept in a six-man pyramid tent. No matter where you were, every night a German aircraft would fly over. We called it "Bed Check Charley," checking the beachhead for the Luftwaffe. Their bombers flew over and dropped bombs on us. If the bombers didn't get you, it would be one of our antiaircraft, spent rounds, or lots of shrapnel on the way down. All our antiaircraft fired and I could see hundreds of little shrapnel holes in the top of my tent. I really believed that I was safer on the front line than I was on the beach. So the next morning I asked the GI in charge, "Can I get a ride back to the front? It's safer there." He looked at me and said, "I know what you mean." I jumped on a truck, went back to my outfit, and when they

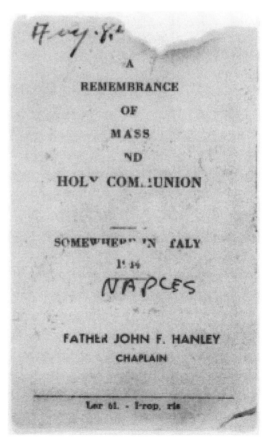

Figure 39. Author's Communion Card.

Anzio

asked what was wrong, I said it was safer being at the front than on the beach.

I later found out that each day 750 other men from the front were given their 48 hours, put on LCI's, and taken to Caserta near Naples for rest and enjoying the good life. Why were some GI's sent to the beach on Anzio for their 48 hours? I wonder why those men were picked and I wasn't. Why not all, for that matter, like me?

My sergeant asked for volunteers to demonstrate a new weapon and like a dummy, I volunteered. There were 12 of us. We marched to see the monsters called "Battle Sleds" pictured in *Figure 40*. The person in the middle, walking, is Gen. O'Daniels, 3rd Infantry Division Commander. The one on the left is Gen. Clark, 5th Army Commander. The one with his hand on his hips is Gen. Truscott, VI Corps Commander.

We trained for 5-7 days on these sleds that were designed by

Figure 40. The sled team at Anzio (The author was a member). General Clark, left; O'Daniels, right; Truscott, with hands on hips.

Russia for their attacks in the winter. Our Gen. O'Daniels copied them for Anzio. The sleds were six feet long, all welded on runners of flat steel. Each was chained together and they were very flexible while moving. These were built out of about half inch thick steel plating like a big piece of pipe cut in half. A GI would lie in each 12 slots and be dragged by a tank. Our squad leader was in contact by telephone with the tank commander. We had three sleds in my regiment and I don't know if there were more. In order to break out of Anzio the Germans had their positions well fortified. It was our job to be pulled by the tanks up to their positions, get out, surround the enemy and destroy their positions. This was a good idea and maybe it worked well in Russia, but it didn't on Anzio. We tried to get out of this battle sled. Our sergeant in charge said, "You've had training, now you're gonna use it." We were stuck. Oh well.

At suppertime the night before the break out, a GI walked up to me and said, "Hey, DeAngelo!" I looked at my friend Larry, the GI who volunteered to go overseas with us. He was assigned to the 34th Infantry Division. I asked him what he was doing here and he said he had come to see me. He had spoken to our friend Daniels (he was the one who had that ear problem), who was in basic training at Blanding with us, and Daniels had told Larry were I was. I invited him to have something to eat with me but he said no.

I asked, "You don't look too well, are you sick?" He replied, "Nah, I'm not sick, but I'm going to die, DeAngelo." GI's will always call you by your last name. I questioned him, "What do you mean you're gonna die?" He said, "Well, I know it." I said, "Come on, I'm probably gonna die before you; I'm in the battle sled team." He said, "Oh no! Are you in that? Oh, that's real bad." I said, "So whatever happens, happens–don't feel you're gonna die." I tried to pick up his spirits but could not. He said, "If something happens to me, and if you get home, will you go see Jackie, a girl I love, to let her know I loved her? She does not live far from your parents, DeAngelo." I said, "Yeah, I'll do it for you, Larry." I asked, "Are you sure you won't stay? You know, tomorrow morning is the break out."

He said, "That's why I'm getting back." He said goodbye. Soon he left. *Figure 41* shows Larry, my friend, who looked like Harry James, the band leader. In another chapter more about Larry.

Sometimes, if we had to go from one Company to another we would pick up our phone line wire and run with it in our hands from one location to another. What they did, those German suckers, was they cut our wire and moved it to their position, where their machine guns were set up. When our GI's were running with the wire, some would run smack into a machine gun and were killed. We were very careful running any wire; we'd stop once in a while to make sure we were traveling in the correct direction.

Figure 41. My friend Larry, killed at Anzio on June 1, 1944.

At times the Germans always set up their machine guns to hit us around the knees. They did this because they figured if they hit us in the knees it would take around 15 people to take care of each of us: doctors, medics, nurses, etc. If they killed us, well then we'd be buried and that was that. If we were wounded, we'd spend time in the hospital. In their minds, wounding us was better than killing, because it would take so many to care for the wounded.

There were 1,525 GI's killed at Anzio and 6,877 wounded. 3rd Infantry Division suffered 955 casualties in one day, with 1,154 missing in action.

Below you will see Figure 42 of our breaking out of Anzio for Rome.

Figure 42. The 5th Army breaks out of Anzio for Rome. May 23rd, 1944.

Chapter Six

Rome

We had a problem as my squad was ready to climb into our battle sled for the break out at Anzio on May 23, 1944. One of the sleds became twisted and was destroyed as it went around a corner, so one squad had to stay behind. Our Sgt. Baldwin won the toss and the other two squads went on as planned. I understand those two squads were chewed up going into combat. Fortunately our squad was ordered to another operation. Sometimes it works out for the best when you volunteer.

Figure 43 shows Anzio Annie after capture. This monster gun was a 280 mm and was one of two we faced on Anzio. Our Air

Figure 43. Anzio Annie captured by the 3rd Division.

GREETINGS FROM THE PRESIDENT

Corps was never able to find it.

Soon we were pushing the Germans back. We started climbing some hills where the German's Tiger tanks had been before being knocked out by our P-40 fighter bombers. From where they were, they had an excellent view of us below. They knew exactly what we were doing even though we used smoke generators to cover our movements and water trucks to dampen the roads and stop the dust from rising when we were traveling or moving equipment.

Figure 44 shows a German weapon called "Nebelwerber" which we called "Screamie Meamie." It had six or seven rockets of 80 pounds each with a range of four miles, but it was not very accurate. After they were fired they made an awful lot of noise flying through the air. The result was mostly concussion but they did have the power to destroy. When they were fired they generated pink smoke and

Figure 44. A German weapon called the Nebelweber. The GI's called it Screamie Meamies. A rocket with 6 or 7 rounds. Used on Anzio.

Rome

the Germans would have to quickly move them to another location since our aircraft would easily pinpoint them.

After breaking out on Anzio we moved toward Rome. *Figure 45* shows Cori, a town C Company passed through. When I walked to this town's church, I fired at the church bell with my M-1. I heard it go bing, bang and I'm certain my bullet's mark is still on it today. I don't know why I did it, I guess it's just the way things

Figure 45. The town of Cori, Italy, captured by C Company where the author shot at the church bell on May 25, 1944.

happen. I captured about 15 prisoners at Cori. When we captured prisoners we had to personally walk them back to the MP's at the rear. As I was walking with these prisoners a couple of GI's asked, "Hey, are you taking them to the MP's?" I said, "Yeah." "OK, here're two more prisoners ... here're three prisoners." I ended up with about 40-45 prisoners. One of the prisoners I was given was at the end of the line and he was wearing a long overcoat. I called him a sad sack.

He was short with a coat down to his ankles, definitely not the cream of the crop.

Another prisoner was brought to me along the way and he was tough looking, strictly German Old Army veteran, perhaps in the service 15 or 20 years. I figured he was going to the rear of the line, but instead he walked up to the front of the line. I ordered all of them to march and soon discovered that they would follow the new guy's lead, almost as if they knew him. If he marched in step, so did they; if he marched out of step, so would they. Whatever step he took the others followed him. This little guy at the end had to take long strides, being short legged. His overcoat was dragging him down. I don't know what rank this lead prisoner held, but he may have been a high-ranking officer. The German SS were known to switch uniforms or remove identifying items from the clothing if they were about to be captured. I finally delivered everyone to the MP's and then turned to walk the several miles back to C Company alone.

Figure 46 shows the town of Rocca Massima on May 26, 1944, captured by C Company. This town was built on a mountain of rocks and all of the homes were built from rocks. There I met a father and his two daughters, one was 16 the other was either 14 or 15. I learned that the oldest was pregnant by a German and that her father had disowned her. Her sister told me she slept with a German cook to feed her family. The father now would not take his eyes off his younger daughter, who was not wearing any shoes. I asked her why she wasn't wearing any shoes and she told me they didn't have money to buy them. I gave her all the money I had in my pocket (what did I need the money for?) and her father became suspicious immediately. I reassured him that the money was for shoes. She was very sweet and nice to speak with. I enjoyed her company for a short time.

Later that day, I came across a "lady of the town." She performed services men wanted. Many towns had one, two, or three prostitutes called "Puttana." She walked up to me and asked, "Would you like to spend some time with me?" I asked her in Italian, "How much do

Rome

Figure 46. The town of Rocca Massima, Italy, captured by C Company on May 26, 1944.

you charge?" I think she answered about 5 or 10 dollars. I told her I'd have to think about it since I didn't have any money left. One of my GI's came in the house where we were. He asked, "Are you going to go with her, DeAngelo?" I said I didn't know, and that I didn't have any money with me. He said, "Why don't you go with her? I'll pay her for you because I want to see what you do with her." I asked, "Why?!" He replied, "Because I want to do it with her." I responded, "Well, why don't you do it." He said, "Because I've never done it before. I want to see you do it, so I can do it." I asked, "So you're gonna pay for me." He answered, "Yes." He paid her. Some minutes later I asked him, "Do you see what I'm doing?" He said, "Yes." Afterward I told him to go ahead and do it. I looked to see how he was doing. He asked, "How am I doing?" I replied, "Great, keep going," and I left him there. I was walking back down the street when I ran into Pfc. Walker, a married man from the South. I said, "Hey, Walker, there's a female giving some samples at a house up the street. He replied, "Not me, I'm a married man and I'm true to my wife." I responded, "Well, I'm sorry, Walker. I was kidding." Before I turned to walk down the street, I saw Walker running up this street like the devil was after him. He soon took care of her. I'll never forget Walker saying he was married. That was Rocca Massima.

Many times we were so exhausted that we fell asleep while marching. We only woke up when we ran into the back of the GI who had stopped in front of us. Often, he too was asleep and we'd have like a chain reaction. This happened to us a number of times and often some GI would break rank. Others would follow. We wondered what happened to GI's behind us. We go looking for them.

As we were marching toward Rome there wasn't much fighting, just some rear guard action. Sometimes the Germans would place three or four men in a good position to hold us up. This gave the Germans more time to build a new defense line or to get their equipment out. These men probably did not know they would be killed or captured. Along the way, my company commander sent a GI to tell me that I was now a Buck Sergeant. That was fine with me. About 5 or 10 minutes later, this was early evening, we were 10 or 15 miles south of Rome. I was ordered to see my company commander and walked in to find him and another lieutenant sitting at a table covered with a map and some booze bottles. It was obvious that both of them were drunk. The company commander looked at me and said, "DeAngelo, I want you to take two men on patrol. Go across as far as you can to raise a ruckus and then come back to report what went on." I said, "What do you mean–raise a ruckus, Lieutenant?" He said, "Use your rifles, start firing, see what happens." I walked back to my squad and picked out two new replacement GI's who had just signed on. "You and you, come with me," I said. "We are going on patrol and I want both of you to pay strict attention to me. You're new and you need to follow my instructions." We moved out, walked about 200 yards and stopped to look around.

I took them down to the bottom of a hill. Some Italians had dug deep pockets in the side of a hill where they would put a cow or horse so they wouldn't be killed by artillery. We found a few that were empty and took them over. I told both GI's, "Go in and get some sleep. When we awake we will leave together. I will report to our company commander." We went to sleep without making any ruckus. I was not about to listen to some lieutenants who were drunk. When we woke up, we returned to C Company (Command Post).

Both lieutenants were still at it–only worse now. They asked me what had happened. I said, "I went as far as the railroad track and up on the hill there's a telephone or power line. I didn't see any enemy." He said, "OK, that's great, you can go back to your squad." But before returning I looked to see a railroad track and power lines for my report. I rejoined my squad. I wasn't back five minutes when we were ordered to pack up, move out and into reserve. We didn't move forward, we walked back to our rear. As I look back, I still think they were idiots. They wanted us to start a ruckus and maybe have some GI's killed. For what reason? Was it necessary? I didn't pay attention to them. If they had asked me about it, I would have told them off. I didn't take orders from any officer who was a drunk, giving such orders.

We were in reserve for a couple of days. We'd take a short rest then get back on the road to the front. Soon we noticed a flight of twin-engine bombers above us. I don't remember if they were B-26's, B-25's, or A-20's. I noticed one of them was hit and this plane is on fire. Soon one or two crews bailed out. It was sad to see this happen to a GI, who might be a friend or relative. But we'd just keep on moving up. That is life and these things do happen. We had to be very careful on the roads because our P-40's patrolled the area. They always had a 500-pound bomb under the fuselage or one 250-pound bomb under each wing. If they noticed enemy troops they would dive and go after them. That's what took care of those Tiger tanks on the side of the hill before we got off the beach.

I was a BAR man for some time but when I became a sergeant, my assistant Pfc. DeBello took over. DeBello was a nice kid. One day we were walking down a hill when we passed a cherry orchard.

Just then, a sniper fired on us. We couldn't tell where he was since the Germans always used smokeless powder, which made them hard to locate. (We did not have smokeless powder. I understand it was invented in 1889 by the US. It was not issued to the Army in WWI or WWII.) It was very quiet and we were waiting for orders to advance or whatever, but no orders came. "What do we do, do we go across now or call for P-40's?" asked DeBello. I had no idea what we should do. We waited for a while and I remembered the cherry trees about 200 feet away from us. "I think I'm going to get some of those cherries for us. Stay put," I told him.

He replied, "OK." It was very quiet, we were waiting for orders to advance or whatever. I have no idea, nobody tells us anything.

I walked to those cherry trees, climbed up a ladder and started picking cherries. I picked a helmet full for us, then walked back. I asked one of my GI's, "Where is DeBello?" They said he was over there. I said, "Over where? What is he doing?" The GI pointed and said, "He was killed." I asked, "What do you mean he was killed? How?" He replied, "A sniper shot him from across that hill." I felt real bad and there was nothing I could do. Some snipers had powerful telescopic sites on their rifles. Through these powerful scopes you could see a mile away. That sniper may have been the same one who shot at me when I was operating the machine gun some months before on the beachhead.

I never went to view his body. Poor DeBello, after his mother died, he was not the same. He was refused to go home for her burial and he always talked of missing her. He told me he didn't care if he went home or not after her death. I guess maybe he did something he wasn't supposed to do like leaving his position and was killed. I felt bad; he was a nice kid. I left the cherries. Only about an hour before he had said to me, "You know, DeAngelo, a guy can get killed." Smokeless powder caused us to lose a number of GI's, like DeBello. I recall when DeBello was given my BAR, in a few days he called out to me to say he had shot and killed a German with a single shot.

Many times when we were out marching we would come across

Rome

large tomato patches and grape vines. We would clean them out in a hurry. But the Germans were pretty dirty. They started booby-trapping the patches. Pretty quickly we realized what they were doing and became very cautious when stripping a tomato patch or grape vines.

One day our mail Jeep came by. I must have received twenty packages; a number of them had probably been stored up somewhere. I sat down to enjoy opening my packages when we received orders to move out. I looked at all these packages, many still not opened, and I grabbed the ones from my family. The rest I gave to any GI's who wanted one. The ones from my family had uncooked spaghetti, salami, and cans of hot peppers and olives. They were great! My mother knew I loved licorice and she always sent me a box of licorice if she could find it.

We were walking toward Rome one hot day in May of 1944 and two of my men were about to pass out from heat exhaustion. Each was carrying a BAR that weighed 19 pounds with ammo. I was carrying my 45 Colt and to give each one some relief, I carried both of their BARs, one on each shoulder, and marched on. When the men felt better I gave them back even though I felt as though I could have carried them much further without any trouble. I know they appreciated that I was there for them, no matter what the problem. When I was wounded in a minefield many months later, two of my men said they were coming to get me. I told them not to because it was too dangerous. I heard them say I would do it for them—what wonderful words to hear from my men and I still hear it today.

We were getting closer to Rome, an open city, and there was no fighting. The fighting seemed to be taking place north of Rome. We walked on the Appian Way, which was the first highway built in Rome. It was lined with Lombardy trees that shaded its marching Roman soldiers from the sun. Once 6,000 victims were crucified by the Romans on both sides of this road, facing each other. Our company commander (I don't recall who our company commander was, we had so many come and go due to sickness, wounds, etc.) drove up in his Jeep and asked if I spoke the language. I said I understood the language and he told me to jump in. We had been walking for days, so I jumped in happily. I was given a map of the city of Rome and a hand-held radio called a walkie-talkie, BC-611-C. *Figure 47* shows what it looked like. This radio had an antenna on top. We had to unscrew its cap to uncover the antenna, which we then pulled out about five feet. Its cap was attached with a chain to its body. We always needed to carry extra batteries for this walkie-

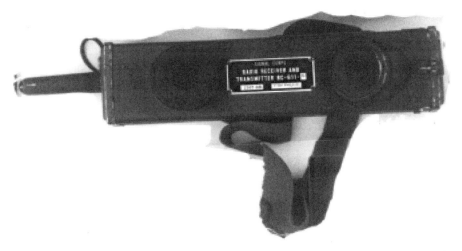

Figure 47. Photo of Model BC-611-C, a Walkie Talkie radio. This type was used by the author going into Rome, at times. It gave the Germans our position.

talkie. When I operated it the Germans would zero in on us with their radio direction finding equipment. I wasn't too happy with this radio since I always felt it gave away our positions somehow. I didn't have it long because soon after I got it set up an artillery barrage would come in. There was a possibility the Germans were able to trace its position.

The Germans were retreating and we were really charging through. With my pack, my rifle, map, and radio, I was about 100-150 yards ahead of our two scouts. My orders were to walk into

Rome and find our bivouacked area by the Tiber River where C Company was supposed to stay for that night. As I turned the curve in the road, I came upon a German leaning over his rifle and ready to take a shot at me. I went for my M-1, but he didn't move or fire. What I didn't know was that he was already dead. I learned later that he had been shot several times by some GI's, after I went by him, who were also surprised as they rounded the bend in the road. I don't know what killed him, but it could have been a heart attack just before I came upon him.

I finally reached the outskirts of Rome on the south side. For 2,000 years, history tells us Rome was never captured from the south. If this is true then I may have been the first to march into Rome when it fell. I noticed its pastel-colored buildings with balconies were quite interesting with a lot of aluminum and marble entrances with balconies on each floor. The first thing I heard was a woman's voice yelling to me, "Hey, I'm from Chicago, when is our food coming up?" When I heard her, I just sat down on the street curb. I waited for C Company to walk by and pointed the way to the Tiber River just down the street where we were to bivouac for the night. I stayed in a room on the roof of the Palace of Justice, which was just like our Supreme Court. I don't know what exactly the rooms were used for, maybe to keep prisoners. I stayed there every night for two weeks.

The 3rd Infantry Division became MP's in Rome for two weeks. They gave us that privilege for the hard fighting we did on Anzio. This was our rest period. Time to regroup, and receive new equipment and replacements. Pope Pius XII had requested Rome's water supply and electricity be turned off. He figured by requesting Rome's water and electricity to be shut down, Roman women wouldn't fraternize with our GI's. The 3rd Infantry Division wouldn't have any water to drink or wash with and move on. We were given MP armbands to keep the peace, but there was little to do. I found a liquor store and bought a bottle of champagne for 25 cents. I took it up on the roof and drank it then went to sleep. The next day I did the same thing, but this time it cost 50 cents, the next day 75 cents. Finally I decided not to buy anymore. I don't recall where I ate, or what I ate, and, frankly, I don't remember too much about this time. We just enjoyed our leisure and slept as long as we wanted. I was getting plenty of rest; we GI's needed it.

One afternoon I teamed up with Sgt. Krug. We walked along the streets and met two Italian girls who said they were sisters. One was husky with dark hair with a dark complexion. The other was smaller, more attractive and had a light complexion, blonde hair and blue eyes—the one I wanted. The 3rd Infantry Division had taken over a small official building and the blonde and I went into a large room with a large table. I was just starting to get some pleasure out of her when I heard a commotion at the door. I heard somebody say, "You can't go in there, it's a restricted area." I was dumbfounded. I peeked out and saw a lieutenant I didn't know guarding the door. He wanted me to have my time with this girl and was stopping every GI trying to get in the room. I thought it was great of him to try to give us some privacy. Unfortunately I was not able to enjoy her. She told me she tried to have sex a few times before but was unable to because she was "crossboned." It was a difficult time for both of us so we did nothing. When we left the building I thanked the lieutenant.

Later on, we met her sister with Sgt. Krug. We talked to the girls about giving a party the next day and they gave us their address so we could pick them up.

The next day Sergeant Krug and I went for a walk. I am sorry, and ashamed to say that we were walking up some street with a bottle of booze in our hands. They say if you're drunk you can't remember, but I remember what happened and it should never have happened. We were having a good time singing, making noise, and feeling great. The MP's left us alone because our division was the MP's and the 3rd Infantry Division was in complete control of Rome. We came across a watch repair shop and inside there were two Air Corps GI's arguing with the proprietor about a problem of some kind. Sgt. Krug went inside, pulled open the door of the window showcase, picked out a watch, set the time to the store clock, put it on his wrist and walked out. I saw him do it; no one stopped him. I too picked one up, put it on my wrist and walked out. We continued walking, singing and having a good time, I said to Sgt. Krug, "Do you know what we just did? It was theft and we could have gone to jail for that." Finally the Air Corps GI's came running after us. "Hey, did you GI's just pick up a watch back there?" "Us? No." I hate to put this in the story but it is true. "Go back there and look for it," we told them. They ran back and we, of course, disappeared. The next morning I asked Sgt. Krug if he remembered what we did. He looked at me and asked, "You have a watch too?" I said, "Yeah, let's get rid of them." We threw them away. I don't know how good they were, or what they were. He and I were really upset and embarrassed we had done such a thing. We never did such a thing again.

Later that day we went to pick up the girls and met their parents, who looked to be in their late 50's. I don't think they were sisters, but they were probably cousins or friends. The girls had rooms of their own and each took us to them. I was going to try to continue what I had tried to do the day before but I tried and tried and still couldn't. She laughed and giggled and told me her doctor had said that sex would be impossible. Sgt. Krug came in and asked, "What's going on?" I explained it to him and he replied, "That's the trouble with you young GI's—you don't know what your doing. I'll show you how it's done." I replied, "All right, be my guest." He disappeared into the room with the blonde. I didn't want to be with his girl, who I wasn't interested in. She tried to steal my sunglasses. They were not expensive and I told her, "No, no, no." When Sgt. Krug came out, he said, "I guess you were right, impossible!" I laughed, I said, "I told you." We told the girls we would be back to pick them up for the party. More drinking and other things to do.

But we didn't pick up the girls like we promised. We were all drinking. Even though everyone knew the restaurant where the party was going to be, when the 6x6 trucks picked us up we ended up driving around for about two or two and a half hours, completely lost. We found the place long after the party was to have started. We were supposed to have women waiting for us when we got there but many had left. It was a mad house. Every GI was drunk. They beat up the band, destroyed their equipment, and broke tables. I guess they were frustrated it didn't pan out the way it was planned. After being cooped up for so many months on Anzio just the mention of death hurt us. The GI's went to sleep wherever they could find a space. Yours truly was feeling good, but not too drunk. It was time to go back to our bivouacked area so we dragged our GI's out of the bar. They were so drunk that it took two GI's to pick them up by their arms and legs and throw them like sacks of potatoes up onto our truck's steel bed. These beds were muddy and dirty and some slid all the way down to the back of the cab. It took a while to load everyone, but we finally made it back to our bivouacked area. All were indeed dead drunk.

Well, our GI's were so drunk they didn't have any clothing except what they were wearing the night before. They were muddy and dirty. We brushed off as much as we could, washed up, and shaved. Dombrowski, the one I had a fistfight with when we were building the latrine, woke up and went out to wash his face. Our helmets were lined up outside our tents with water in them to use as a basin to wash. He put his hands into his helmet to put water on his face, and ran his fingers through his hair. He found his head didn't have any hair. He looked in the mirror and saw that his head was completely shaven clean. He didn't have a strand of hair on his head and his eyebrows were also shaved off. He wanted to know who did it and picked up his bayonet, saying he was going to kill whoever shaved him. We had one GI who was a barber and I don't know if he was the one who did the deed, but he sure made himself scarce when he heard that Dombrowski was prepared to go after him. Fortunately, an order came down telling us we were ordered to go on parade within the hour. We cleaned up as best we could. *Figure 48* shows on August 6, 1944, with Gen. Patch reviewing 3rd Infantry

Rome

Figure 48. General Patch, our new 7th Army Commander, reviewing the 3rd Division troops and singing the division song. August 6, 1944.

Division's 15,000 men singing "Dog Face Soldier." *Figure 49* shows this song.

    Many things were happening, but we were not told exactly what was going on. The 34th Infantry Division went north with three new Divisions. The 10th, 85th and 88th Infantry Divisions came up and went past Rome. They were assigned to the 5th Army. The 3rd, 36th, and 45th Infantry Divisions were reassigned to the 7th Army under Gen. Patch. Gen. Clark was still commander of the 5th Army. Gen. Truscott was with VI Corp.

    We had been in Rome for only two weeks. The Pope had made sure everything was turned off, trying to keep Roman women from getting tangled up with American GI's. Of course it didn't happen that way. I'm sure a lot of grown adults today have fathers who were 3rd Infantry Division soldiers. Not me, but Sgt. Krug probably.

There were a lot of things which went on in the Infantry that were never recorded and what I'm trying to do is let people know about some of the funny things that happened to us GI's at times. One company commander had to put in requests for supplies or rations based on the number of GI's in his command. This commander was told he had two extra GI's and he discovered that some of his men had dressed up two women as GI's. His GI's had smuggled two women into the company for some nighttime pleasures. They had disguised them as GI's, dressing them up with combat boots, rifles, etc. I understood that they even went into combat with them for a while. Very quick, these two women were gone.

I remember saying sometimes that when this is over I am going to write a book of my time in the army. I am sure that I was not the only one who said these very same words.

We were now off to Naples by truck.

Rome

THE DOGFACE SOLDIER

Moderato (Traditional)

Burt Gold Ken Hart

I WOULDN'T GIVE A BEAN TO BE A FANCY PANTS MARINE — I'D RATHER BE A DOG-FACE SOLDIER LIKE I AM —; I WOULDN'T TRADE MY OLD OD'S FOR ALL THE NAVY'S DUNGAREES FOR I'M THE WALKING PRIDE OF UNCLE SAM —; ON ALL THE POSTERS THAT I READ IT SAYS THE ARMY BUILDS MEN — SO THEY'RE TEARING ME DOWN TO BUILD ME OVER AGAIN — I'M JUST A DOGFACE SOLDIER WITH A RIFLE ON MY SHOULDER AND I EAT A KRAUT FOR BREAKFAST EV'RY DAY — . SO FEED ME AMMUNITION, KEEP ME IN THE THIRD DIVISION, YOUR DOGFACE SOLDIER BOY'S O — KAY.

Figure 49. The 3rd Division song sung by 15,000 troops marching by General Patch. Rome, Italy on August 6, 1944.

Chapter Seven

Naples

We were bivouacked at a new area around Naples for training. The cold wet winter on Anzio had caused a problem with my feet and while in training, the insides of my feet broke open with puss and blood oozing out. I didn't know what it was. It was hard for me to put my shoes and socks on, much less walk. I was hospitalized, my feet were bandaged and I was put to bed. A nurse bathed my feet with warm water and Epsom salts through my bandages every few hours. The doctor said, "Boy you have a bad case." "A bad case of what?" I asked. They said it was trench foot. I don't know if it was really trench foot, but I got a bad infection of some kind. I spent the next two weeks in bed at what I think was the 51st EVAC. It was near Naples by a racetrack where our replacements came in. It was a nice building, very modern, and I think it may have been a hotel at one time. Soon after my bandages were removed, both feet looked healed.

Then on July 8, my birthday, the doctor came in to say I wasn't going back to my outfit at this time. "I'm going to send you to a place called Pozzuoli. There are some other GI's with foot problems there. At the beach, I want you to walk. Go in the surf without shoes or socks. I want your feet in the hot sand on the beach to get your feet back into condition." Of course, I got out of training and I spent my time recuperating.

A 5th Army truck took us to Pozzuoli which, incidentally, is where a famous actress was born. She may have been one of the many children who came to us GI's for candy. I hope she found the young GI who was good to her, his name was Charlie. Maybe he was one of the GI's who was also recuperating at Pozzuoli like I was. He might have been in the same tent with me.

We stayed on the beach and did nothing. Each morning we would walk with shoes and socks a quarter mile for breakfast, lunch and supper. Then we walked back to run up and down the beach without socks and shoes. We did only what we wanted to do; we didn't have to report to anybody. When I wanted to swim, I walked into the Mediterranean Sea. We didn't have bathing suits, so we usually wore boxer shorts. They had a ribbon on each side to make them tighter. At times we wore a pair of green denim long pants and nothing else, only my dog tags, my St. Christopher medal, and my black prayer beads. (I don't know what happened to the beads–they may have been lost or taken off when I was wounded–but I'm pretty sure my mother sent them to me.)

While I was there at the beach, I recall the little boys and girls who came by hoping that we would give them some chewing gum, candy, and maybe cigarettes for their families. I hated to see kids want something so badly. We always gave them something. That was the American GI, never wanting to see a little kid go hungry.

Figure 50, July 14, 1944, on the beach at Pozzuoli. (On this particular day, Hitler's meeting room was bombed and he was nearly killed. This was big news and we all hoped this war would be over. If he had been killed, I'm sure the war would have ended, but it wasn't to be.) In the background are a railroad line and a road to Naples. *Figure 51* is another photo taken the same day. It shows me with a little dog I found. The puppy stayed with me for a couple of days and then was gone. I don't know if someone stole him or if he just wandered off. I am wearing a cheap wristwatch that I think I picked up from one of the Italians for two bucks. Yes, I had a moustache.

That photograph of me standing in front of a building was mailed to my parents. My family knew I was in Italy but they didn't know where. When they showed the photo to my maternal grandfather, he said, " I know where Frank is, he's in Pozzuoli." He said he recognized its buildings. The town of Qualiano is about a

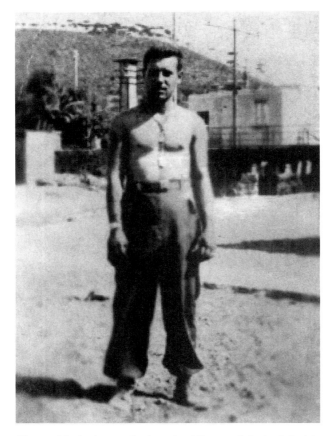

Figure 50. Author at the beach of Pozzuoli, Italy. July 14, 1944.

mile behind me in the picture. Qualiano is where both my parents were born. When I was growing up I always heard my family speaking of the town of Qualiano, Qualiano, Qualiano and thought I would remember it forever. But here I was, recuperating just a mile from my parents' birthplace and I could not remember the name Qualiano. It had just disappeared from my memory. I still do not know why.

There were some families in Pozzuoli who would make sandwiches for us for about $1.00. They were delicious–made of cut and fried potatoes mixed with eggs- and, by golly, they tasted really good. We were tired of eating GI rations.

In some towns there were some attractive ladies who didn't work,

Naples

Figure 51. Author at the beach of Pozzuoli, Italy. July 14, 1944.

except on their backs (Puttana). I was standing by the road on the beach one day when a very attractive woman riding in a horse-drawn buggy stopped. Her parasol was spinning and as she stepped down from the buggy she said, "Are you staying on the beach?" I replied, "Yes." There were some little beach bungalows that rented for about a quarter a day where you could change your clothes. They were not for us to sleep in. We had six-man tents pitched on the beach a little ways up for sleeping. Since I spoke the language, I became friendly with her and we shared a bungalow for a few hours.

Later in the day I had to leave to report back in but I told her I would return to spend the night with her. When I came back she was gone. The next day I saw her on her buggy again, heading out of Pozzuoli. It was the last time I saw her. She waved to me and I guess she was moving on to find more work again, spinning her parasol. As a young man, my grandfather drove a horse and buggy, taking the town's people of Qualiano to the beaches at Pozzuoli. Could it possibly be that this buggy was the very same one my grandfather drove from Qualiano to Pozzuoli? Was the lady with the parasol a relative?

On the beach, they sold lemon ice. I went to buy a cup and asked the owner for one in English. A young man next to him said in Italian, "He's an American soldier so charge him more money because they have a lot of money." I turned to him and said in Italian, "If you don't get off the beach, I'm going to kick you all over the place." He said, "You speak Italian?" I said, "Damn right. If I hear of this again you are going to get it." He took off, I never saw him again.

Down the road, not too far from where we were staying, there was a club called the Allies Club. It sat on the top of a hill. Every day and every hour a fight would break out among the Navy, Coast Guard, Army, British, and Air Corps, maybe Marines. The beaten ones always ended up being thrown down the hill. It seemed that those of us GI's in combat never had ribbons on our shirts, but our rear echelon GI's had lots of ribbons to show. They were always walking around with polished boots and clean clothes. They always had a crease in their pants, while we were likely to ask, "What's a crease?" If you ever saw Bill Maudlin's "Willie and Joe" cartoon, you know what I'm talking about. Bill Maudlin was with the 45th Infantry Division at the same time I was with the 3rd Infantry Division. In fact, a writer for some newspaper in Indiana, Ernie Pyle, was writing great stories of the infantry GI's. He was seen with the 45th Division always carrying his small portable typewriter, talking to many GI's and asking to tell their stories for the people back home to enjoy. I do not recall seeing him, but I am sure I had seen him from time to time.

After the war my grandfather told me about a building behind Pozzuoli. He said it was a terrible place, but I don't know what he meant by that. He was born in 1860. He said that back in the 1880s to 1890s, he used to hear the sound of people screaming in the building, like they were in pain or being tortured. He said he also remembered that there was a Nuns' Home near Pozzuoli. Nuns who became pregnant were sent there to deliver their babies. He said, "I don't know what happened to those babies–maybe they were put up for adoption."

The day finally came when our doctor visited us. "You are all healed, DeAngelo, you are going back to your unit." This meant C Company, 30th Regiment, training again and combat very soon. The Army trucks drove us to C Company area where we received new equipment and replacements. I walked around one day and came across an Italian farmer selling walnuts. I bought a whole basket of about 25-50 pounds for $5. I dragged that sucker over to my tent and told everyone to help themselves. They went pretty fast. GI's came in to fill up their pants pockets. Unfortunately, we ate too many and most of us got diarrhea, including me.

One day in early August 1944, I was walking down a street in Naples and saw a member of K Company, the first company I was assigned to. I was walking up one side of a street, and walking down the other side, toward me, was a GI named Pfc. Fox. He had a face like a fox with a mustache, and when he saw me he yelled, "You're dead! I know you're dead! I saw you dead!" He turned and ran from me. When I heard what he said I didn't know what he was talking about, so I ran after him. He just kept running, looking back over his shoulder and yelling, "You're dead! You can't be chasing me, you're dead!"

I finally caught up to him and asked, "What are you talking about, Fox?" He said, "Didn't you get killed on Anzio?" I said, "No, I didn't get killed." "But I saw you dead," he insisted. I said, "You didn't see me dead." He calmed down a little bit and seemed to understand that I wasn't a ghost. He then told me that he thought I had been killed on the hill after our K Company went to counterattack the Germans who had counterattacked and pushed F Company back. I said, "No, Fox, I was transferred the next night to C Company of the 1st Battalion. That's the reason you never saw me again." I explained, "The person killed was DeAngelico, our names were similar." He realized his mistake and added that another GI, Dannic, had also been killed that evening. These two GI's and I were on the same LCI when we crossed the Mediterranean Sea to Naples. DeAngelico and Dannic had been killed the same evening. DeAngelico's body was buried, but Dannic was missing in action. Possibly a large shell came in. I made Fox relax, we enjoyed our conversation, and then had drinks. He went back to K Company, I went back to C Company and we never saw each other again. The list of members in the 3rd Infantry Division book listed two Fox's, one in E Company, one in A Company. I don't know if he was transferred, or if it was the same Fox. Both were listed killed in action.

Once a GI came around with a nice Smith and Wesson revolver, a 32. I wanted the gun so I bought it for $35. Even though it had a broken spring I thought maybe I'd run across somebody who could fix it. I should have found someone who could. Later I sold it, still with a spring broken.

One beautiful day, August 6, 1944, we noticed twelve C-47's flying overhead. Out of the clear blue sky our GI paratroopers were jumping out of the planes around 500 to 600 feet. All at once we heard "Don't fire! Don't fire! GI's, GI's! Paratroopers!" I don't know why they jumped over our training and bivouacked area. They landed on our pyramid tents, our kitchen, and it's a wonder they didn't land on our fires. I don't know if they got a bad signal to jump or what. God! There must have been 300-400 of them. We always had to watch for German paratroopers (Fallschirmjager) dropping on us, but when we saw these aircraft most of our GI's knew they were our C-47's. Some GI's were trigger happy and ready to fire at anything.

We were training on the beach by the Mediterranean Sea near Pozzuoli. We were always training and even though we had learned how to throw a grenade in basic training, here we were grenade training again. This time we were sitting on the beach in front of barbed wire, facing the sea. Some of us were sitting on or in our helmets. This sergeant picked up a phosphorous grenade and, pointing to its pin, said, "Now, GI's, you can remove this pin anytime and hold it in your fingers as long as you have the grenade handle in the palm of your other hand. Once you remove this pin, and as long as you have this handle in the palm of your hand, the grenade won't go off. You can replace the pin anytime." We GI's knew that. So what else is new? He said, "Now, if you remove this pin and you hear a POP, get rid of the grenade, fast. That means it is a faulty grenade." Then, he pulled the pin and we all heard the grenade go POP. You talk about GI's going through barbed wire behind us! The sergeant looked at the grenade, then looked at us, and just dropped it in front of him. Of course it went off and phosphorous was all over us. It didn't fall on me, but many GI's were burned. We got mud to put on some spots. That was an experience not many GI's have gone through, I believe.

We also had rifle grenades fired from .03 Springfield rifles, later from M-1's. Every time a GI put a grenade on the end of his rifle to fire, he had to make sure there was a blank round in his rifle. If you had a loaded round, well, you had problems. One morning, this GI forgot to put a blank in his .03 rifle. With a live grenade on the end of his rifle, he pulled the trigger. That live round went right into the grenade. I don't remember too much about it, but saw a big explosion in front of him. I don't think he ever put another live round in his rifle to fire a grenade again, and I don't know what happened to him.

Later that morning we had rifle inspection. A lieutenant walked up to us and we each brought our M-1 rifles up and pulled the bolts back without clips or rounds. He took it from us, looked through its barrel to see if it was clean or not, said so, and then threw it back to be caught by the GI. This was not the case with a BAR. A GI standing next to me had a BAR at the side of his right leg with the butt on the ground, a clip in place, and its bolt back. This lieutenant came by, bent down to look in its barrel, and said, "OK." As he said OK the GI bent down and pulled the trigger and two rounds were fired. That clip was full of 20 rounds. The Lieutenant had his face right next to its barrel, and he turned every color in the book. He never said anything to that GI; both were frightened.

One or two days later there had been a notice on our bulletin board that said that any GI who wanted to transfer out of the Infantry could do so by signing up for the paratroopers. All they had to do was take a one-week course on the island of Sardinia. They would still be considered Infantry but would receive $50 more per month after joining. I know some GI's did, but I wouldn't join since I'd rather take my chances on the ground. But for $50, a lot of our GI's transferred. I think the loss of paratroopers over Sicily was the reason for this request. After training he became a paratrooper and received the Parachute Badge to be placed near his Combat Infantry Badge.

Later we were ordered to Naples to get on LCI's for training. When we heard LCI's we knew there would be an amphibious landing someplace, but where?

This was August 9, 1944 and we knew the Normandy Landing was completed on June 6th, so we all wondered where we would be going—landing at what beach. We trained again, staying offshore, sailing in, hitting the beach early in the morning and walking in. We got new equipment and replacements, and got to know each other. Soon our amphibious training was completed, we learned that our landing would be somewhere in France.

But before we were ready to leave on August 12th, 1944, for France, we heard a rumor that disturbed those of us in the Infantry in Italy. We heard that our Air Corps gunners on bombers refused to fly. I don't know if this was true or not, but we were all upset.

Here we were struggling down on the ground while these gunners were flying (which was not a good deal either), but if there was bad weather they did not fly. If our ground troops had bad weather it was time for a German counterattack. Our Air Corps got to sleep on cots, in warm buildings or in tents, while we slept on the open ground with or without a blanket, cold, wet or both. Several GI's, I heard, went over and asked to be transferred as gunners. It never happened.

We went aboard our LCI's and stayed off the Island of Sardinia. I had met a couple of GI's I knew when we were tied up next to another LCI. One was named Daniels and I don't remember what Company he was with, but he was the one at Camp Blanding who had a great big infection on the lower lobe of his right ear. He told me that some of the GI's we had known, Jimmy for one, had been killed. I wished him luck. It was the last time I saw him. Daniels was listed twice, once in the 30th Regiment book and once with the 7th Regiment book, and in both books the spelling of his name and his rank are the same. It shows no wounds, missing, or killed? Strange to be in both regiments of the 3rd Division.

I received mail that day. A letter I had written to Larry (the young GI who came to see me on Anzio and who told me he was going to die) was returned. It was marked deceased. His premonition was correct. I'll never forget him; he was a nice kid. He didn't have to go overseas with us, but he wanted to go to be with us, and yet we were all separated. I don't recall how close I was to him, but it's strange how you become friends but don't always become close. I don't know, I think it is your mind that does that to you.

If you recall the number of times I heard of this town of Qualiano when I was growing up. Well, OK, it came out of the clear blue sky, like a big bolt of lightning. It hit me between my eyes—*Qualiano*. Well, of course, I would never be in Italy again. Now I was on my way to France. Why in the world would the name Qualiano slip my mind all those months I was in Italy? I was there for ten months, especially the last one or two months when I was close by around Pozzuoli. I could have walked to this town, it wasn't far. In fact, when we walked for breakfast, lunch and dinner, it may have been another half mile or less from me. Yet, its name came back to me just like it was yesterday. Bang! Qualiano. You figure it out, I can't.

The 3rd Infantry Division was a great division. What makes a Division great are its GI's. All I can say is that I enjoyed my time with them and they seemed to know what was going on all the time. I don't recall hearing anything bad about the 3rd Infantry Division.

The Division was staffed three times because of all the wounded, missing, captured and killed. More than 40,000 men came into the Division as replacements. Remember what happened to L Company of the 30th Regiment. When they tried to capture the town of Cisterna, L Company was just about destroyed. Its company commander, Capt. Britt, lost his right arm. I think if we had had three or four full divisions landing on Anzio, we would have gone past Rome in a matter of a couple of days. I felt a big hurt on Anzio when we were unable to help Col. Darby's rangers when they tried to capture Cisterna. We just didn't have the manpower. We heard the gunfire and action only a few miles away from us, but we just couldn't do anything except stay where we were and not move up to help them.

Chapter Eight

France

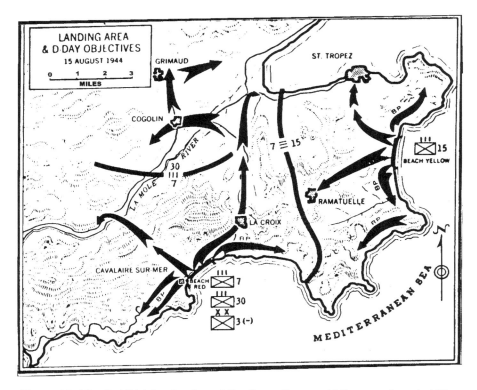

Figure 52. The 3rd Division landing at Southern France. All three regiments hitting the beaches, it was called Dragoon by the 7th Army under General Patch.

Figure 52, our landing in Southern France on August 15, 1944 (called Operation Dragoon) on Cavalaire Beach near Toulon. Toulon is on the left side, St. Tropez on the right. Our LCI's never went full bore to run onto the beach. The thinking was that if they stayed far enough off the beach, they could back off more easily and evade the enemy. This time, when we walked down the ramps we were supposed to be in water up to our knees or chest. Unfortunately, the first GI who walked down went under and didn't come up, which meant we had about ten feet of water under us. The rest of us refused to get off with our heavy equipment that included 60 mm mortars, machine guns, and ammunition–over 100 pounds of gear. We knew our life preservers could not hold us up. A few other GI's stepped off and disappeared below. They got rid of their gear and some floated back up. The top brass knew we couldn't get off our LCI without drowning, so they brought some Higgins boats LCVP to us. We got on board and went to shore. I blame all this on some LCI commanders who refused to go full bore onto the beach to unload us without drowning us. This had happened before. If a LCI got stuck on a beach, it was at the enemy's mercy, and would be shelled or dive-bombed. If these Naval guys had been under proper command, they would have been court marshaled for murdering some GI's. Nobody pressed this issue, but to me it was sinful. It left a bad taste in our mouths. I'm sure many GI's who were to get off their LCI's safely, found themselves in ten to twelve feet of water and in deep trouble.

We came upon the first towns pretty fast. We noticed some of those fighting for the Germans looked Oriental. I feel they were of Russian blood, probably from Mongolia. I recall reading that when German troops crossed the border into Russia, the Russian people were glad and some joined the German Army. They were tired of Stalin's way of getting rid of his people. But when the German troops went deeper into Russia, they began to kill many of its people and the Russians, who were now German soldiers, got peeved off and rebelled. They deserted and joined the Russian Army. Most of the Germans we met on the beaches were probably low grade soldiers. If you recall on Anzio, they brought 10-11 divisions from Southern France and Northern Italy down to fight us. The Germans we faced now in southern France were not the quality of fighters we faced at Anzio. They didn't really want to fight and many gave up without fighting. But the fighting became much harder as we moved north going toward the towns of Montelimar, Lyon, Besancon, Belfort, Colmar and Strasbourg.

In the town of Aix on August 21, 1944, we saw pregnant women having their heads shaved clean. They were collaborating with the Germans, either living with them, dating them or married to them. When the Free French (FF) took over some towns they shaved these women's heads so they would be noticed. Some were killed. I don't know what happened to them or their children. They were spat on and cursed at, probably disowned by the family. Why they took up with the Germans, I'll never know. I guess they had their reasons.

We often walked 30-40 miles on the dusty, hot roads and needed drinking water. In the center of each town was a fountain with cold running water and we would all fill our canteens. The fountains ran all day an all night, which I feel was an incredible waste. To this day I do not let water at home run any longer than needed. Now at this point our GI's were fighting rough and hard Germans. The Normandy GI's were pushing the enemy toward the east; we of the 7th Army were pushing up from the south, and to the east.

On August 31st, 1944, near the town of Montelimar, we came across three miles of German 19th Army wreckage. They were caught by our P-47's. Fighter bombers, horses and vehicles were destroyed and lay on both sides of the road, as well as in the foxholes that the Germans had dug. If Germans were driving or marching nearby when our P-47's flew over, they would jump out of their vehicles or break rank and dive into these foxholes. I'm sure if they widen these roads someday, they will dig up bodies. Many bodies in fox holes were probably filled over by earth from a bomb crater. I know many are still buried on both sides of these roads in some parts of Europe where the war took place. An unknown number of Germans were killed and approximately 1,000 horses were killed. The horses were used to pull weapons when it was hard to get fuel for the vehicles. Fuel was getting short.

One day we captured a Renault car. I didn't have a license but we climbed in the car and I just drove it up and down the hill without knowing where any of the gears were in the transmission. I ran into a wall. We just left it there; it wouldn't run anymore.

Many times GI's would climb up on Sherman tanks and M-10 Tank Destroyers to chase after the Germans. One day we were all standing up on 6x6 trucks. We saw our P-47's flying above us and knew they were looking for German vehicles to blow up. Usually a few GI's carried a yellow smoke grenade to throw out to inform our pilots we were friendly troops. On this day no one had a yellow smoke grenade and, boy, did we jump off our trucks. At last a GI found a white smoke grenade to throw out. The P-47's were beginning to dive down on us, but when they saw white smoke they pulled up and away. I am sure a yellow smoke grenade was on hand always from that day on.

We were moving fast on foot and came to a field filled with many cantaloupes that were in big piles on both sides of the road. As we were walking by we took a few but kept on walking. We cut one open, took the seeds out and enjoyed the cool, wet fruit. The poor farmer lost most of his crop, but I am sure our government paid for it after WWII.

At times as we were advancing, we chased the enemy for many miles. Our company Jeep, with its trailer, would stop in the middle of us while we were walking on both sides of the road. They handed out K-rations as we marched by, but we didn't stop. If we were lucky we would be allowed to stop to eat. We didn't eat as much as people might think. It seemed our stomachs had shrunk so it didn't take much to fill us. The lemonade powder was good and we also had cocoa and coffee, but no tea. Our C-rations were canned and we liked the meat and beans and hash the most. Nobody liked the stew.

The 10-1 rations were great. They were usually issued to the tankers, tank destroyers, and other ground-moving vehicles that were able to carry a couple of cartons of 10-1 rations. Each came packed with an extra can opener inside.

On September 8, 1944, we walked to the town of Besancon.

France

Figure 53. 3rd Division GI's using ladders at the Doubs River at Besancon, France. The author used the one on the right.

Figure 53, GI's from the 3rd Infantry Division walked down into the Doubs river and climbed up these ladders since its bridge was blown. One of the three ladders was used by yours truly. The one on the right hand side, the Bailey Bridge in the photo, was installed soon after. There were three hills around Besancon and we had a very hard fight there. On top of each hill was a fort and each fort protected the other fort. When we were trying to capture one fort the other two forts were firing on us. It was a situation where we thought, "Which one do we capture first, or can we get all three at the same time?" Every time we tried to take a fort it became impossible. Finally someone suggested, "Well, we'll do what we have to do." Good old American thinking. Soon a 155 mm Howitzer was brought up to fire on the Citadel. C Company began to flank this huge fortress with A Company following in the rear of the lead platoon. This 155 mm Howitzer was placed on the main road, and yours truly had seen this action. They fired point blank at this fort and kept on firing at its wall. We were so close to the fort that they sighted the Howitzer through its barrel. It hit the wall of the fort many, many times. Finally at around 6 p.m. the white surrender flag went up. That ended the fighting. That is how we captured the town of Besancon with its three protective forts. It was really something to be there and see our 155 mm Howitzer at work.

While fighting at Besancon, I was walking up a road when a Sherman tank came down from the opposite direction. I was right next to the tank and about 4 feet in front of its muzzle when it fired its 75 mm. It's OK to be behind one when fired but definitely not in front of it. It was nerve shattering; I had a headache for several hours.

As a buck sergeant, I ordered my assistant, Cpl. Williams, "Get on the other side of some dirt road. We are going into some woods and," I said, "make sure you aren't in front of our GI's." I had a Tommy gun and soon began to fire. Afterwards, I found Cpl. Williams lying down. I said, "What are you doing here?" My assistant replied, "I'm shot." I asked, "Where are you shot?" He said, "In the rear end." I told him I didn't understand why he was in front of us and added, "I was the one who shot you." He said, "No, no, no you didn't do it." I said, "I can tell you I did it, because you were in front of me when I fired." Cpl. Williams was a police officer in Pennsylvania before the war. He did return to C Company after a few weeks.

Soon the 3rd Infantry Division was to relieve the 36th Division in the Vosges Mountains. When we arrived at their positions we were told that the enemy was across the valley on top of a hill. The 36th Division was OK. It was not like the 45th Division, our other sister division. When the 45th Division was on either side of us we slept. When the 45th Division knew we were on either side of them, they slept. It got to the point where we thought something was not right with the 36th Division. I think the commanders of this division probably weakened its combat abilities. During the night the 36th Division moved out and left behind their rifles and some personal items. We figured they wanted to move out fast. That morning, as

France

Figure 54. Author was shot at with this type of German machine pistol., MP-38. With his Thompson, killed the shooter.

we were shaking our blankets, there in front of us were Germans, also shaking their blankets. Question, when did the hill move closer to us? Talk about diving for your rifle. We began to fire. The next moment it was quiet. They had disappeared. I don't know if it was a forward observation post or what. Much later I learned the 36th Division was going to lose their colors. I don't know if that was true or not, but if it was it isn't in any records. It would be a disappointment to the GI's of the 36th Division, who were like us. I still believe their top leadership was lacking in many ways.

Figure 54. The MP-38 machine pistol was well used by German troops. They had lots of them and they were very destructive weapons. As I was giving instructions to my GI's, a corporal came to see me. He said, "DeAngelo, First Sergeant wants you." I replied, "OK, fine. Why don't you stay here and make sure these GI's dig in, we might get a counterattack." As soon as I turned to walk away a German with a machine pistol let go a burst and hit the corporal across his chest. The German took off back into the dense woods and I ran to the corporal and tried to comfort him. He became delirious and started talking about some guy and then asked for water. I asked our medic what he thought and he replied that he didn't want to give him any water since he had chest wounds. " I'm afraid he's not going to make it," said the medic. The corporal died within a few minutes.

I felt pretty bad, I think that German was shooting at someone with stripes and the corporal was wearing stripes. I think if the corporal hadn't come to see me I might have been shot instead, but I was not wearing my stripes. If you were hit in the chest with one round, others followed. The spacing of the rounds was very close when hit by an MP-38.

A few minutes after that shooting, a 4th platoon GI assigned to a light 30 caliber machine gun placed his weapon, in position, cocked and ready to fire, facing the enemy. When I saw this GI in charge of his machine gun alone without his weapon, I asked, "Where's your weapon?" He replied, "It's up there." I said, "What do you mean it's up there?" He said, "We fell back." I said, "Do you mean to tell me you left your machine gun up there so all the enemy has to do is turn that damn thing around and fire at us?" There had been no retreat, nothing. "What you should have done was pick the darn thing up and bring it with you, tripod and all. You'd better go and get it, it's your responsibility." He said, "You're kidding me, DeAngelo." I said, "No, I'm not kidding. Go get it!" This machine gun was about fifty to seventy-five feet away. Again I ordered him, "Go and get your weapon." He said, "No, I'm not going." I had a Tommy gun (I used to swap weapons) and I pulled back the bolt, "You'd better go back and get it." He high-tailed, got it and brought it back. I said, "Don't ever do that again, understand?" Some time later this GI was killed in action. It was dangerous for any GI to leave his weapon with a couple of boxes of ammo where the Germans had an opportunity to turn it around and wipe us out.

When my company commander or someone in charge gave me an order to do something, I always did the best I could. That's the way I was and that's the way I wanted our GI's to be. I didn't want anyone who was wishy-washy. I mean this was a serious business, a dead business!! If you screwed up, you died or someone else died. I made sure my GI's did not die because of someone else's mistake or by some accident, but by situations out of our control.

About 45 minutes later we were ordered to move forward. My

BAR man, Pfc. Riddett, was a young kid about nineteen and very funny. He always carried a frying pan on his belt. Whenever he sat down he fried something. We moved forward with Pfc. Riddett on my right side. As we were going through some dense woods right where that German with a machine pistol had killed our corporal, I had my GI's move up in a straight line. We were lying on the ground and there were GI's on both sides of me. I was telling them to straighten out the line when I guess this same German fired at me with his machine pistol. I was behind a small tree, the leaves in front of my face went PRRRRR which meant he hit the leaves. Afraid he would fire again, I rolled from my stomach to my left side, and as I did I pulled back the bolt of my Tommy gun and momentarily rolled back to my right side. There he was standing up in front of me, without his helmet, but wearing his M-43 folding cap. I fired a clip of 15 rounds of 45 caliber at him. He never fired again. I knew I had hit him hard. We were pulled back and I never heard anything more about it. I never checked to see if I hit him. I know I killed him.

Figure 55. This German weapon, called STUG-44 "Krummlauf," shoots around corners at 90 degrees.

Figure 55 shows a German rifle, accurate up to 200 yards, that could shoot around 90-degree corners. In fact, they had two other rifles–one that could shoot at 45 degrees and another at 35 degrees. I was talking to a couple of ex-Marines some years later about these rifles, and they thought I was smoking pot. I told them there were such rifles. You just had to see it, they were called "Krummlauf."

Figure 56. This was something, a new M-1 Grease gun. A 45 caliber, it replaced the Thompson, the old gangster-type weapon.

Figure 56. US Army's new weapon called by the GI's "The Grease Gun Model M-1. The author was given one and it was then given to another GI.

This was a cheapy, probably only cost twenty bucks to make. The thing of interest was its barrel, which could be removed. Its barrel was more precision made than some other components. They issued me one and told me this was to replace my Tommy gun. I don't know why they wanted to replace the Tommy guns. This new weapon was what I called a piece of garbage. I took it into combat and fired it a few times. I gave it to someone else.

In combat I never associated myself with one particular weapon. I used Carbines, M-1's and the 45 caliber Tommy gun. When I used the Carbine I had a clip in place with two clips mounted on the stock. I would also have four clips on my pistol belt and a lot of ammunition (maybe 200 rounds) in a bag. It was harder to get ammunition for the Carbine than it was for the M-1. With the Carbine, one of our GI's using it shot the German twice in the body as he was advancing toward the GI. The German went up to the GI and tried to take the Carbine away from him. Both men fought for it. The German lost his life from his wounds. Now with the M-1, getting hit just once will knock one down, and you stay down. We could use ammunition from our machine gun belts and would take out the rounds to put it in the M-1 clip but save the clips. When we went into combat with the M-1 we had a full belt of ammo with ten clips, eighty rounds, plus two bandoleers with five clips. Each had forty rounds for a total of 160 rounds.

Incidentally, with hand grenades, we unwrapped the tape from around the containers, removed the grenades and taped the handles down. Then we put the grenade handles through the metal loops of our suspenders. This way if we went through dense woods it wouldn't pull the pin out. It was a safety precaution even though we bent the cotter pins so they wouldn't come out, but you never knew. It was a situation where it was safer to take this extra measure of precaution and know the tape was on. We always used caution to stay alive.

As a buck sergeant I was told I would be getting an ex-sergeant back into my squad. This was the GI who gave me trouble when I first joined K Company at Pietravairano, Italy. He was the one who told me to go down to the road to pick up firewood and bring it to his tent. He and I were transferred to C Company one rainy night. On Anzio I had wanted to kill this GI. He had been transferred to the MP's from C Company. Somehow he accidentally (or otherwise) shot someone. The MP's busted him, and sent him back to C Company. When a GI screwed up, they were always shipped to the Infantry. So when he came back to my squad he made a big speech in front of my GI's saying, "I used to be a sergeant before this GI ever became a sergeant; he was nothing but a replacement." On and on, he went, "And I'm not gonna do nothin'!" I said, "If you are gonna be in this squad you are going to work like the rest of us, you understand?" I treated my GI's very well. Many sergeants delegated orders to other sergeants under their command. I also delegated, but stayed involved. If we needed to go to get rations, I would go and get rations, if we needed water, I would go for water, if we went on patrol, I would go on patrol, if we stood guard duty, I stood guard duty. My reason? I gave our GI's extra time to rest and sleep. Other sergeants just didn't do this, and I think that's the reason some sergeants and GI's wanted me back in their platoon a few times after I was busted.

The next order I received from my company commander was to send out two GI's on a contact patrol. I picked one GI and said, "You'll go with me. When we return I want you to go with another GI to show him the way." I wanted my men to go with somebody who had been on that contact patrol before. When time came for this GI to go, he refused and I agreed to send another GI in his place. As I sent him off, I told him, "I'm going to send you in his place. I'm not finished with him, but if anything happens to you, I'll take care of this GI real good. I want you to understand that." He said, "OK, DeAngelo." Fortunately all my GI's came back that night. The next morning the GI who refused to go on patrol said, "Well, I told you I'm not gonna do nothin'." I said, "I'm taking you down to our company commander." I dragged his tail down to our company commander and explained what had happened. "This GI is a problem. He should be taken out of my squad and put in some other outfit." He refused to do anything. He refused to go on patrol, to fight—everything. I just told the company commander that he had to go and that was it. The company commander chewed his rear end. It was the last time I saw him. I don't know if he was transferred or put in the stockade. My gut feeling about him is that at that time the 3rd Division had a GI who was to be executed. Some of the officers from the 3rd Division had attended the execution of Private Slovik. After Slovik's execution our Division did not execute the GI. The timing was correct and it's possible he was the GI who was to be put to death for refusing all orders.

From time to time when we advanced, our rations were short and the Jeep was not able to deliver supplies. It was a real bonus when we'd come across a dead German with some German black bread, and margarine or butter in tubes. It looked like a very large tube of toothpaste, except the opening was much larger. We spread this on the bread and enjoyed it. We were told that bread was made out of sawdust of some kind. I wonder if this was true?

France

Figure 57. 3rd Division GI's, this is the way we looked in the Vosges Mountains.

We came to the Belfort Gap, a tough place to go through. It was mountainous with dense woods. One day I was looking down onto the plains and noticed a P-47 landing in the distance. He had his landing gear and flaps down, flew in and stopped. A perfect landing. The plane didn't catch fire. I don't know if he was shot down or his engine failed. I never saw the pilot climb out of the cockpit. I bring this up because I recently read a book of memoirs written by some pilots and it described a P-47 pilot who was killed landing in just such a situation. I spoke to the writer, a retired Air Force colonel, who told me the pilot hit a tree. I don't recall him hitting a tree but think he had been shot down. There was no abrupt stop, it just came in and landed and nothing moved after that.

Figure 57 shows 30th Regiment GI's eating hot food after weeks of combat. This is my outfit off the line. Notice our M-43 field jackets are packed with mud. We had a couple of weeks' growth on

GREETINGS FROM THE PRESIDENT

Figure 58. 3rd Division, 4.2 Chemical Mortar Crew firing on German Troops at Vosges Mountains.

our faces, and we were dirty. Our poor 3rd Division GI's. This was the way we usually looked as we fought in the rain, snow and cold through the Vosges Mountains. This was at a rest area at the town of Bult. We were sent there to rest, shower, and get some clean clothing. Most of the time when we had our first hot food, we upchucked. We were used to eating cold rations and our stomachs were not used to eating hot food like Spam or creamed beef, also known as SOS, which stood for shit on a shingle.

Our GI's were firing 4.2's, chemical mortars. *Figure 58* shows what these looked like. They fired a round about the size of our 105 mm, about 32 lbs. When you had a good crew firing them, one GI was on each side picking up the round, putting it in the tube and going back to pick up another one. This was all in the matter of one minute. Each 4.2 could fire six rounds, maybe more, real quick, depending on how well the crew was trained. I have seen GI's pull these 4.2's mortars on carts with bicycle-type wheels. They would pull the carts from behind a big T-bar handle, one GI on each side. Soon we captured some Germans after firing about forty or fifty rounds of 4.2's and the prisoners wanted to know where our automatic 105 mm cannons were. They wanted to see one in action. They all thought it was an automatic 105 mm, when it was our 4.2 chemical mortars. They did a lot of damage when they exploded. We told them it was a mortar, but they did not believe us.

On one particular day I captured about 45-50 prisoners. I found them in a barn and when they came out, they didn't have any fight in them. They wanted to get out of this war. I searched the prisoners, hoping to find a wristwatch. I still didn't have one and needed one for when I was on guard duty. I ended up with about 40 pocket watches. Now they were pretty cheap ones, probably costing only a couple of bucks each. But one of them was very big–about 5" in diameter– and was more of a clock than a watch. It had a glass cover about a quarter of an inch thick, and it had a key with which to wind it. This German soldier had it in his jacket pocket. I removed all their watches. Then I asked every GI if they wanted a watch. I gave each a watch. I finally gave some GI the big one. I didn't want to keep that darn thing. He kept it for a while. Later he gave it to another GI because it was heavy. I'll never forget that big sucker. I would have loved to have kept it because today it would have been a nice conversation piece. The MP's were always after us. We were not supposed to take such things off the prisoners. They wanted them. So, we took them ourselves because MP's were hard to deal with at times. We thought some MP's were in some other army.

As we were moving to the front, about 50 feet away we saw a young GI sitting on the ground, his back against a tree. We all had heard a rifle shot up in front of us a minute or two before. As we walked by, this GI shot his left foot. No one stopped to help him. We were as scared as he was, and we all looked down on him for doing this to himself. I do not recall what happened to him.

We were moving awful fast in those days, climbing on trucks, M-10's and Sherman tanks to chase the enemy. Somehow, we must have bypassed one of their 120 mm mortar observers. We lost some men to this mortar. Early that morning, about 6:30, I heard a grenade of some type go off. I was wondering what the hell was going on. I didn't know if it was one of ours or one of theirs. I looked up to the top of this hill, about 200 feet in front of me, and I didn't feel good about this. I got out of my protected position below ground and rose up onto my knees, but I couldn't see anything. I stood up and saw a stonewall at the top. Seconds later, two young Germans came and set up a tripod for their MG-Lafette 42 machine gun. They were about ready to load, cock and fire it. This Mg-42 machine gun was called a "Hitler Saw" and it fired 1500 rounds per minute. I knew they were getting ready to fire on us below and standing up, with only five rounds left in my M-1, I pointed my M-1 up in their direction, fired all rounds and then quickly reloaded. But I didn't fire again since the Germans never returned fire. It was kind of strange (as I mentioned earlier), for it was not typical for the enemy to have their machine guns placed this way. They always had one, two, three or four riflemen for protection of their machine gun. If there had been riflemen around that day, they would have picked me off. I was lucky to have destroyed this machine gun and its crew. It was the same on Anzio when I was alone, not having men around me to protect me when I was manning a light machine gun one morning, many months ago.

Soon afterward, I walked down the hill and didn't bother to tell anybody what I did—it was my duty. Sgt. Hohmann called us together and told us that we had lost some sergeants and corporals. He said, "DeAngelo, you are now a staff sergeant." As soon as he said it, a 120 mm mortar came down and landed no more than ten feet from us. These mortars were concussion more than anything else. The last time I saw Sgt. Hohmann, he was running on a road down the hill. I don't know what happened to him; he may have been reclassified or sent home. I believe he cracked up and left. When that mortar hit I knew I had to get out of there and figured the next round was going to be a direct hit. I knew then that we had overlooked an observer. All he had to do was correct some degrees and fire again. I started to run downhill to our CP. There were two roads—I was going to take the one to my right that Sgt. Hohmann had taken. Another GI called out, "DeAngelo, you're on the wrong road! It's going to enemy lines." I jumped off that road and onto the other road on my left. I ran towards the house our CP was in. As soon as I ran next to this house, a 120 mm mortar dropped nearby, behind me. Then Sgt. Schamma wanted to know what was going on. Before I could say anything another mortar dropped right in front of a doorway where Sgt. Schamma was standing. It didn't get either one of us. I ran into a house and down to the basement where our lieutenant was. "What the hell happened to you, DeAngelo?", he asked, "You're white as a sheet." He gave me a big shot of booze and my next words were, "That mortar has eyes, and he's trying to kill me." To make a long story short, he sent me to a hospital for observation. I was taken to see a doctor who said, "You're in pretty bad shape, DeAngelo." I told him, "I lost most of my GI's." He said, "Why don't you go to Room #3 and stay there until I call you." For the next three days I ate, slept and watched movies. Finally on the third day he came to see me, "You know, I forgot about you, DeAngelo", he said, " I'm going to send you back to your outfit." I said, "I feel I shouldn't be going back to the front, I feel pretty bad, I've been fighting since Anzio, I'm just tired." He said, "Well, you're going back up there, they need sergeants." He told me to pack up my stuff; the Repo-Depo truck would pick me up. I thought, "To hell with him." I was not going to any Repo-Depo again. I was willing to give up my stripes so I went AWOL from the hospital. At the time I was a Buck Sergeant, but acting Staff Sergeant.

When this doctor had told me to go to Room #3 it reminded me of a movie I had seen as a young boy. The two actors were Laurel and Hardy. As I remember, both were in the Army overseas during WWI. An officer had told Laurel to stand guard duty and not to leave his post until he was relieved. Well, 20 years went by and he was still on guard duty walking in a very large circle. He stood five feet deep in this circle and behind him was a pile of empty cans of food he had eaten during those twenty years. Then one day he fired on a plane flying over his post, and was found. His friend Hardy, in reading the newspaper, found his friend had not been killed as he thought. He was told the war had been over for many years. Just think about this. I could still be in Room #3 at that hospital today, if the doctor had not remembered me in that room.

Concerning the Repo-Depo, there was an officer named Maj. Frye who I was told had many paratroopers plus a lot of other GI's after him to either kill or get rid of him. I heard he was in trouble because he may have been involved with the paratroopers who were dropped over Sicily. They were shot down by our Navy and Army antiaircraft. The story I heard was that he gave orders for our paratroopers to drop at a certain time when they should have been in another area. Later he was assigned to be in charge of a Repo-Depo. All troops who came from hospitals or furlough had to go to a Repo-Depo. From there they might be sent back to their outfits. Many times when a German counterattack was made while GI's were in a Repo-Depo and when GI's were needed as replacements, they would go in and clean out the Repo-Depo and a lot of GI's ended up in new outfits and were never sent back to their outfits. This is one of the reasons why I went AWOL from the hospital. I didn't want to go to a Repo-Depo because I was there once when I first made a buck sergeant. There was this private first class assigned to the Repo-Depo that was telling me what he wanted me to do. I told him I was a buck sergeant, he said, "It doesn't make any difference what you GI's ranks are; we are in control here." There was no respect for anyone. Once again, were these GI Repo-Depo GI's in a different army? We GI's understood the problem — its commander was Maj Frye.

All frontline GI's hated any Repo-Depo's. I can assure you many who were assigned to the Repo-Depo were the most miserable people

France

to work with. They thought it was their God given right, no matter what we were, sergeants or what, to tell us what to do. Many GI's who were released from the hospital went AWOL rather than go to Repo-Depo, so I was not the first one to refuse to go to a Repo-Depo, and I wasn't the last. Ask any GI about the Repo-Depo and he will say it was very bad, and that's the plain truth.

My outfit was 60 miles up front. I started walking and would get a lift once in a while. I came to a field where some GI's were eating and asked the mess sergeant if I could have something to eat. He told me to get myself a mess kit. As I was eating, I heard a voice that I seemed to recognize. Sure enough, it was Armand, a neighbor of my Aunt Mary, the mother of my cousin, Sgt. Frank (with the pigeons), whose parents were undertakers. We talked for a while but then I had to leave and continued walking into a town. There I ran across some C Company GI's and asked them what they were doing there. They told me they had taken some time off and I replied, "Hey, that's not right, we have to return to our company." It was getting late and we were still about 30 miles from our front line so we all agreed to leave in the morning to rejoin our company.

So the next morning I was staying with a French family. They were cooking breakfast when I noticed the wife looking out the window. She showed me there was an MP coming our way. I didn't want the MP to find me because I knew it would go against my Army record. I ran to hide in the attic and when I looked out, then I saw a GI helmet sitting on the windowsill. It wasn't my helmet, it had been left there days before I arrived, but I knew the MP had seen it. There was nothing I could do—no exit to get away. I was sitting on the attic steps when the MP came up and asked, "What are you doing up here, soldier?" I replied, "I am waiting for you." He said, "I saw your helmet." I answered, "No, that's not my helmet, I'm wearing mine." He said, "Come down with me." I tried to explain, "I'm working my way up to the front where my company is. I am AWOL from the hospital." Big deal, he put me in the stockade anyway. I don't remember if other MP's picked up our other GI's, since I was the only one in that house. The other GI's were in some other homes. I guess all returned later to C Company somehow.

In the stockade, I was put in a room with a bunch of German prisoners who wore large tags around their necks. An MP Pfc. came in and said, "You GI's are to be treated just like these prisoners of war. What is good for them is good for you." In this room were about five other unknown GI's. Nobody said anything. He left and returned in five minutes with some tools, axes and saws. The Germans were taken out to be fed and watch movies of some kind. We were given cold rations, but no movies. He told us to pick one of the tools and go out and cut firewood. There was one saw left. He looked at me and said, "That means you, too. Pick it up and go get some wood." I said, "Only a few minutes ago you said we were supposed to be treated like enemy prisoners, am I correct?" He said, "That's right, what's good for them is good for you." I said, "Well, our Army Soldier's Handbook says if you're a captured enemy soldier, you must do manual labor when requested. Not so if you are an NCO." The handbook stated that a sergeant is to be in charge of men under his command (like private, private first class, and corporal) and is to tell them what to do. It states that he does not do manual labor himself, but is in charge of directing others to do what is requested.

"Well, I know now you didn't read your handbook, but I did," I told him. "For your information I am a buck sergeant, acting staff." He replied, "Well, I don't see any stripes on you." I said, "We Infantry don't sew them on. We never do, when we become sergeants we are known as sergeants by our GI's." He went out to get a buck sergeant. A big fat MP came in a few minutes later and asked, "What's going on?" I repeated what I had said and he scratched his head, saying he would be back. Within five minutes a lieutenant returned with him. He asked, "What's going on, soldier?" I explained the situation to him. The lieutenant said, "Well, you're right, soldier, but our Provost Marshal wants to see you right now." He took me out to the Provost Marshal's office. I knocked and heard a voice say, "Come in." I walked in and closed the door gently. I came to attention and gave him a salute which he didn't return. After some seconds I put my arm down but remained at attention. He never said at ease. He asked, "What's going on, soldier?" I explained it all again and he didn't say boo or anything in reply. The whole thing took two minutes. Then he said, "You're dismissed, Private, you may leave." Still at attention, I gave my salute, and he didn't return that salute either. After a length of time, I put my arm down, made an about face still at attention, opened the door and walked out. I gently closed the door and walked back to the stockade.

About an hour later our C Company Jeep came to get me. After driving 30 miles, the driver said, "Well, the whole Division heard what happened, DeAngelo. The Division got hold of Regiment, Regiment got hold of Battalion, and Battalion got hold of C Company Commander. He wants your tail back to C Company." I said, "Isn't it strange for him to send his Jeep to pick me up?" He said, "You're damn right!" Each company has two Jeeps, one for the commander and the other for use by supply and mess. As we were driving back to C Company we came upon 20-30 officers walking on the road going in our direction. Were these officers replacements? In this group was my future company commander, Lt. Murray. We arrived at C Company, and my company commander (unknown) said, "DeAngelo, I don't mind you taking a few days off, but why the hell did you have to get in trouble like this with the MP's?" I said, "Lieutenant, I had nothing to do with it. I was trying to get back to C Company and this MP caught me. They made a big deal out of it." I explained what took place. He said, "Well, get back to your squad, do your job. I'll get your stripes back soon, maybe in a week or so." The C Company Jeep driver at Bruyeres, France, was H.H. Huggins. Some years later I read about a Four-Star General who picked up a GI paratrooper who was also AWOL from a hospital. He was going to be sent to the Repo-Depo and was afraid he would not get back to his outfit. The General said, "You must inform your outfit to remove your name from the missing rolls. Give me your name, serial number and outfit, and I will turn it over to G-1 Corps., saying you're safe and returning to your assigned outfit." Now this happened to me the very same way and I was busted by a low-life officer, one who should never have been an officer, but then the other GI had a four star General giving him a ride and his help.

Later that evening, I was called for guard duty. We were on top of a hill and down in the valley, near the town of Letholy, a cheese factory was burning below. About 3 a.m., I heard somebody walking up behind me. I said, "Halt! Who goes there?" He said, "Lt. Murray." I replied, "Lt. Murray?" He said, "Yes, I'm your new third platoon leader." I asked, "What are you doing up so early this morning? Nobody gets up this early except us GI's." He said, "I heard about you, DeAngelo. I said, "What can I do for you, Lt?" He said, "This is all new to me and I want you to show me as much as you can so I can be a good officer." I said, "You're kidding me, Lieutenant, no one has ever asked that of me or anyone I know." He said, "Well, I'm telling you now, I want you to show me everything I need to know so I can be a good platoon leader." I asked, "Are you really serious Lt.?" He answered, "Yes." We shook hands. He and I became very close from that morning on. There was a time later when he became C Company Commander. The third platoon wanted to get rid of a squad sergeant and Lt. Murray asked me to take over, saying they had requested me. I told him no. I was happy where I was. I was tired of leading men into combat and losing them. I said, "I'm just tired of it, besides the actions taken by the MP's Provost Marshal." He appreciated my honesty. Twice Lt. Murray asked me if I wanted to become a Staff Sergeant. Each time I said no, but it was a good feeling to know that our GI's appreciated me and knew I was their type of Sergeant. Another time he wanted me to be a Tech Sergeant in one of his other platoons. They also had requested me, but I told him no again. Another time he said he wanted to do something for me some day.

That day came when Lt. Murray called me to his CP and said, "I would like you to go to Paris to receive a 'Battlefield Commission' and become an officer, but you will need to be transferred out of C. Company." I said to him that Lt. Audie Murphy after receiving a commission was still servicing in the same company. I have known others who received a commission, were transferred and then killed; in fact, one had turned down going home for a commission and a few weeks later he was killed. My gut feeling was to stay put and sweat it out. Lt. Murray felt I would be a good officer and thought the GI's at my new company would have had a good officer whom the men would appreciate serving under. Like before, I turned it down.

I also thought, with a name like DeAngelo, that if I were an officer, some higher officer might give me a great deal of trouble because of my name. Like the one who was so drunk at Anzio and told me to go out and raise a ruckus when there was no need to seek trouble. As I look back, I was on KP and guard duty so many times. As I understood it, KP and guard duty was to be once per month. Was it because I was an Italian/American and could not be trusted?

I recall the doctor who forgot me for three days and another doctor who refused to tell me about my heart. He was also the other GI doctor with bad feet like I had. Yet, I heard he was shipped to England and maybe "ZI" (Zone of Interior), while I was sent to the front. It makes you think, why? Maybe it was like going to school in Providence as a child. No kids to play with because I was an Italian/American. Now, being in the army, was it the same?

Chapter Nine

Vosges Mountains

One night while in the Vosges Mountains, one of our lieutenants (I can't remember who, like I said, they came and went) pointed to a spot where he instructed me to dig a hole for four men. He left and I looked at the area. I figured the Germans were in front of us and on either side of us and maybe the only place they weren't was behind us. I had turned some dirt but I didn't dig where he ordered me to. I looked at a large tree and started digging behind it. I was down a foot when the lieutenant returned. He asked, "Why are you digging here, DeAngelo?" I said, "Well, Lieutenant, I just feel like this is a better place to dig one." He said, "I want you to dig where I ordered you." I went back to where he ordered me to dig and I started digging. Soon he left for a briefing. I went back to where I wanted to dig and finished a hole large enough for four men to sleep in. When he came back he said, "DeAngelo, you have disobeyed me again." I said, "I have no reason for why I disobeyed you. The hole is dug, Lieutenant." The four of us went to sleep that night and the Germans fired about five rounds of 105 mm into our area. One dud landed just where he had wanted me to dig; the next hit five feet off the ground and smack in front of the tree we were behind. The next morning the lieutenant saw both, a dud in the hole where he had ordered me to dig and the place in front of the tree where the 105 mm round had exploded. He looked at me and said, "DeAngelo, from now on you can dig anyplace you want to dig." "Right, Lt."

Early one evening Lt. Murray said, "I don't have any water in my canteen, DeAngelo, see if you can find some water." I heard running water some where above us, we were high in the Vosges Mountains, I found some GI's getting water. I had heard their canteens being filled because they had a plastic cap with a chain. Both were hitting their aluminum canteens. I put both canteens in this small stream and filled them. I put one Halazone pill in each canteen to make sure the water was safe to drink within an hour. The next morning the Lt. again said, "I'm out of water DeAngelo, go back and refill my canteen," I said, "Sure Lieutenant." The creek was about two feet wide, with cold running water, nice and clear, except for some awful looking algae on its sides. I told the Lt. there was a lot of algae in the water. I didn't want to fill our canteens with it again. He said, "OK DeAngelo."

The Lieutenant loved hard candy. It didn't matter what kind it was as long as it was hard. He ate it all the time. One day I received a three pound box of hard candy, I gave it to him. He would keep candy in his trench coat pockets. Every once in a while he'd get a piece to chew on. I kept him supplied. I think this kept him going on all the time. I scrounged for candy constantly. We had charms which nobody liked because there were so many. I would pick them up when they were discarded in a 10-1 Rations box. GI's would throw everything they didn't want in this box. Then some GI would pick up the box and give the stuff away. I already picked out the charms and put them in both pockets of my jacket to give to him when he wanted candy.

Once we were shot at with wooden bullets. They were dyed red. Once hit it was hard to find all of it's pieces. Soon the wound became infected. This type of wound was well known years ago on wooden ships due to sea water that had gotten into the wood. When the ships wood was hit by canon balls, it found it's way into the bodies of men on board these ships. Soon it caused the wound to become infected and many of the wounded died.

One late afternoon, Lt. Murray received orders that said there was a town which may or may not be occupied by Germans and C Company was to check it out. Lt. Murray took the 1st and 2nd platoons; a lieutenant that was with the 3rd and 4th platoons stayed behind with a Sherman tank. I went with Lt. Murray since I was always with him. As we approached this town we began receiving small arms fire. The Germans were still in town having supper we were in their line. Lt. Murray ordered me, "Go back and bring up the tank with the rest of our men, DeAngelo." I said, "OK, Lt." As I was walking away, it was just getting dark, some of our GI's were just laying up on the right side of the hill. I said, "What are you GI's doing? Why aren't you on top of the hill to see if the Germans are going to counterattack us from that side?" I was not a sergeant at that time, so to wake them up I fired into the Germans left flank on our opposite side. I received return fire. I said, "Do you understand now what I mean?" Boy did they ever run up to the top of the hill quick, they started acting like soldiers. As I was walking to reach the Sherman tank and our two platoons there was some gun fire. It came from below my left flank. I didn't pay too much attention because it was down a slope. When I reached our GI's I said, "Lt. Murray wants the two platoons and tank to move up." We were walking forward when I heard something below my right flank. I said, "Halt Lieutenant, let me check out what this is." It was my responsibility for I was leading them. I asked, "Who's down there?" He started speaking German. Of course, I didn't know what the hell was going on or what was said, it was too dark to see. I did not want to take any chances.

Remembering the gunfire that I'd heard on my way past the slope, I quickly fired one round down the slope with my Carbine. I heard someone fall and not move. I ordered our GI's forward and in a short time we reached Lt. Murray. He said, "DeAngelo, there is someone firing at our left flank, go and see if you can get him." I asked, "Well, Lieutenant, have you heard any firing from that area in the last ten minutes? He said, "No, but they had been firing for a while and I was getting a little tired of it." I said, "I think I got him, Lieutenant."

Then the lieutenant I had just brought up to Lt. Murray said, "I want to file charges against this GI." Lt. Murray asked, "What do you mean file charges? Is that what you said Lieutenant?" He said,

"Yes, this man killed a German back there." Lt. Murray replied, "He killed a German? Did you not hear what I just ordered him to do? I told him to go out and get that German. Come over here, Lieutenant, do you see that body lying there? That is Lt. Smith, who came from an antiaircraft battalion to C Company. He walked over to ask the person in the foxhole if he was a German and was killed. Of course we killed the German! Do you understand what I'm talking about? If you don't like what we're doing, I'll get you transferred, but in the meantime keep your mouth shut and do what you are told. This soldier you want me to court-marshal is the best I have." He then dismissed him. I don't know what happened to that lieutenant; he was not in C Company very long, maybe a week or less. Where do these people come from?

The next morning I went to see the German I had shot. He was on his back and I had hit him through the heart. He had a square, pockmarked face. I didn't search the dead; I never did that. Once in a while I think about him lying there dead. It's one of those things that I guess one thinks about at times. I still do after many years.

When Lt. Murray would go on two or three-day leaves, he left me in charge of C Company. Believe it or not I was just a private. Boros, our 1st Sergeant, never said anything to me about it; he just left me alone. Did Lt. Murray see something in me he didn't see in Sgt. Boros? I have no idea. This happened on more than one occasion.

Once again when Lt. Murray was away, one of our GI's came in to say, "There is an Air Corps GI who wants to see you, DeAngelo." The GI came in and told me he was looking for a particular GI, Pvt. Frank Mosses, who was with the 3rd Platoon. I said, "I'm sorry. He was killed a few days ago." He said, "I've been wanting to meet up with him but it has taken me this long to come visit him." I said, "I'm sorry, do you want me to tell you how he was killed?" He said, "Well, tell me." "He never knew what hit him. A mortar came into his foxhole and he was killed instantly, he never knew any pain." Lt. Murray had two or three bottles of whiskey on his desk and I poured him a big glass. I said, "Here, drink this." He drank it.

The day before he was killed, Mosses said, "DeAngelo, do you want this pocket notebook?" I said, "No I really don't need it." He said, "Go ahead and have it." He gave it to me. I said, "I have something Mosses gave me. There's nothing in it, you can have it." He said, "No, I'll go and find where he's buried." Again I said, "I'm sorry. We GI's in the infantry, we see death everyday. We see it so many times, when we say he's dead it doesn't mean we don't care, we just see so much of it." He understood and thanked me for being kind. I was very sorry. Then, before leaving, he told me it was his older brother Frank. I told him to see the Grave Registration Officer to learn where his brother was buried. If he's alive today he may be wondering, "Who the hell was the GI behind the desk without any stripes, or showing any officer rank who gave me a drink?"

One day going on patrol there were two GI's in front of me, it was raining. I heard a shot, it was fired at the first GI, missed, and ricocheted off the road. He quickly jumped to the left of the road into a gully and to safety. The second shot hit the second GI, Pfc. Radcliffe, in the back somewhere. As he fell, "Oh God!" he cried out, and died. I laid down on the right side of the road in a gully. All I could do was to stay put because of this sniper, with rain water running down the gully into my clothes. These snipers had beautiful rifles. They were one of a kind with a powerful mounted scope. They could literally see all of you. Put you right up front. I stayed in this gully. I was ordered not to move until a tank came to help. A tank came up and protected me from getting shot. I was in a bad situation—I was wet and cold. I'm sorry we lost a nice GI. I don't know where that bullet hit him either, in his back or head.

On November 3, 1944, we were in a home in a town called Saucerray when several rounds from a self-propelled gun or a tank slammed into the roof where our CP was located. I was standing up and some GI's were sitting around in a circle. I was in the middle of the circle when the roof blew off. Some GI's were killed, some wounded. I received a cut on the back of my neck and was treated by our medic. He took my name down and said, "Well, you're getting a Purple Heart." I never received it.

I always made our GI's move up fast in order to take over the position of the enemy because German artillery and mortar fire would not come down on their own positions. When we were advancing we always made sure German positions were taken and then we rested while waiting for our next orders. German artillery and mortar always exploded at our rear since they thought we were advancing when we actually had finished advancing and were forward in their positions. The closer we moved to the enemy the safer we were. We still had to worry about small arms fire like machine guns and rifles but the majority of our wounded and deaths came from artillery and mortars rather than from small arms fire.

We often wore the same clothes for months at a time, so when we finally got a shower and a change of clothes, it was a real treat. Again, I recall my mother telling me to make sure my underwear were clean, but I can tell you that some of our dirty clothes were so filthy they had to be destroyed instead of cleaned and reissued to the next GI. Our long johns, after months of wear, were completely out of shape and almost always had holes in the knees, our socks with no bottoms.

Later, we walked around a town to visit the Red Cross building for some free coffee and donuts. We were upset when we were told the donuts were fives cents each. Anyway, I saw a line of GI's standing by and I went to the end of this line. Soon some Red Cross women asked it they could pass through us to get to the large building on our left side. On the right side of another building I noticed a door open and a MP standing halfway inside, counting 15 GI's and then closing the door. A little while later, he would open the door and count 15 more GI's. I was then number 16, so now I am number one—first one at the door. When the door opened, I was let in. I was told, "Pay the two dollars and take the first one coming down the stairs." To my surprise we had entered a house of prostitution. I said to the MP, "Do you mind if I pick the one I want?" I waited until one came down whom I felt I would enjoy and we went upstairs. After completing my encounter I walked down the back stairs. I was told by another MP to sign my name, outfit and serial number. I was told to take a syringe, fill it up with an antiseptic called Argyrol, stick it into my penis, hold the fluid for a few minutes and let it drain into a trough. Then I went in line a second time, and another $2.00. Again, the Argyrol treatment. Later I was told it was set up by a Captain who was with our regiment as a doctor. He was sending too many GI's to the hospital having no major problems. A few days later we were ordered back to the front having been showered and fed, and received clean clothes and had some fun.

Again, sometimes cold hamburgers and cold coffee were brought up to us late at night. Even though both were cold, we enjoyed them anyway. At times we saw the townspeople butchering dead horses. They would take the rear quarters off to eat later. As soon as the hindquarters were cut, the heat of the dead horse was seen rising if the weather was cool. The Germans used many horses to pull weapons of all kinds.

Soon the Germans were applying their 20 mm antiaircraft weapons against us ground troops. We in turn applied our Half Tracks with four 50 caliber M14, or twin 50's, with a 37 mm in between, M15 A1. I know these were not liked by the Germans and they soon did not apply their 20 mm's again. Each Infantry Company was assigned a Half Track to combat their 20 mm. I understood it was against the Articles of War to use 20 mm weapons against ground troops. They did it first; we finished it with M14 or M15 A1.

Later, we went deep into the Vosges Mountains, having heavy dense woods. These woods were always very difficult for any Army, including our GI's to go through. We tried to bypass these woods. It was very hard fighting in them. We climbed up to 2,000 feet or more on some of these mountains.

A few GI's would find a place to sit at the back of a tank to keep warm, but when the tank's engine was started, they'd have to get out

Vosges Mountains

of the way quickly since they didn't know if it was going to move or if it was just using the radio or charging the battery.

From time to time in the mountains, we would come upon a dead German laying in the road or trail in the woods, crushed into the ground by some tank rolling over him. Moving through the Vosges one morning, I came upon a very young German who was in pain and shock. I noticed his hand had a few fingers missing and bleeding and seeking some kind of help. As we were moving up in those days, we would cover many miles and our medics were not able to help him. I am sure someone, after we moved on, did help him. As the Germans were moving back, we always would get on a Tank, or Tank Destroyer or truck to keep contact with them and later did the same the next day, keeping the Germans from digging in and trying to hold us back from moving forward, as we were each day, going after them.

Then, one night I ran a fever of 100 degrees. Our medic took my temperature and said I could not be sent to the hospital unless it was 101 or higher. So I slept in a barn where there was hay and other stuff around me. The next morning my temperature was normal. Was there something in the barn that did it?

Figure 59, November 17, 1944. This photo shows my old K Company being decorated. Later C. Company was called—and my name. Gen. O'Daniels, pictured here, was the one who presented me with my Bronze Star. He complimented me on an excellent job and while I stood at attention, he pinned the star on me. Again, we then saluted each other. It was a nice feeling for this 20 year old as I was walking back to C-Company.

The day I received my Bronze Star, 283 Bronze Stars and 157 Silver Stars were issued to the 30th Infantry Regiment. I understand that at first I was put in for a Bronze Star, but then Battalion and Regiment suggested I receive the Silver Star. Division turned it down to a Bronze Star. Why?

One morning I was on patrol about one hundred to three hundred yards in front of our lines. I recall that the patrol consisted

Figure 59. My old K Company receiving citation by Gen. O'Daniels, 3rd Division Commander, the author received his Bronze Star by the General, November 17, 1944.

of me and three other GI's. I heard a shot and immediately one of my GI's fell to the ground. I asked, "What the hell is wrong with you?" He said, "I'm shot, DeAngelo." I said, "What do you mean shot?" He said, "Look!" A bullet had gone into the left side of his right foot just below his ankle. It was sticking half way out of his boot. I had a pair of pliers that I always carried with me in case I came across any German telephone wire (plastic orange color). I never knew if the wires were open or not so I cut them just in case. I pulled the bullet out with the pliers and then took his boot and sock off. Blood with clear fluid was seeping out. I took his First-Aid pack off his ammo belt and put sulfa powder on the wound and bandaged it up.

Looking at this bullet I said, "That's a M-1 bullet." He said, "You're kidding me." I said, "I'm going to take it back to find out who the hell shot at us. As for the other GI's, I do not know what

Vosges Mountains

happened to them but assumed they returned to C Company in a different direction. I told him I would get him back. The road was sort of S-shaped and I said to the GI, "I know you can't walk, so what I'm asking you to do is put your arm around me and I'll put my arm around you. I'm going to run, you take big hops with your good foot. Just hop, it's the only way I can get you back. No one is going to come in daylight to get you so just do what I say." He said, "No, let me go, send a medic." I said, "I'm not going to do that, I won't leave you here, we are too far up front." He put his arm around me and I put mine around him. I ran; he hopped. When the Germans saw us running and hopping they started dropping mortars on us. They fired about six or eight mortars trying to hit us and the whole time he was saying, "Let me go, let me go, DeAngelo." I said, "No, no, we're either going to get killed together or wounded together." We finally made it back and I went to our company commander and said, "Lt. Murray, who the hell is the GI who shot at us?" Lt. Murray said, "What do you mean, DeAngelo?" I said, "Well, look at this, this is an M-1 bullet." He said, "I don't think anybody from here shot at you." I said, "Well, if I ever catch the GI who did it I'm going to break his neck. We were on patrol and we got shot at." I'm sure someone had forgotten our patrol was out in front. I should have been notarized for helping that GI, but nothing ever came of it. At times I wonder, again—why?

Every once in a while when we moved to a new area I could smell fish oil. We knew the Germans used fish oil to clean their weapons, so whenever we smelled it, we knew they were around. We would stay on our toes in case of a counterattack or something unexpectedly. I will always remember the smell of fish oil. It was on their clothing and equipment, it was always present. But the smell didn't keep us from liking canned fish. I remember one day when we came upon a fish cannery, took as many sardine cans as we could, and ate them on our way.

I received a letter, believe it or not, from a manufacturer in the United States who manufactured condoms. I wondered why this company would write me a letter. It read, "Dear Mr. DeAngelo, we are sorry you have been unsatisfied with our product, please be reassured we will do our best to improve the product." I don't know who did this, it was kind of funny. I should have kept it, it was a serious letter, I had made a complaint. I had not complained. This is what happened when we were in the Army. Some characters will always be characters. GI's did things like this from time to time. Me, writing a letter to a company that manufactured condoms of a complaint. It was strange to receive such a letter apologizing about the quality of their product. I don't know if their product was good or not, I never used one.

Late one afternoon as we were walking through the Vosges Mountains we glanced to the left. We were not on any road we were walking on the side of this mountain. We noticed on our left on a road was a large column of Germans walking. There were a thousand, or more with their rifles over their shoulders, walking toward us. We stopped and very quietly, set up our machine guns, mortars, and bazookas. Very soon we were given orders to fire, we fired into that group of Germans. Afterwards we did not stop to view the outcome. I know we destroyed many German's that day. They were caught dead. We had a couple of companies of GI's firing, you couldn't help but hit somebody with all the ammunition we fired. I don't recall reading anything in our regimental book of this action.

In the Vosges Mountains, I came upon what looked like a hole dug 10 feet below the ground. It looked like there were 1 or 2 rooms. Using a ladder, I went down to see if there were any enemy. I came upon this big crate of Schnapps, too big to carry out. I took a couple of bottles, I told others if they wanted any to go and get it. I don't remember if they did but I know I had 2 or 3 bottles of Schnapps. I mean those Germans could have lived in it for weeks, and drink forever. It was something to see, it might have been a command post of some kind with all that Schnapps.

Around the top of some mountain we came to a listening post built of concrete. I remember reading the year 1914 carved out over the entrance. It had been used during World War I. The Germans were retreating quite fast from this area and we were close behind them. I don't know if the Germans even knew this post existed. It was strange to read 1914, wondering what took place there in WWI.

In the town of Thann, around Alsace Lorraine, we came across this house. I met a cute lady there. She must have been in her late twenties. I guess you don't know the ages of some of these people, they seem to be worn down by the war. She was wearing wooden shoes like the Dutch wear. I became friendly with her. Soon I asked if she wanted to make zig, zig, the French word to make love. She said yes. At the time I was carrying batteries for our back pack radio, for the company commanders' SCR-300. I don't know how I got the job of carrying these batteries. She and I went walking up some steps, you could hear her wooden shoes clicking each step she took. It was strange to hear. We found a room. Soon I heard Lt. Murray call, DeAngelo, DeAngelo, where are you?" I replied, "I'll be right down." I completed our zig, zig and walked down, "What do you need, Lt.?" He said, "I need batteries for the SCR-300 radio." Following me down the stairs was this lady with her wooden shoes, click, clack, click, clack. Lt. Murray didn't say anything, he knew what took place some minutes before. I understand recently at some speech, Murray had spoken of that episode. Why I do not know. It was fun to relive it all over again when he told me he had spoken of my lady friend and her wooden shoes.

The people in Alsace Lorraine spoke English, French and/or German depending on which government they were under. We captured the town of Rosheim in Alsace Lorraine on November 26, 1944. The Germans had not turned off its water or electricity, so I guess we out flanked them very quickly. I was asked by Lt. Murray to look for some Schnapps. I went from house to house and everybody was so kind they gave me a glass of Schnapps. I didn't want to be rude and refuse it, so after five houses I was feeling pretty good. But I still didn't have a bottle for the lieutenant.

I walked on and stopped at the Unger house on Hitler Strasse

(Street). They had three daughters and a son. Their son was put in the German Army and had been sent to the Russian front. He was still alive at the time. They were a wonderful family and I hit it off pretty good with the youngest daughter, Odette, who was about fifteen. I was beat because of all the Schnapps I had. The lights were still on, we were in the house talking. We were sitting on the couch then my head just dropped down on her lap. I fell asleep. Too much Schnapps plus being tired I guess. I slept for about two hours, finally I woke up. My head was still in her lap. I said I was sorry. She said it was all right, now the lights were not on. They were turned off, only an oil lamp was burning. At some time the power was turned off. The Ungers invited me to spend the night in their son's room. They took me upstairs and I crawled into the bed, which must have been five feet high, and slept until morning.

They served me coffee and some great homemade bread for breakfast. I thanked them and left in search of Lt. Murray. "What happened to my Schnapps, DeAngelo?" he asked. I told him, "I couldn't refuse the glasses everyone offered, so I drank it all. By the time I got to the fifth house I was out of it." He laughed, but I did finally find a bottle for him. I visited with the Ungers for a couple of days and gave them what little I could in return for their hospitality. GI's didn't like 20 Grand or Raleigh cigarettes, so I gave them some of those along with some crackers, coffee, toilet paper, chewing gum, cookies, biscuits in a can, and some rations GI's didn't like. I put them all in an empty 10-1 rations box and took it to the Unger's, they were happy. Odette gave me a photograph of herself before I left. The Unger's were really nice people.

The next day I was given an extra loaf of bread our bakery had baked. I took it to them. We had plenty plus nobody wanted this extra loaf. The Unger's always made me coffee. That night they invited me to supper, so I stayed. A young man in civilian clothes, very nice and polite, was seated next to me at the table. Odette said to me, "Did you know that he's a German soldier?" I said, "You're kidding me? Where's his uniform?" She replied, "Well, he's a friend of my brother and lives in town. He didn't want to go with the Germans, so he stayed behind." I asked her again, "Where's his uniform?" She said, "It's upstairs in one of our rooms." I said, "Tell him to go upstairs, put his uniform on and let him come down to me." He went up to put his uniform on and came down to where I was sitting. I said, "Now sit down and eat your supper." He sat down. Then I noticed he was carrying a bag of 9 mm rounds and a machine pistol, MP-38. Here I was sitting down having supper with my M-1 in the next room, against the wall. He put the machine pistol against the back wall along with the ammo, near me. I said, "When you've finished supper, I'll take you to our MP's. I told you to put your uniform on, because if you were out of your uniform you could be shot as a spy." He understood. I asked him if he had anything of value on him. He had a watch plus a fountain pen. I told him, "Take the watch off and give it with the pen to Odette, she'll hold them for you until you return." That's what he did. I marched him off to our MP's and turned him over. Of course Odette was very happy I took him as a prisoner. I explained, I had him give her his pen and watch because he might lose them or they may take them from him. This way he would get them back from her when he returned.

 Later that night Odette and I were getting friendly. She took me outside and showed me where they kept chickens and rabbits. I got real close to her, which I wanted, but I didn't penetrate. She became afraid and pushed me away. I didn't say anything; she didn't say anything. She smiled and I was happy. That night I told her I had to leave the next morning and asked if they would be so kind as to set an alarm clock for me. Some hours later, her father came to tell me it was time. I dressed and we had breakfast together. The last time I saw the Ungers they were at the top bedroom windows waving and crying. I waved and told them I would be back. I blew a kiss to them. Before I left I gave them more food I had accumulated. I returned to my outfit and we walked forward to the next town on the way to the front.

Then, at the next town, I tried to sneak back to Rosheim to see the Unger family. As I was walking back down the road, who came walking up the other way but Lieutenant Murray. He asked, "Where are you going, DeAngelo?" All I could say was, "I came down to find you." Which of course was not true, I was on my way to Rosheim. I think if I had reached the Ungers I probably would have been AWOL for a few days. Later I told him what I was doing, he just laughed and said, "I understand DeAngelo." I said, "They were a nice family, I enjoyed them very much. They made me feel like a son, because of their son being away. They were very wonderful, and very nice. I'm sorry I never contacted them, I should have .

There were 1,277 3rd Division GI's killed in the Vosges Mountains.

Chapter Ten

Colmar

At daylight on the morning of November 7, 1944, we walked down the side of a mountain toward the town of St. Die, which had been burned and gutted by the Germans. I never knew why they did this, probably to take revenge on the civilian population. It was quite light and we were getting close to the bottom of this hill, when a few German tanks started firing into nearby trees. We were having tree bursts all around us. All GI's are petrified of tree bursts, and some lay down on their bellies and wouldn't move forward. The tanks, which must have been Tiger tanks, kept on firing into us. Lt. Murray looked at me as though he was trying to figure out what we should do. I said, "You know, Lieutenant, we have to get these GI's off the ground so we can move forward and take over the German position. It's the only way to protect us from tank fire. Pretty soon they'll be using mortars and then we'll be up a creek." I saw a fallen tree in front of us and said, "Here's what we can do, I'll fire my M-1 over our GI's heads, you fire your Carbine." We started to fire, then reloaded. We were both yelling, "Let's get going! Let's move and take over their position."

Then I saw a tracer round flying over my head. Lt. Murray received a round that went inside his right trench coat pocket. I quickly reloaded my M-1. I had seen where that tracer had come from, rested my M-1 on top of the fallen tree, and fired all eight rounds in that direction, reloading again. Then we both walked forward and I found a dead German with a bullet hole through his upper chest. I turned to look at where I had been standing when I fired and saw that there was a direct line of fire from me to him. I knew I had been the one who hit him. Lt. Murray was in front of me when we passed a foxhole. I called out and asked if he had checked the foxhole out. He said, "No." I said, "All right, I'll check it out." I did and out came a German with a grenade in his hand. "You see what I mean? You have to check every foxhole." He said, "You're right, DeAngelo." We captured and killed a few and took over the German foxholes for protection.

At that time, one of my friends, Pfc. Avala, was shot through the right hip. I walked over to see him and asked, "How are you doing?" He said, "DeAngelo, I'm hit. Can you get me to a medic?" I told him I would get some of the captured Germans to carry him out of there. The last time I saw him he was being carried up the hill by four Germans. The 3rd Infantry Division book states that he was killed and missing in action. I don't know what happened and wonder if an artillery barrage caught them. It's possible the German prisoners carrying him were also killed. We kept mopping up each town, always on the move and going forward.

We were told our next town to capture was called Neuf-Brisach. This was February 6, 1945. The town was built in 1472 and was first destroyed by the Germans in 1870. It was built with bunkers and moats to withstand a siege. We were told the town was supposed to be a division objective, then a regimental objective. When we arrived, our trucks came up with long ladders similar to the ones the Crusaders had used to climb castle walls. We asked, "What are we supposed to do, climb these walls?" We ended up not using the ladders. *Figure 60* shows the bunkers that people lived in or used for storage. The 3rd Platoon of C Company, of First Battalion, the 30th Regiment, captured the town on this day. *Figure 61* shows an aerial view of Neuf-Brisach. You can see why our GI's called it Waffle City.

Figure 62 shows the author in front of C Company CP carrying a 45 Colt with combat knife and two clips for the 45. You'll notice I'm not wearing my helmet, I'm wearing an overseas cap and a blue scarf. This photo was taken at Neuf-Brisach by Pfc Harry L.

Colmar

Figure 60. 3rd Division captured Neuf-Brisach with its deep bunkers. Our CP was posted.

Figure 61. The town of Neuf-Brisach, called by GI's Waffle City. Viewed by air.

Figure 62. The author standing in front of C Company CP in Neuf-Brisach, Alsace Lorraine.

Rothstein, who was born in Germany of Jewish parents and spoke both languages. He found a camera with film and took my photo. Years after being discharged I was at home talking to some friends when I heard a voice. I called out, "Rothstein," and he turned to see who called his name. We spoke, he said he had the photo and that I should visit him in the Bronx. I did and he gave me the photo. When he joined C Company he did not have anyone who would speak to him. I felt he needed a friend and I became that friend. I helped him fit in, as a new replacement.

Figure 63 is a picture of my platoon taken on February 8, 1945, in Neuf-Brisach. It was a squad from this platoon that captured the town. Pfc. Walker, Sgt. Baldwin and half seen is Lt. Lombardi, who was killed a short time later. They were all outstanding GI's. I enjoyed each one of them very much.

Figure 63. C Company, Third Platoon at Neuf-Brisach, the author was with this platoon since Anzio. One squad captured this town.

Recently when I was having the above photo made, I requested it be done over because the Lt. on one end was left out. I wanted it to show this was Lt. Lombardi in the photo. Strange, as it was shortly thereafter that I received a call from someone whom I do not know, asking if I knew this Lt. Lombardi by saying his name. Yes I did know this Lt., he was killed after I was wounded. Then he told me it was his dad. He never knew him. I said, "I have a photo of your dad." As I look back, why did I want to have this photo made over again of this Lt. not seen at one end of the other photo? I made a copy of the photograph showing half of Lt. Lombardi and mailed it to his son, no reply of any kind. Very strange—no reply.

In the town of Neuf-Brisach I met a young mother and her 5-

month-old son. Her husband had lost the restaurant they owned and was not well emotionally. I felt sorry for her and her child and gave them coffee and food. Her husband did not like GI's for some reason and he was not around at times. Nothing was going on between the wife and me.

For capturing the city we were told, if we wanted, we could ship a German rifle home. We had to cut the stock. Then we placed it in a wooden box, no more than 30" x 6" x 6" and gave it to our Supply Sergeant. I had found an Italian rifle called Mannlicher-Carcano, this was the type of rifle that killed President Kennedy. The one I had, had a bayonet attached as part of the rifle that swung out from underneath. To use it you pulled the bayonet from it's position to place it up in front and locked it. This rifle's workmanship was so bad, I wanted to trade it with some one who wanted it, so I did. My trade was a German rifle, manufactured in 1944, having machined parts. It was not possible to exchange rifle components with other year models before 1943. The first rifles, manufactured before WWII, and up to late 1943, were fitted by hand. It was not possible to exchange components with another, even if the two were manufactured the same day and by the same person. So it became impossible to hand manufacture these rifles, after late 1943 rifles were machine manufactured. I cut the stock of this German rifle 92 mm Kar 98k the standard German service weapon of WWII. It was received at home in good condition. It was machine manufactured in 1944. I gave it to a salesman when I purchased a new car in July of 1946.

We had a GI who was a loner, and he would take off from time to time. I had noticed him taking some APC tablets (something like very strong aspirin called "All Purpose Capsules") with some strong drink and wondering why this GI was doing this, he was a strange one. Around the Colmar he was killed, how, I do not know, but when searched the Grave Registration, people found a small bag, one would buy with tobacco to roll one's cigarette, it was found with gold items.

Colmar

Figure 64 shows Sgt. Vasion nearest to the camera with Sgt. Hohmann. Vasion was the GI I had my third fight with on Anzio. Our 30th Regiment was being decorated by the French for capturing Neuf-Brisach. I don't remember seeing Sgt. Hohmann after this photograph was taken but Vasion was still with us.

Figure 64. 3rd Division receiving the French "Croix de Guerre", February 20, 1945. The S/Sgt nearest to camera is Vasion, whom I had a fight with at Anzio. On the other side of him is S/Sgt Hohmann.

A few weeks after, I had captured a prisoner. *Figure 65* shows the automatic pistol I found on him. It looked like our automatic 45, either made into a 38 Cal or 9 mm called a "Star." It was a 9 mm in excellent condition. It was manufactured in Spain, and shipped to Germany. Every time I thought I was going to be captured I threw it away. When everything calmed down, I'd retrieve it. It was well known that if you were captured and they found any German equipment on you, you would be killed. They would assume that

Figure 65. My Star Weapon, manufactured in Spain for the Germans, captured.

you must have killed a German to get it.

I placed this "Star" automatic in my "A" barracks bag, each GI had one. I told our Supply Sergeant, Ducy to hold it for me. Weeks later I wanted to clean my weapon, it was gone. I asked, "Sergeant, what happened to my automatic?" He replied, "A Lt. came by, he said you told him he could have it." I said, "That is not true." I was peeved off. I asked, "Is that true?" He said, "Yeah, he came by a couple of weeks ago and said you told him he could have it, he has it now." I marched to our CP. I went in to see that Lt. There were other officers and the 1st Sergeant, with some GI getting reamed over something. I said, "Lt. I understand you have my Star." He replied, "Well yes." I said, "Tell me something Lt., I never gave you permission to go to the supply sergeant and say I gave you permission to have it." He didn't say anything. I said, "Lieutenant, I'm going to tell you something. I want it back." I received it within twenty seconds. Nothing else was said. I feel this Lt. and the other officers did respect me. I was willing to take them on, I didn't give a damn, what could they do to me? Put me in the Infantry.

I always got along with my officers; we had fun. One was Lt. LaBelle, a French-American. When I received a package from home, there would often be a jar of hot peppers in it and he and I would sit around and eat the peppers, joking and laughing. Lt. Murray didn't care for this kind of food, I believe, but hard candy was another thing.

I got my second case of frostbite and Lt. Murray told me to go down the hill to First Aid. I could barely walk it was so painful. As I was walking down I heard an explosion behind me and I learned that Col. Armstrong was killed. When I arrived at First Aid, the captain asked what was wrong with me and I told him my feet were really bad. He said, "You must go back to your outfit." I thought "OK, I'm not gonna fight him; he thinks he knows more than I do." As I was walking back up to my outfit, guess who was being carried down the hill on a stretcher? Lt. Murray. He had been hit in the rear end. They stopped and he asked me where I was going. I told what the captain had said and he asked if anyone had even looked at my feet. I told him, "No, I think he thought I was gold bricking." Lt. Murray got off his stretcher and put me on it since I was unable to walk any further. They carried me back down to First Aid and Lt. Murray told the captain, "This is the best man I have in my company. I want him to be sent to a hospital, now!" My company commander's wounds were not bad, but he did receive a Congressional Medal of Honor for his actions that day, December 16, 1944.

I was bedridden for two weeks trying to get my feet cleared up. A full colonel came by, asked a couple of questions, and I noticed on his report he had written that my heart was not "remarkable." I didn't understand this so I asked him, "What does that mean? Does it mean there is nothing wrong with it or does it mean that it isn't anything good? Tell me." He wouldn't answer my questions. The more he didn't answer my questions the more aggravated I became. If my heart was bad, I should be told about it, and perhaps taken out of combat. All he said was that I was being sent back to the front. I said, "OK, but I'll tell you one thing, Colonel. I'll be back and you'll never send me back to the front again. You have not explained to me about my heart. Remember what I say, I'll be back and you'll never be able to send me back to combat, no matter what you do." One of the GI's who was sent to the hospital with me also had problems with his feet. He was not bedridden like I was; he was a walking patient. The colonel sent him to England and "ZI", Zone of Interior. I don't know what the hell was going on. Soon the ambulance came to take us to the Repo-Depo. About two blocks from the hospital we had a collision with a truck and one of the GI's was hurt. Of course, we had to return to the hospital. The colonel saw me but I didn't say anything to him. It wasn't time to say anything because he was uncaring. Another ambulance came to take us to the Repo-Depo and then later on to C Company.

I was not afraid of combat; I was tired of it. I saw too many GI's wounded or killed. I saw just too much of it in the fifteen months I spent in a front line company. Death in the infantry is a very short time, a matter of days, maybe minutes, or seconds.

Sometimes Lt. Murray would ask me, "Where would you put a BAR (Browning Automatic Rifle) or the light machine guns, DeAngelo?" I would reply, "Well, I'll check from what direction we might have a counterattack." I found some good locations and he would tell me to make sure they were set up exactly where I wanted them. We didn't have any counterattack that night or the next night, but you never knew. It was always good to be prepared for anything that would pop up on us at any time.

Around Christmas 1944 at the Rhine River, we heard some Germans singing Christmas songs. It was strange to hear them singing while there was gunfire in the distance. I know for sure we did not fire across the river where the singing came from. I remember that we also started to sing. Many of our GI's were thinking of home and family. When was the last time each one of us had spent Christmas with our loved ones? Our cooks always made sure we had Christmas and New Years' turkey with all the trimmings. We enjoyed the rest and the food on these holidays, but most of all we were grateful the fighting stopped for a little while.

Figure 66, shows French Sherman tanks in Guemar. These were U.S. Army tanks given to the French. The French never marched; they always rode while we always walked. They had uniforms identical to ours and everything. Many girls were raped in Sicily, Italy and France. Some African-American GI's were being blamed for these rapes. Many French soldiers were from Morocco, North Africa. The U.S. Army ordered us to wear a round button that said "US Army" on our collar to distinguish us from them.

Figure 66. American Sherman Tanks with the French 1st Armored Division at Guemar. The author asked to fire on the Hetzer-38T. January 9, 1945.

We had problems with the French troops attached to our 7th Army. We captured a town, then the French drove in. Then these French troops would take over and eat the food, drink all the wine and have fun with the women while we were on our way to the next town to capture it. As soon as we left for the next town the French troops would move in again and enjoy that town. We GI's were not having fun, the French troops were having all the fun, and not much fighting.

Figure 67 is a picture of a German tank called a Hetzer 38T. We were moving across a field of snow early one evening and this particular tank was in front of us, firing. The tank crew couldn't get its cannon lowered to fire at us as we were moving closer to them.

Figure 67. A German tank, Hetzer-38T, in Guemar. The author asked French tanks to fire on it. One of our men hit it with his Bazooka. It was destroyed.

They started the engine and put it in reverse, but it coughed and died. They kept firing at us as they tried to back away. I don't know where our tanks were. This particular German tank had no turret. Its 75 mm cannon moved up, down and very little sideways. A remote controlled machine gun was mounted on top and its gunner sat inside sighting with mirrors. We moved on and came across some

French Sherman tanks, some were burned up and some of them were just sitting there. I didn't see any French troops outside and figured they were inside sleeping, or drunk. I walked up to one of the tanks, started yelling and used the butt of my M-1 against the hull to get their attention. I spoke English, but no one inside paid attention to me. Then I asked if anyone spoke Italian. Well, a member of one tank crew popped his head out and said he spoke Italian. I pointed to the German tank and said, "Why don't you fire at it, it's giving us trouble." He said they would and went back inside, closing the hatch behind him. He never fired his 75 mm at the Hetzer 38T tank. I believe these French were petrified of that German tank, probably thinking there might be more than one. Did this German tank knock out two or three French tanks? This was a bad situation we were facing. Finally, one of our GI's snuck up on the left side of the Hetzer as they were trying to restart its engine. He fired a bazooka rocket and it hit one inch above the underbody, under the driver. All four crewmembers were killed. This was in the town of Guemar, with snow and very cold.

American GI's were very different from the Germans. I am sure this also applied to the Japanese. Both were trained to follow orders, but when we lost officers or NCO's we were able to take the lead, be in charge, even if we were a private. It is the American Way not to wait for orders but to know what to do in a pinch. We did not wait for an officer or a NCO to be replaced and come to lead us. The Germans and Japanese had to wait for their leadership for orders; we did not wait to be told what to do.

We stayed in the town of Guemar for about a week, resting up, and getting replacements. The next morning I went out to check the Hetzer 38T and pulled out its radio and battery and brought it to our CP. We had taken over a priest's home. Guemar's Catholic Church had been completely destroyed and inside I saw a tremendously large cross of Jesus hanging by just a very thin cable. It didn't fall, but an explosion or something very small could have made the cross fall. There weren't any walls, just a little of whatever was left to keep it from falling, it was strange to view this. We found many rooms in this priest's home. One room had many radios, the next room had silverware and china plates, another had white bread. The next room had salami's and cheeses. One section of a wall in the basement had red wine. Another section had white wine. We ate all the cheese, bread, salami, and sausages. We drank all the red wine, soon we started hitting the white wine. We never washed a plate, we kept going into the plate room to get plate after plate, there were piles of dirty plates in the sink. We searched for the priest who lived in this house. He was captured by C Company. The towns' people complained about him, he was a collaborator. He marched with other prisoners , to the rear to our MP's.

As I was walking down Main Street next morning in Guemar, I came across some activity by our GI's. I asked, "What's going on?" They said there was a barn with a platform inside, a GI had removed a brick from the back wall. They were looking through this opening, they saw snow on the ground and a German helmet having a white cloth over it. Many Germans had white cloth over their uniforms to blend in with recent snow. I asked, " What are you going to do?" They replied, "As soon as he pops up we're going to put a bullet in his helmet." I said, "Let me see what you're talking about." I had binoculars of ten power. Theirs' were six power, I said, "I see half of his helmet." Four or five inches were above the ground, he wasn't sticking his head out, his helmet was moving side to side. I said, "Before you fire let me see what's in the background of the town behind him. I looked once, then a second look. I saw a big tank with its 88 mm sitting facing the road. This road led right down into the town of Guemar. I said, "You know if you fire at him that tank behind him is going to blow us right out of this barn. Don't do anything till I get back." I ran to see our company commander, Lt. Murray, I said, "I know where a tank is parked." He said, "Are you sure DeAngelo?" I replied, "Yes, he's sitting there waiting." "Go upstairs, there is a field observer officer from artillery with binoculars on a tripod." I walked upstairs I said, "Lieutenant, I know where there is a tank." He asked, "Where?" I showed him. "But I can't see it." I told him, "I can point it out." He showed me a map. I saw that road on his map. The end of that town had a wall. "This wall had an opening. He's inside the opening, blending in with the wall. Behind him are a couple of buildings." He said, "OK, I'll take care of it, I see it now." Well, he called for 155 mm Long Toms. These were each a 93 lbs. He called for firing effect. Nine rounds came over and destroyed that tank. We received confirmation. The Tiger tank had been destroyed, as well as the Hetzer 38T from the night before.

GI's are GI's. I noticed a pile of feathers here, a pile of feathers there, and sometimes rabbit fur. An order was received from battalion not to kill any more livestock. About an hour later I heard an explosion. Two minutes later a GI called our CP by phone and said a round had just come in and killed a calf. I said, "It killed a calf? You're kidding me?" He said, "No, it's a shame to let it go to waste." I reminded him that we weren't supposed to kill any livestock and he said, "What do you want me to do?" I explained the situation to Lt. Murray, who told me to go down and check it out. When I arrived I noticed the calf had a nice clean hole was in its forehead and it was obvious some GI had shot the calf and was trying to blame it on the German artillery. I told them I didn't want anything to do with this. I just walked back to our CP thinking, now what? When I returned I told Lt. Murray the story. Some GI's do crazy things at times.

We received a new replacement Pfc Stephens, a pretty nice guy. We had rations called 10-1, which meant ten men could eat out of one carton. We had been off the line for some days when these rations were issued to us. Inside was butter, coffee, tea, cocoa whatever. Soups, graham crackers, a can of uncooked bacon, this GI Stephens had been a chef in Chicago, and he wanted to join Lt. Murray's GI's. He took the can of bacon, fried it, took the grease, dropped the graham crackers in then rolled the graham crackers in sugar, it tasted great. Our company commander, Lt. Murray liked them very much. I told him Stephens would like to join us, which he did. Every once in awhile he would come up with something cooked differently for us, it was a great change eating food cooked by C Company Chef Stephens.

Whenever we opened 10-1 rations, there would be a note with a girl's name and address tucked inside the package of graham crackers. It would read, "Please write." I imagine some GI's did write to these girls. I don't know if a romance or marriage ever evolved from that type of correspondence. It would be nice to know if it did happen. I remember seeing some names of girls with addresses for us to write them. It was interesting and nice to know, someone was thinking about us asking us to write.

Around this time, we had applied large search lights to light up the night sky, called "Artificial Moonlight". We had big speakers pointed toward the front lines, broadcasting in German to give up and come to us, and pamphlets which we floated down by aircraft or by our 105 mm shells firing toward and over their lines.

One morning, in Guemar, I came across a young GI walking with an older German prisoner. I asked, "Where'd you get this prisoner?" He replied, "Well, another GI just gave him to me." I asked, "Have you searched him?" He said, "No, I thought the other GI searched him!" I said, "Don't take a chance that someone has searched him before. I'll search him, you keep your rifle on him." I found a grenade in the prisoner's pocket. The prisoner looked at me sternly. He was probably SS but his uniform didn't indicate that. I had told our GI's not to trust anyone and to make sure all prisoners were searched. I looked down at the snowy ground and noticed the prisoner was wearing a brand new pair of combat boots–ours! They were in better condition than the ones some GI's were wearing. I asked him, "Where did you get these?" He told me he got them from another place up north. I said, "What place?" He couldn't tell me. I said, "Take them off." He didn't want to do it, so I took out my knife, cut them off him and threw them down in the snow. Then I said, "Now, you walk in the snow like the GI you took them from." Some GI from antitank said, "If you weren't a lieutenant, I'd beat the hell out of you for making him walk in the snow barefoot." I said, "What do you mean? I'm not a lieutenant." He said, "Well, what about the bars on your jacket?" I looked and realized that I had taken Lt. Skeahan's jacket by mistake. I explained this to him and said, "Look here, buddy, I'm just a private like you, so let's fight if you want to. Let me tell you something, you don't know what we in Infantry go through; so don't give me any of your crap. For your information those combat boots he was wearing were probably taken off another GI, who is either dead or walking barefoot in this snow someplace." I told him that if he wanted to make an issue out of it, he should report it to battalion. I heard nothing. Earlier the Germans had captured a bunch of GI's. I believe that pair of boots was taken from some GI, either dead or a prisoner, possibly walking without boots in the snow. Now this prisoner was doing the same, walking back to the MP's.

Two new replacements joined C Company. They had spent Christmas 1944 at home and when they came to C Company their M-1's were unloaded. They asked me when they should load their M-1's. I told them, "Load immediately for we are on the front line." I am unable to recall their names, but the very next morning both were killed, this was mid January 1945. I don't know why they were not told to load their M-1's. That was a problem with the Repo-Depo GI's, they didn't care or worse.

Figure 68 shows a bridge at Maisson Rouge on January 23, 1945. It collapsed and one of our Sherman tanks fell into the Ill River near Guemar. I was in the woods in the background and saw the tank fall when it broke through the bridge. I understood they were told in advance that the bridge was too weak for a tank, but some lieutenant ordered them to proceed; he was later broken for giving the order. When the bridge collapsed, the Germans counterattacked from where those trees are in the background. A small river called L'Orchbach River ran nearby. Right behind there was sort of a lean-to built half into the ground and half out of the

Figure 68. Our Sherman Tank falls into the Ill River at Maison Rouge. The author saw it happen while standing at the trees on the far side.

ground. I got into the lean-to. We started receiving machine gun fire from German tanks in front moving toward us. I said to myself, "I'm not going to stay in this." I told some GI's, "We better get out of here because those tanks are going to start firing into this building." They said, "No this is a good place to be." Nobody would go with me. I got out and behind it there was a plank across the river. I walked over the river. I was getting machine gun fire over me, under me, and on both sides of me. As soon as I walked off the plank, I ran into some lieutenant I didn't know. He asked where I'd been and I told him. He then asked where I was going and I told him I had lost track of my company and was trying to get back to join them. I don't know if the lieutenant walked over the plank to get the other GI's.

I walked through an open field to the next town, where I found a bunch of GI's. We had no way of protecting ourselves from German troops once the bridge was out. The Germans came into town and captured some GI's. Some GI's who wouldn't give up were in cellars and the Germans poured gasoline into the cellars and burned them. An order came down from our generals and colonels that now there were no holds barred. We could do whatever we wanted to do in

Colmar

retribution. We took off and started to go to town on the Germans. We did as we were ordered, plus more.

Figure 69. It was cold in the Colmar section. Our feet were wet and cold (I always carried a pair of dry socks and would change them when I could) and some of the GI's were wearing shoes called snow packs. There was no ventilation in the snow packs and perspiration built up. When it was cold our feet were cold. Resting, I took my snow packs and wet socks off. I tried to warm up my feet by rubbing them with "Barbarsol" shave cream. I put my dry socks

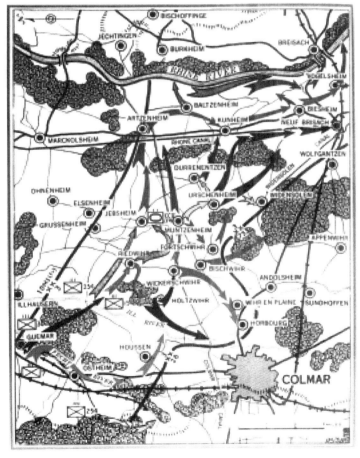

Figure 69. The town of Colmar with the Rhine River, with the town of Guemar.

on. Suddenly we received orders to move out immediately! I just couldn't get the darn snow packs on since my feet had swelled up. It was a bad time to be caught with them off. It was something I avoided from then on. When we slept, we slept with our boots on, because you never knew what was going to happen. The only time we slept with our boots off was when we were in the rear, in reserve, for training. There is a movie called "Battle Ground" that shows what I am talking about—taking your boots off can cause you plenty of trouble.

January 29, 1945. *Figure 70* shows crossing the Colmar Canal. When we reached the canal, we came upon some big barges that people lived on all year around. These barges traveled from one end of the country to the other. I went on one and it was beautiful inside. The living quarters were all mahogany and polished brass. I noticed over the fireplace on one end was a bust of Napoleon as a brass bell. On the other end was another brass piece called the "Manneken" or the "Brussels Boy." I sort of borrowed these two. I still have them today. The story about the "Manneken" boy goes like this: the King of Belgium lost his son around 1469. He proclaimed that when his son was found he would build a statue of him in the position he was found. They found his son peeing. So if you go to Brussels you'll see this boy's statue in the middle of the town, peeing. *Figure 71*. I don't know how old it is, its brass screws are handmade, so it must be pretty old. Now it's about 58 years older. I am told that on special days some kind of uniform is placed on the "Manneken." I understand there are around 15-20 sets to be used on certain holidays. The brass bell has Waterloo on its side. I don't know how old or valuable they are.

Colmar

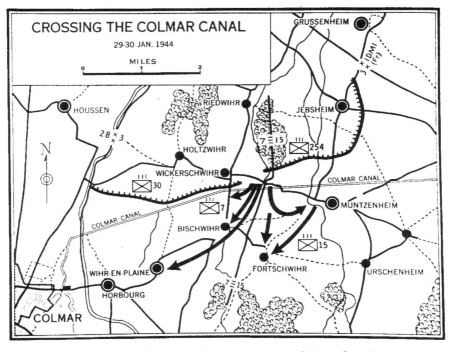

Figure 70. The 3rd Division crossing the Colmar Canal.

Figure 71 The above two items I collected on the Rhine Canal.

Chapter Eleven

Paris

I was getting tired of fighting. So I told my company commander Lt. Murray, "You know I'm getting tired of fighting, I haven't seen a movie, haven't had a drink, I haven't been with a woman, I haven't done nothing, all I do is fight, fight, fight, I'm tired of it." He said, "What do you want me to do DeAngelo?" I said, "Lt. maybe you could get me a four day pass so I can have some fun." The next day he said, " DeAngelo I've got you a four day pass, being you have seniority you have a choice of either going to London or Paris." At that time we were bivouacked around the town of Nancy. I said, "Lt., I'll take Paris." He said, "Fine, the other GI will go to London." I replied, "Great Lt."

I dressed in clean clothes and put on a new reversible olive drab jacket that had imitation fur inside. I think it was around 6 a.m. when I jumped on the back of a 6x6 truck. We drove the 100 miles from Nancy to Paris, and even though it was cold when we got there I was glad to be away from the front. I got a room from the Red Cross for 50¢ a day. It was nice and had both a commode and a bidet. I went to my room, took my new jacket off, and put it on the bed to wash my face and hands. I walked downstairs and met up with another GI who had ridden in on the truck with me. We hit the streets and walked around for a while. Finally I said, "We have to find some action. I don't know Paris." Neither did he. We stopped the first GI who walked by and asked. "Hey, GI, would you like to make five bucks?" He said, "How?" I said, "Why don't you show us the highlights of town, where to go?" He said, "You don't really need me to do that, but I'll show you around for about an hour." I said, "Fine."

As we were walking down a street a good looking blonde in a fur coat, high heels, and nylon stockings passed by. She winked at me. I looked at her and thought, "Gee, not bad." I asked her where she was going and she told me she was going to her apartment. "Would you like to see it?" she asked. I said, "Well, yes, but what about my friend?" She said, "I have a friend for him." I told him. He said, "Great!" I told our guide, "I guess we don't need you." I gave him five bucks. He said, "Thanks, go on and have a good time." He walked away.

She explained, "Don't walk with me, but walk behind me." We followed her to her apartment. Her girlfriend was ironing and my friend paired off with her. I noticed a photograph of an actress on a nightstand. I asked, "Where did you get Betty Grable's picture?" She said, "That's not Betty Grable, that's me." I looked at her, "That's you!" She said, "Yes." Again I looked at her. I could see that in her younger years she could have looked like the actress. Now she was probably in her early thirties. She took her fur coat off and all she was wearing underneath was a slip. That's it. There was only one small sofa bed, so our friends went into the bathroom. Of course I enjoyed both her and the bed. She didn't tell me how much money she wanted, but I gave her $10 and she smiled. She asked if we were going to come back and I told her we would take them both to dinner later, but first my friend and I were going to explore Paris for a while. We probably would have returned if we hadn't found other things to do.

There were so many bars to visit, places to go, and things to do. We walked to the Grand Hotel and stopped at the bar there. In the corner was an attractive lady who looked to be around forty plus. Between her and me were three medical officers, all majors. She was looking at me and giving me the eye as if to say come on over and buy me a drink. I noticed all three medical officers were looking at me and giving me a thumbs down signal. I thought, "Hmmm!" She wasn't paying attention to them or vice versa; I think they probably knew she had a medical problem. They had warned me she was not a good choice to associate with. They didn't say a word, just gave me their signal she was bad to know. I don't think she was aware of what they were doing because they had their backs toward her. We had a few drinks and then left, seeking some fun.

In one cafe I ran into a GI from the 1st Division, the Big Red One. He was short and he was very drunk. He made a speech saying the Big Red One was the very best Division overseas and could lick any outfit. I turned to look at him and wanted to tell him the facts of life or, better yet, lay him out to sleep it off. There is always one like him, talking loud so all could hear.

Now concerning the 1st Division called "Big Red One." It had seen some combat in North Africa. For some reason most of its GI's were transferred to other divisions in Africa, Sicily, and Italy to the 3rd, 34th, 36th, and 45th Infantry Divisions. A few thousand were then left and were shipped to England. With many new GI's going to England, I think many replacements were put into the 1st Division and it became a full Division once more. In the meantime, those of us in Italy were in combat for many months, while the 1st Division saw no combat for well over a year and a half before going to land at Normandy on June 6, 1944.

As we walked around Paris, I noticed some people behind a partition of some sort, and only their heads and feet were showing. I learned that this is where men peed. It was set up on a street corner, with a trough that ran down into the sewer. It was kind of funny to be standing on one side and directly facing the guy on the other side of the partition. For women I think there was a small building nearby.

We walked around and came upon two girls about our age. One was very attractive and the four of us stopped for a drink. The attractive one said, "I'm going to walk around town, do you want to walk?" I said, "OK." We walked around for a few minutes and then both of the girls ran into an apartment building and never returned. We waited about a half hour before saying, "The hell with this, they are not coming out." We didn't know what happened. We went on and did other things.

I got on the underground subway called the Metro alone, and since I didn't know the names of any of my stops, all I could do was count the stops. I got off and counted them riding back. If you didn't know Paris, you didn't know what to do, or see. I don't remember if I ate food or not, but I know I did a lot of drinking. I guess the best places for food were expensive, where officer's dined.

The next day I met the GI again. We continued to walk around Paris. I had not slept in my Red Cross room–I slept with some new woman in her room. We ran across the two girls who had ditched us and took them to a bar for drinks. Again, they ran into another apartment building and disappeared. I ended up with another woman that night.

I was having a great time, but I would have liked to have gotten to know that girl who disappeared. She said she was from Brest on the coast of France. I had to leave the next morning and didn't think I'd see her again when I ran into her in the afternoon. I said, "I've been wanting to be with you for two days but every time you disappear. I'm leaving for the front tomorrow morning. I won't be back." She looked at me and asked, "Do you want me to stay with you?" I said, "I would have loved you to stay with me every day but you always disappeared." I couldn't figure out why she was always running away, but thought she might have just been playing hard to get. She said, "OK, I'll stay with you tonight." She took me to a small hotel and went to ask the landlady for an alarm clock. "Great!"

I waited about 30 minutes and was wondering what had happened to her this time. I went down the hall to look for her and saw the GI I had been exploring Paris with trying to get her into his room. He was drunk and trying to force himself on her, which really peeved me. She was relieved to see me and we returned to our room. I was peeved with him, wondering where her girlfriend was since she wasn't with him. She must have walked out. I had taken my dog tags off and put them on the nightstand because they didn't have a rubber edge around them to keep both from hitting and making noise. That night we made love a couple of times. When the alarm went off, I got up and dressed to leave. I told her how much I liked her and she replied, "I loved to zig zig with you." It was good to hear that. I was sorry we spent only one night together. I kissed her and told her to take care. I didn't tell her where I was going or what outfit I was with. There wasn't any reason to because we didn't know what could happen to us. Being in the infantry, things did happen. I had some money, maybe $40, and put every cent of it on the nightstand for her along with some chocolate and candy, but no

Figure 72. The author in Paris, looking old and tired, but had a few on that day.

cigarettes. As I was leaving I looked back at her and saw that she was crying. I forgot to take my dog tags with me and every once in a while, I wonder if one day someone is going to knock on my door to say, I'm from France, I'm your son or daughter. Since I didn't use any protection, there is a very good possibility that I may have a child somewhere in France; then again, maybe not.

The chocolate I left her was called Tropical Chocolate and it wouldn't melt if you left it in the sun. I don't know what they had in that chocolate, but it must have been concrete. In our emergency rations, we had a larger "D" type chocolate bar that you were supposed to just nibble on for energy. Some GI's ate it all at one time. We also had a fruit bar with raisins, dates, and grapes, a good one to eat, but hard to get.

I climbed on our truck and rode back to C Company. *Figure 72* shows the way I looked in Paris. When my parents saw this photo my mother said, "See how tired my poor boy looks? They're working him to death." She didn't know I was drunk. I told her the truth about the picture when I came home and she gave me a dirty look like she always did.

The GI who went to London stayed there and never came back. He was "Z. I." to the United States. "Zone of Interior."

Chapter Twelve

Strasbourg

The objective for the 36th Infantry Division was to capture Strasbourg. We had settled down after we captured Colmar and were going to have a couple of days of rest. Lt. Murray went to battalion for a briefing and came back shortly. "DeAngelo, get the men ready, we're moving out," he ordered. I said, "We just got here, Lieutenant." He told me that the 36th Infantry Division had failed to take Strasbourg and we were going to have to take it. A few days later Strasbourg fell to the 3rd Infantry Division. It is possible the 36th Infantry Division did not go into combat again as of that time, that I know of.

My company commander called me and told me to contact B Company. Like I said, we always picked up a phone wire and ran with it in our hand. B Company was about one or two miles up the road, so I had to walk through the dense woods alone. I was very careful, not knowing if I might run into the enemy. I saw a lot of dead Germans along the road. I was twenty years old, alone, and it wasn't always easy, especially when I thought about what might happen. I arrived at B Company area safe and sound, relayed my message, picked up the same wire, and returned to C Company.

One day we received orders that we would be detached from the 3rd Infantry Division. I don't know if it was the whole battalion or just my company that was assigned to the French 2nd Armored Division. The French were unable to cross the Fecht River; they had tried it a number of times but the Germans beat them back with artillery and mortar. The Germans had destroyed the bridge earlier. We walked to this river and crossed in small boats without any

Strasbourg

trouble. We found that the Germans had flooded both sides of the road, so we were forced to walk on the road. Of course, the road was zeroed in on because that's the way the Germans did things. Did the French know of the flooding? I think they did. We walked for a few miles and stopped for the evening.

I was on guard duty that night when I heard the sound of hob-nailed boots coming toward me. I knew that the Germans always wore hob-nailed boots and we could hear them whenever they walked on a hard surface. I quickly called for some GI's to assist me, then I yelled, "Halt, who goes there?" A voice called out, "French Lieutenant." I commanded, "Come forward and be recognized." He came forward, I checked him over, and sure enough he was a French lieutenant. He was from recon and told me there weren't any Germans forward. I asked him what time it was, as I needed to be relieved. He lit his cigarette lighter so he could see his watch and talk about everybody diving for a foxhole! We thought his flame would be seen by the Germans, who would then would drop mortars and fire artillery. But nothing happened. Now back for some sleep, if we can.

During the night we heard a heck of a noise coming up from our rear. The Germans had blown down many trees on both sides of the road to block it. Like I said, the French always rode vehicles, and an American French Half-Track with a big saw blade on its front came up the road. The driver would drive it up against a tree to cut it in half, then push the two halves aside. I thought we were going to have problems, like mortars or artillery coming in on us. But again, nothing.

The French lieutenant told us there was another bridge forward. Early the next morning we heard something strange high over that area. It was a Messerschmitt 262 Jet diving and bombing the bridge. Hitler had requested this first jet fighter aircraft be manufactured as a fighter bomber. He ordered it to be a bomber more than a fighter– a big mistake. As we pulled back, the Half-Track was still cutting trees forward. There were many French Sherman tanks with M-10's waiting to move up. We stopped to ask the French for water, but since they didn't carry water, they offered us some wine, which they carried in a 5-gallon Jerry can. Soon the Germans heard all these tanks and M-10 commotion. They started dropping artillery and mortar rounds. We jumped into a ditch, water and all, but still lost a couple of GI's. The French closed the hatches of their Shermans because a mortar couldn't do any damage to one unless it's an M-10 tank destroyer with the top of its turret open, as I recall one day on Anzio.

Walking back across a newly installed pontoon bridge I noticed a dead GI. I didn't know who he was, a replacement? I asked a couple of GI's nearby, "What happened?" They said, "He just came by to join his outfit and was killed." I asked, "How?" They both pointed to a GI standing nearby and said, "He thought the dead GI was a German and shot him last night." As I walked up to the GI, his back was toward me. I turned to face him, and saw that he was one of our men. Some months earlier, when we were walking through the woods, I had noticed that he was not keeping up with the rest of us. He kept falling back, as though he was looking for a place to hide. At the time, as a Sgt., I had said to him, "We must all move forward. Your doing this will one day cause someone to get hurt or killed and you'll have it on your conscience the rest of your life." Then I asked him, "What happened?" He replied, "I heard him come up behind me; I shot him." I asked, "Didn't you say anything to him? Did you not halt him?" He said, "No." I said, "I recall one day telling you you were going to do this. Do you remember? Every time we went into combat, you always took off to the rear. I told you one day you were going to cause somebody to get hurt or killed and you would regret it the rest of your life." He looked at me strangely.

February 20, 1945. Soon we detached from the French to rejoin our 3rd Infantry Division. For helping the French cross the Fecht River and take their objective, we received the French Croix DeGuerre with Palm Medal and a green and red Fourageres cord worn on our left shoulder.

We were also awarded the Presidential Unit Citation Badge at the same time as the French Declarations. We had crossed a number of rivers: Colmar, Meurthe, Moselle, L'oignon and the Ill. We were experts in river crossings and amphibious landings, and I wonder if this was why the French requested us to cross the Fecht River for them? Then, maybe not.

All of my orders were taken seriously and I did a lot of things an average GI probably would never do. We all have to take chances. My responsibility was to save lives and I did my best each time. I'm sorry about the people I killed and when the subject comes up, I'm reminded that if it wasn't him, it would have been me. I hope their families forgive me, especially the one with the pockmarked face.

If I was given an order to move a mountain I didn't say, you're crazy. I'd ask the captain or lieutenant how far, and in what direction. I have to admit the first time I was under artillery barrage, I was very frightened. We were always frightened each and every time. But the longer we stayed in combat the more aware we became of what was going on and what could happen. One particular time, I remember about three 80 mm German mortars being fired on us. I heard them coming out of the tube, and I counted, 1,2,3,4,5, up to 10. I would run around giving my GI's orders and then I would jump in a foxhole. Then these mortars would hit and explode all over the place. I guess some GI's probably thought I was nuts, I just wanted them to know there was no fear as long as one listened and used their head.

In our platoon, we had a GI by the name of Horseface MacDonald. He was an older, weather-beaten GI, who had been in the Army a long time. When his best friend, Vasion, was shot in the stomach (I think he had two or three rounds in him), Old Horseface told him, "Aah, all you got is a little scratch, don't worry about it. In fact I wouldn't mind getting a scratch like that if I got shot." Vasion went to the hospital and returned to our outfit after he recuperated, but he was never the same. I don't think they should return any GI to the infantry after being wounded so seriously. They should have been given a non-combat job. To me it was uncalled for. There were a lot of GI's who could have been saved from getting killed or wounded a second time.

Now the 3rd Infantry Division was ordered to spearhead the 7th Army attack through the Siegfried Line. On March 13, 1945, we began moving to an assembly area near Schmittviller in Alsace Lorraine. We were going forward across the Siegfried Line on March 14, 1945. We were near the towns of Epping Urbach and Ornersviller when we came into a large minefield. Our two scouts were out in front, Lt. Murray was behind them, and I was behind him. The first three missed this mine, but I stepped on it. It happened at about 6:30 p.m. When it happened, the other three pulled back. I was down and I knew what would happen if I touched another mine. I heard some soft voice say, "Don't crawl, the war is over for you, you're going home." Was it my guardian angel whose voice I heard? I immediately took my pistol belt off. I tied a tourniquet around my right thigh. I took out my canteen, drank all my water with all my Sulfa tablets, and just relaxed. Every once in a while I released the tourniquet. Then some GI's were yelling, "We'll come to get you, DeAngelo." I yelled out, "No, no, no don't come, it's too dark and someone will hit another mine. I can't move. I don't know where these mines are." I laid there for about an hour or so until a couple of GI's were coming to get me. I yelled again, "I don't want you to come to get me." They said, "No, you would do it for us, DeAngelo." These two GI's were brave to come to get me out, but then, we were all afraid we could hit another mine for it happened many times before.

I was not in pain. There weren't any stretchers so they sat me on an M-1 rifle, and had me put my arm around each shoulder. In the dark, they carried me over some low bushes and what was left of my right foot became tangled. At that point there was some pain. I said, "Wait, let me untangle my foot." With my left hand holding on to one GI, I reached down with my right hand and untangled what was left of my bloody foot. They finally put me down near our CP. I thanked both GI's. Lt. Murray tried to get medics, but they

Strasbourg

couldn't find us. I lay there still with no pain. Later a lieutenant came by and nearly fell over me. He asked, "What are you doing here, soldier?" I replied, "I stepped on a mine." He asked, "Did you get a morphine shot?" I said, "No, sir." He said, "I'll give you a morphine shot." I said, "Thanks, Lieutenant." I do not know who this lieutenant was. Still, I had no pain.

I knew what was happening at the time. Eventually our medics arrived with a stretcher and took me to a house where a medic did a good job of bandaging what was left of my right foot. He said, "Oh, in a short time you'll be walking, DeAngelo." I said, "Don't give me any of that baloney; I know it's gone." I knew this medic, but I do not recall his name. Apparently, he did a nice job of bandaging what was left of my right foot. Later that night I was moved to the middle of some town where they laid me down on a crossroads. I got a hold of some medic and said, "You know, this is a hell of a place to put me, right in the middle of the crossroads where a truck or a tank could come up and run over me. Get me off this crossroad!" Finally I was mad, "Get me off the road and put me on the shoulder, now!" I was moved. I didn't see C Company again. I know I had thanked both GI's who came into that minefield to rescue me. I'm sorry I can't remember the names of the two GI's and the medic who attended me, plus the lieutenant, for I knew their names at one time.

I do not know if the two GI's who came into the minefield ever received any medals for rescuing me. I know I would have made it my business to see that they got something for the chance they took. I hope their lieutenant did the right thing, if not, I am disappointed he overlooked such an important life-saving risk these two GI's took.

Much later at another First Aid station, my pulse wasn't great, my color looked bad, plus my blood pressure was very low. A medic called, "Captain, this GI here is in pretty bad shape." Many hours had passed since I was wounded and the captain said, "Give him plasma, it will make it easy for him. He'll go to sleep and that will be the end. We can't do much for him." I was conscious and could hear every word but I didn't say anything. I just thought to myself, "I'm going home!" This medic gave me the plasma and as soon as it went into my vein, he said, "Captain, this GI's blood pressure is good, his heartbeat has improved." The captain said, "He's not going any place, give him another plasma but keep an eye on him." From there I went to a field hospital to be operated on. First a C Company medic helps you, then you go to First Aid, and next to a field hospital nearby. Many GI's had a lot bigger problems than mine and had to have surgery first. I was okay and relaxed. I wasn't concerned about it, after all a soft voice said, "The war is over and you're going home," so why worry about it. My regiment, the 30th, had around 50 GI's wounded by Schu mines that same night. Sometime later Lt. Murray had requested our Battalion Commander for another route because of the high casualties which were mounting from Schu mines on that night. He was given another direction the next morning, moving forward, going deep into Germany.

At the field hospital, a medic came in and said, "Well GI, we're ready for you now. I'm going to put this rubber tubing around your thigh." It was now 20-25 hours later and I was starting to hurt. He asked, "Is it hurting you?" I said, "Yes." He said, "It will be over soon." They took what was left of my foot above the ankle and placed a tube in for a drain. As I came out from under the sodium pentathol, a nurse said to me, "So when are we getting married?" All the doctors and nurses around us were laughing and told me that I had told the nurse that I loved her and wanted to marry her as soon as possible. It went around that I was the one who raved to marry her and I noticed that a lot of the staff had smiles on their faces each time they came to see how I was doing. Today I wonder what she looked like.

After the surgery, I was moved to a bed and noticed that the GI next to me was a medic I knew from our company. He was delirious and I asked the nurse what was wrong with him. She told me he had gone out to help a GI who stepped on a mine. As he was putting his arm under him to pick him up, he hit a mine and his right arm was blown off. He was a very nice GI and we used to talk all the time. His name was McDavid and I enjoyed being friends with him for the short time I knew him. I was sorry to hear of his wounds.

I asked the nurse for a P-38, which is a vessel to pee in. She brought one, and I found that I was all bandaged up down there. Here I was laying flat on my back, how was I going to use this P-38? I pulled some bandage away and finally bent it over to the right and was able to pee. A doctor came in short time later and asked, "Well, DeAngelo, how's your foot?" I said, "To hell with the foot, what about this down here?" He said, "Unfortunately we had to remove your right testicle because a stone destroyed it, but it missed your other testicle by a sixteenth of an inch. You're fortunate to have one good testicle. You will be able to perform and have children." That's great, I said, "OK to know, thanks doctor."

The next morning McDavid's bed was empty. The nurse told me he passed away during the night. I was sorry to hear of his death.

The next day they sent me to the 23rd Station Hospital. I don't remember where it was located, maybe at Ribeauville. I was lying in bed when who should come along but the same colonel I had met when I was in the hospital with frostbite. He looked at my chart, read my name, he said, "DeAngelo, it seems to me that I remember your name." I said, "Well, Colonel, you should remember. I'm the one who told you I would return and you couldn't ship me to the damn front again." He turned around, walked away, and I never saw him again. Guilt was written on his face. I told him off good. What could he do to me, send me back to the front line again, it would be a joke. I had a smile on my face knowing it felt good to tell him off—a real asshole.

I noticed a patient in a red Army Hospital bath robe who would walk by my bed, then turn around and walk back again. He never stopped to talk. Finally I said, "Come here, I want to talk to you. Why are you walking by me and looking at me all the time?" He said, "Are you the GI who lost a foot?" I said, "Yeah, I lost my foot!" He asked, "You also lost your right testicle?" I said, "Yes, I lost my right testicle. What has this got to do with why you are looking at me?" He said, "Well, I had three testicles, did they give you one of mine?" (Early organ transplant?) It turned out he was a mental patient and a medic told me there were quite a few patients like him. I don't know if this was a put on or what. Later that same day I was given a blood transfusion and broke out in hives. The medic gave me a shot and soon the itching stopped. The blood I was given was a bit off to match mine.

I want to explain one thing to all readers, I've never had any regrets about what happened to me. I've never bitched about it, in fact I tell stories about it, always with a smile.

My stay at this hospital was very short, perhaps less than a week or so. I think that colonel was anxious to get me shipped out of there quickly. On April 15, 1945, I was put aboard a C-47 Douglas Aircraft DC-3, and flown to Paris. I was taken to the 51st EVAC hospital and put in a room with three patients on each side of the room. My bed was closest to the window. We heard President Roosevelt had died, but we didn't think too much about it, for we had other things on our minds.

A GI was in a bed near the door and when he heard me speak, he asked, "Hey, are you a Yankee?" I turned to face him, "I'm from New York City, why?" I could tell from his voice that he was from the South, and then he called me a nigger lover. Here we were, him with a leg amputation and me with a foot amputation, and he was picking a fight with me. This GI started to call me names for no reason at all. I didn't know who the hell he was or what outfit he was with. I said, "I'm not a nigger lover; I like all people. As long as they treat me right, I'll treat them right. If they treat me bad then it's a different matter." He started cussing at me. Out of the clear blue a thought came to my mind and I asked, "Tell me, big shot, how many blood transfusions have you had?" He answered, "About ten or twelve." I said, "OK, chances are at least one or two of those transfusions came from black donors." He looked at me with a stunned expression, "Naw, they wouldn't dare do that! They wouldn't give some black donor's blood to a white man." I said, "Well, I think you better check it out, big shot." It wasn't even two minutes later when a medic captain walked into the room. The GI grabbed the captain as he came through the door and asked, "Captain, can a nigger's blood be put into a white man's veins?" The captain looked at his chart and said, "Yes, it's a possibility you got one or two pints yourself." The big shot yelled, "If you think I have nigger's blood in me, bleed me! Get it out of me and give me some white man's blood." Every GI in the room was either laughing or snickering. I'll never forget it as long as I live. I tell this story when discussing the war and everyone gets a good laugh. I'm not sure if it was correct that he had received blood from a black donor, but assume it was a possibility. Why not? After all, blood is blood. Sure would like to know what happened to that GI. I wonder if he bled himself to death after being discharged. It's possible I might have had a pint or two myself. As for me, so what?

Chapter Thirteen

Army Hospital

In a few days, on April 20, 1945, I was taken out of the hospital and carried aboard a C-54, which was a DC-4 Douglas four-engine transport aircraft. There were sixteen stretchers on board and we had two nurses. We took off and six hours later we landed at the Azores to refuel and have some food. Our nurses were great. It took us about 9-10 hours to reach Newfoundland where we landed and refueled. Then we flew another 4-5 hours on to Mitchell Field, N.Y. As we were coming in to land, we were waved off just as the pilot was to touch down. He put the coals to the engines, went around and landed the next time. We arrived on April 22, 1945. When he walked by I said, "I'm glad you landed okay, Captain." He said that someone had been taking off or landing in front of him and he had to avoid a collision. That's my experience flying across the Atlantic ocean; with a great pilot and two great nurses aboard.

We stayed at Mitchell Field for a couple of days. We had a very attractive lady come in to sing the song, "Dreams" written by Johnny Mercer. Pretty soon a doctor came to ask how I was feeling. I told him I felt fine. I had been getting penicillin shots regularly. I said, "I've got a little problem on my left calf. I have a wound that gets a scab and drops off, then it gets another scab and it too drops off. I may have something in there." He probed around, put his thumbs on either side of the wound, pressed hard, and out popped a stone. He put some powder on it, ordered extra penicillin, and told me to let him know if I still had problems. It healed fine after that. A few days later we took off from Mitchell Field aboard a C-47, a DC-3 Douglas Aircraft, twin engine. After about an hour of flight we landed in Atlantic City, New Jersey on April 24, 1945.

Army Hospital

We were taken to England General Army Hospital. It had once been a hotel called Hadden Hall and was located on the beach. It was a large hotel and they had removed the doors to all the rooms. There were both hot and cold salt water taps in the tub, ice water to drink and all the hot water we wanted. I understand there were 5,000 men in this hospital who had arm or leg amputations plus other wounds. We used up all the floors of the hotel. The paraplegics on the fifth floor were given beer to drink to help them go to the bathroom.

The Hotel Strand had a large glass dome with a great big dance room below. Once in a while our paraplegics on the fifth floor above would throw empty beer bottles out. They would crash through the dome while people were dancing. It just got to those GI's when they heard the hotel guests having a good time dancing, laughing, and partying. Remember, these were kids, 18, 19, 21 years old, totally disabled in wheelchairs or beds forever. One night the hotel featured bandleader Joe Reisman. His band played great music and since we had no air conditioning, we could lie in bed and listen to it through the open windows until 2 a.m.

We had many GI's with double amputations, some above the knee, others below, and some were missing an arm. A majority of the GI's was independent, and some were really terrified of facing the reality that they lost a limb. While others were pretty stubborn, they thought nothing of it. One particular GI, a double below-the-knee amputee, used to get a pass to go home to Pennsylvania. He had one of the newly designed collapsible wheelchairs. He would get in his chair, roll up to the bus stop about three blocks away, jump out of the wheelchair onto the bus steps and land on his knees. In seconds, he had folded his wheelchair and walked on his knees up into the bus, carrying the chair. This sounds funny but it was really something to see. He got to know the bus drivers since he went home often and they would go out of their way to drive to the top of a hill above where he lived (down below). He would reverse what he did getting on the bus, open up his wheelchair, get in and roll down the hill. There wasn't anything to hold him at the hospital, and most of us could get a pass every weekend if we wanted one. It was funny to hear how he did it.

England General Army Hospital was situated on the beach and our wounded GI's would be taken out to the boardwalk in wheelchairs. They also had special benches installed on the boardwalk where we could sit. It was nice. Fresh sea air helped the wounded to heal quite fast.

Some GI's were not only hurt physically, but mentally as well. When their wives came to visit them, some would tell their wives to go home to start divorce proceedings. They felt they were a different person than the one they had married because of the wounds they received. It shook up a lot of families when some GI would make that request. Some didn't bother with their wives because they were drinking, and didn't care. I imagine some GI's thought about committing suicide since they felt they were not whole men anymore. A special eye was kept on those who were quiet, withdrawn or didn't bother with anyone.

Then there were others who were having a great time, running around and laughing and thanking God they came home alive. Maybe not in one piece, but they came home period.

Figure 73, photo was sent to me by Col. Murray, my Company Commander. He visited Germany and found the location where I had stepped on the Schu mine.

Figure 74, April 30, 1945, shows Sgt. Schamma and Lt. Murray near the end of the war. If I hadn't been wounded I would have been in the photograph.

Figure 75 shows Lt. LaBelle, right side of Lt. Murray in Salzburg, Germany, on May 6, 1945. The war is over.

Figure 76, taken on October 15, 1945, shows Lt. LaBelle, a nice guy. Whenever I received a package from home he would sit down with me and help me eat whatever my mother sent (chili peppers, olives, etc.) As an French-American he particularly enjoyed the sausages, salami, and the cheeses. Lt. LaBelle was a Grave

Army Hospital

Figure 73. Photo sent to the author by Murray, possible field where I was wounded by the mine on March 14, 1945, on the border of Germany.

Figure 74. Sgt. Schamma on the right side of Lt. Murray in Munich.

Figure 75. Lt. LaBelle and Lt. Murray in Germany. May 6, 1945. Two great officers.

Figure 76. Lt. LaBelle in Germany, October 15, 1945. A nice guy.

Army Hospital

Figure 77. Sgt. Poenchar in Germany, May 6, 1945, a great GI.

Registration Officer for a while and it was his responsibility to pick up the bodies of GI's, Germans, and civilians. I think it got to him, seeing so many GI's and friends killed. I can understand that.

Figure 77 shows Sgt. Polenchar, a policeman from Bethlehem, PA. after the war, some years later. I asked him if he was one of the two who got me out of the minefield but he said no.

Not long after, my cousin Joe drove my mother, father and grandmother down from New

Figure 78. Calvin Knotts, left, with the author and WACs at the 500 Club in Atlantic City, New Jersey. May 10, 1945.

York City to visit me. As soon as my mother came to my room, she started to cry. I told her if she didn't stop crying she could go back home. I said, "I want you to be happy I came home rather than not at all." She stopped crying and enjoyed her visit. I asked my grandmother about my Grandfather Frank. I was told he had passed away some months earlier.

Figure 78 shows Calvin Knotts, me, and two WACs at the 500 Club in Atlantic City, New Jersey. It was just about this time that Jerry Lewis and Dean Martin first started performing together, right at this club. This photograph was taken May 10, 1945. We were both using crutches and you'll notice that Calvin is wearing all his ribbons. I didn't have any to wear. We never saw the two WACs again.

The purpose of being hospitalized at England General Army Hospital was to recuperate and rebuild our bodies. The hospital was to try and repair our wounds and to take our mind off of what we had gone through. I was facing an operation that would get me ready for my artificial limb and couldn't get out of bed when I was ready for the operation. I was in room 224 on the second floor of this hospital. In this room was a Greek kid, Nicholas, who had lost both legs below the knees. Calvin Knotts lost his left foot, Robert Hall (who was the only one married) lost an arm and a leg. Nicholas was in a wheelchair all the time. Around June 7, 1945 we were ready and grounded for an operation; Knotts, Hall and me.

Knotts, Hall and I were all prepped for surgery on the same day, June 11, 1945. They gave me a spinal. I was conscious the whole time, but I didn't feel any pain. I was operated on by two crazy doctors, one of whom was named Smith. They had this thing over my chest that looked like a small tennis net. I couldn't see anything. What was going on? I was able to listen to their conversation and hear them tell jokes. I remember one of them saying as he was cutting away on my leg, "You know, this GI's bones are tremendous. Look at his bones!" The other doctor said, "Well his mother gave him special food because I've never seen bones as strong."

I heard all the sawing and cutting, everything, throughout the operation. I heard one of the doctors throw my leg bone in a medical can to be burned. It didn't go inside, but onto the floor. He said, "Well, you can't get them all inside." They were wonderful surgeons. They did all amputations. I don't know how many more these two doctors did that day, but I know they did all three of us that morning.

There was an orderly for Room 224 who was a pain. We had to stay in bed for weeks at a time and he would always give us a bad time. To pass the time, I built model airplanes and sometimes my balsa wood shavings fell on the floor. As I could not get out of bed, I was unable to clean them up. So he would get upset and would try to get back at us. One day, we four in our room, decided to get even with him. It seemed we had a shortage of bedpans, about four pans per floor. So one of us asked for a bedpan. The orderly had to look for a bedpan, flush the contents down the commode, wash the inside and bring it to us to use. As soon as one of us sat on the bedpan another would ask for a bedpan. He had to look for another one because we'd have a hard and long time doing number two. As soon as he found one, then another of us asked for a bedpan. The last one in the room said, "Please get one for me to use, the other three are still sitting on theirs." He was sure running around trying to find enough bedpans to use at one time. I am sure he was a little nicer to the GI's in our room from that day on.

The boardwalk had a lot of shops. There was a place that sold salt water taffy. It was called "Fralingers." We got to know the manager; she was beautiful, not only beautiful but kind. She always gave money to GI's. If a GI asked her for $5, she'd give it to him. If he paid her back, fine, if not, that was fine too. It made her feel good. She had a young girl working for her. She and I hit it off pretty well. She was from Pennsylvania and was lonely; I don't know what happened to her parents. For my birthday on July 8 she bought me a stainless steel ID bracelet, the kind the military wear. It had my name engraved on it. I told her she shouldn't have spent her money on me. She obviously liked me a lot, but I didn't have the same kind of feelings for her. We had gone to the movies, but there was nothing going on between us. I thought of her as a sister and I told her so. She got very upset because I wouldn't take the bracelet and of course she couldn't return it because it was engraved. In a way I'm sorry I didn't take it since I hurt her feelings. I understand she threw it in the ocean. I think she paid about $12 for it.

Shortly after my operation, while sitting on a bench on the boardwalk, I met a beautiful 18-year-old lady. Her name was Gloria Snell. She and her mother were from Connecticut. I met them on July 28, 1945, the day a B-25 crashed into the Empire State building. I had pictures of her, but I lost them when I gave them to someone to make extra copies. Gloria was very attractive and her mother would never let her out of her sight. I was still on crutches. Every time we went someplace her mother tagged along. Some GI's would come over to me and ask, "DeAngelo, introduce me to your friend." I would introduce them. She gave me their address in Trumbull, Connecticut. She asked me to write to her. I did a couple of times but I didn't receive any response. I don't know what happened. Some years later, at home, I received a card that read, "Dear Frank, I hope everything is OK, Gloria." At first I didn't remember who she was, then it dawned on me when I saw the Connecticut postmark. She remembered me and just wanted to say hello, nothing more, she left no return address.

The thin scar on my stump looked like someone had used scissors to trim it beautifully. Some doctors who have seen my stump since then have commented on what a great job my surgeons did. They put it together with just a small seam and with no excess flesh that could have caused problems. The four of us in room 224 were always raising hell. We were all young and happy to be home and happy to be alive. Yes, we did remember our friends who didn't make it home, the terrible things we went through, saw, and did. One day Nicholas came into the room in his wheelchair. "Nicholas," I said, "You know I'm sick and tired of seeing you in that wheelchair; I'm going to do something about it." Calvin and Robert were looking at me as if I were crazy. I got out of bed and hopped over to the closet door. There were two doors, one for the bathroom, one for the closet, and neither one had a lock. I opened the closet door and picked up a pair of combat boots. I said, "Nicholas, shove your stumps into these boots." He did and I laced them up. "Now, that's better." Calvin and Robert nearly died laughing and Nicholas thought it was the funniest thing. He said, "Do you know what I'm going to do? I'm going down to the rec hall so I can show off my boots." Off he wheeled down the hall looking like a dwarf from the waist down with those combat boots on his stumps. The hospital staff couldn't figure out what was going on but everyone in the rec room got a good laugh. When he came back he said, "That was a great idea, DeAngelo." This was only one of the stunts we pulled on that day.

One of us had a birthday. We called the Red Cross and they showed up with a cake and a small piano that they pushed into the room. Then we all sang "Happy Birthday." About a week later, I requested another GI birthday. They came again. Then a third GI birthday. Finally the Red Cross said, "How many GI's in the same room have birthdays within a week's time?" There was only one person who had a real birthday. The others were fabrications but we got free cake, Coke and songs. They didn't come to sing for us anymore. Even if one of us had a real birthday, forget it.

The orderlies would make our beds and always pulled the sheets real tight. If you hit the sheets with the flat part of your wooden crutch, it would sound like an explosion. Then one of us would yell, "Medic! Medic!" Of course the nurses would run in and find out what was going on. "We're going to break you GI's up; you are the worst bunch in the entire hospital." We were having a great time, not bothering anyone and we weren't doing any damage. Sometimes we'd meet a GI who had been in bed for some months. Maybe he didn't have any company, nobody came to see him; maybe his family lived some distance away. But, whatever, we'd go down to the boardwalk and find a good-looking woman. We'd say to her, "Look, we have a friend in the hospital who's all by himself and real lonely.

Would you go up to visit and say a few nice words to him?" Some of the girls would say yes and we'd give his name and room number. Occasionally a romance would start. It was always great to talk to these women and have them go visit some GI. Some women came from as far away as Philadelphia, sixty or seventy miles away, for a weekend.

I was still on crutches since it was taking a long time for my wound to heal. They had a shop in the hospital where they made artificial limbs. After the swelling went down on my stump they made a cast of my stump to fit for an artificial limb. It took time because they had so many to make. We weren't in a hurry and they would call us when it was ready for a fitting.

I went home for a weekend and when I returned, I found that I had been assigned another room. I was the only one in the new room and it had two empty beds. But soon I saw a GI coming down the hall on crutches who had a right leg amputation above the knee. I said, "There is an extra bed in my room if you want it." He said, "Why not?" He moved right in and Pete LaCorte became my friend. *Figure 79.* The nurses got even

Figure 79. My friend, Pete LaCourt, met at England Army Hospital, Atlantic City, New Jersey. September 27, 1945.

Army Hospital

with the four of us by giving us different rooms.

Figure 80 dated December 2, 1945, shows me in my uniform with my ribbons of the Purple Heart, European Theater, Good Conduct, Bronze Star and Combat Infantry Badge. I also have a Unit Citation with an oak leaf and the French Croix DeGuerre on my left shoulder. You can see that I had a mustache at that time and had put on some weight. I couldn't help but put weight on—the food was great and I was making up for lost time.

Figure 80. The author at England Army Hospital, Atlantic City, NJ. December 2, 1945.

Figure 81. The author with friend Bette. Atlantic City, New Jersey, December 18, 1945.

I wasn't having any trouble walking on crutches. When my artificial limb was ready, they called me in to be fitted. I put it on and immediately felt like I was going to get sick. But soon after I walked right off with it without any trouble at all. The doctors were amazed that I wasn't having any problems with it. Almost right away, I could walk without pain. I asked if I could wear it for a day. They said no, I had to come back a few more times. "When you are more used to it we'll let you wear it for a day." I never had any trouble wearing the first one.

Figure 81 shows a photograph and a very attractive girl, Bette, who was kind and sweet. I had met her as she was leaving the hospital one day after visiting a friend of hers who had lost both arms and both legs (one of two with this type of wounds in WWII). His name was James Wilson. In 1945, the people of Atlantic City donated $100,000.00 to Wilson to help him after getting out of the hospital. The other one was Fredrick Hensel. I do not believe he was at Atlantic City at England Army Hospital. I was sweet on her and tried to get to know her. I invited her to go see a movie that night soon after dinner I was my usual self and tried to get frisky with her. She said, "If you want to see me again you'd better be nice." I promised I

Army Hospital

would be. It was difficult dating her at first. A couple of times I made a date and she didn't show up or call. I gave up on her.

There was a hotel called The Hotel Strand behind the hospital. Their second floor was like our second floor. We had nothing else to do but listen with our earphones to the Breakfast Club each morning. At the hospital, our lights went out at 10 p.m. The guests in the Hotel Strand thought the hospital was vacant at night since no lights were on. With our lights out, we could see into the lit rooms of the Strand. One night an attractive redhead about eighteen years old and her girlfriend checked into their room at the Strand. Their shades were up. The redhead took her clothes off, she walked to the mirror and started pushing her breasts up. You could hear GI's in the hospital rooms, "Oh my! Look at that!" None of the others knew that I took the only phone to my room. I knew the girl's room number so I called. I heard her phone ring and saw her pick it up. I said, "I'm getting out of the hospital tomorrow and I would like to meet you. In the meantime, why don't you pull your shades down? You're getting us all excited." Of course I said that for my own benefit and we had made a date for the next day. Now some GI's were looking for that telephone. I wasn't going to let them know I had it, so I put it under my pillow and pretended I was asleep, otherwise they probably would have killed me, and they would be right to do so. That's what you do in the army—you play games. The next day I met her at her hotel and we went out for a while to talk. She was very attractive and gave me her address in Brooklyn, which I put it in my notebook. One day my notebook was gone and I wonder if maybe some GI found out I made the call that night, and got even by taking my notebook I was never able to contact her though I sure would have loved to.

I went home on furlough for a weekend. Two weeks before, they had transferred me from Hadden Hall to the Traymore. The Traymore was another hotel some blocks from Hadden Hall. This is where we stayed before being discharged. It was a waiting place to get all the paperwork ready for our discharge. When I returned one

Sunday night I was told, "DeAngelo, there has been someone calling every day on every hour for you." I said, "Who would call me?" In a few seconds the payphone rang in the hall and it was for me. It was Bette. She said, "Boy, you're a hard person to get a hold of." I said, "Well, I went home." She said, "I've been calling." I said, "I know, Bette, but I did not know who was calling, you didn't leave your name." She said, "Would you like to see me?" I said, "No way, Bette. Every time I make a date with you, you don't show up." She said, "No, no, I had a little problem to work out. I'd be glad to see you if you want to, Frank." I said, "Well, if you don't show up this time, don't bother calling again." She said, "I'll show up." She showed up, we started seeing each other. She never told me what her little problem was and I never asked.

One very cold night I wasn't wearing my artificial limb because it was being adjusted and I was walking on crutches. I stopped walking and looked at her. I gave her a big hug and a kiss. She said, "It's about time." I said, "What do you mean it's about time?" She explained, "For two weeks you never held my hand. All I'd get was a kiss on my cheek. Then you'd put me on the bus and off I'd go." I replied, "Well, I promised you I'd behave myself." She said, "I know that, I'm glad you came to realize I like you." I said, "And I like you too."

One day I visited her at home and then missed the last bus back to Atlantic City. I'm talking about a sixteen or eighteen mile distance. I was wearing my artificial limb. I was determined to walk from her home all the way back to the hospital. I walked three miles and even though I was wearing my uniform, cars kept passing me by. I might have gotten a ride if I had been thumbing, but I wasn't. I just wanted to know how far I could walk with the artificial limb. I wasn't hurting. Guess who stopped by? A garbage truck. The driver said he was on the way to the hospital to pick up the garbage so he took me the rest of the way and dropped me off at the front entrance. I told my doctors and nurses what I had done and they looked at me like I was crazy. I had really tested my artificial limb, that's for sure.

Thank goodness my stump looked fine the next morning.

Bette and I were going on a date one evening but I stopped by the mess hall for supper first. There were two GI's, one was Asian-American, much bigger than I. I only barely knew them. I said hi to them and the Asian-American responded by pushing me. I was wearing my artificial leg but I didn't fall. "What the hell was that for?" I asked. I could see both were drunk. They started pushing me around and broke my glasses so I hit them so hard they both landed on the mess hall floor. I got on top of them and hit them a number of times. All the other GI's around me were yelling, "Go, go, go, DeAngelo! Go DeAngelo!" Finally the MP's broke us up and put us in the stockade. They put me in one room, the other two in another. Some lieutenant came to talk to me and asked what had happened? I said, "These GI's pushed me and I didn't like to be pushed. They were very drunk so I just let them have it. I didn't want them to beat me up. They have a reputation of beating a lot of GI's when they're drunk. I wasn't going to be part of that. Also, I want them to pay for my broken glasses." I called Bette to tell her I couldn't see her that night. I told her I'd tell her what happened when I saw her the next day.

I was released late that night, too late to meet Bette. The next day when we met I told her about it. She said, "I can't believe you GI's would fight." I said, "It wasn't me who started the fight." As we were walking on the boardwalk a couple of GI's who saw the fight came over and one of them said, "DeAngelo, I'm so glad to see you took care of those two. Nobody would fight them; they were always beating someone up. You really did something for the GI's who were unable to protect themselves against those two." It was a nice feeling knowing other GI's appreciated what I had done. Of course, Bette was happy I was able to protect myself and put the two GI's in their places. Nothing came out of it. I don't know what happened to those two GI's. I never saw them again, maybe they avoided me. I did not go out of my way to avoid them.

There use to be a place where Bette and I would have drinks, sit by a real fireplace, and listen to Bing Crosby sing, "I Can't Begin to Tell You." This was a very romantic song for both of us. It was a nice quiet place to talk, there weren't any fights, and it was just her and me—great times. Sometimes we'd take in a movie. We saw the great movie, *Laura,* with Gene Tierney and Dana Andrews. After each date, I would walk her to the bus stop, kiss her goodnight, and put her on the last bus of the day (around 11 p.m.) to the town where she lived. She never missed a bus and she always took the last one.

I saw her every day for weeks. We went to movies, talked, or went to the luncheonette on Atlantic Avenue for delicious chicken salad sandwiches. Bette liked them. I think they were .75¢. We'd go for a drink, sit by the fireplace and enjoy each other. We had a great time on every date we had.

One morning at the Traymore Hotel, I was sound asleep. Knotts was in the same room, he yelled real loud, "DeAngelo." He took a picture showing my hair standing straight up. I still have his photograph but I didn't include it in this publication.

Soon Knotts met a girl who looked like Jane Russell, by golly she did. Her brother was George DeWitt, a comedian. Knotts liked her very much and she liked him. They were going steady for a while. I don't know what happened to her, but it was just amazing that she looked like Jane Russell's twin, with everything like her. I know Knotts was crazy about her.

Once I took the bus to Bette's mothers house for supper. Bette's mother was a pretty lady who had been divorced for years. She had a gentleman friend who would come over to sit down with us and talk. Bette's brother was a B-29 gunner, nice guy, and she had a sister who worked at our hospital. We all had a good time together that night.

Soon Bette asked if we could spend the night in a hotel. I said we could and we did. I was crazy about her. I wanted to be with her all the time. One day she asked me, "Can you rent a car?" I said, "I don't have a license, but I have a friend who has a car." He loaned me his car. She had a license so she drove. We went someplace and made love. We didn't think too much about the consequences. Many weeks later I noticed Bette wasn't feeling well. She went to a doctor a number of times and I paid all her medical bills. I didn't know what was going on; she never told me why she was so sick. This went on for about two or three months. I said, "I think you should be up front with me and tell me what's going on so I can help you." She said she didn't want to talk about it so I left, saying I wasn't going to see her again. The next day she called, "If you knew what was wrong with me you wouldn't have walked way. Can you come over?" I said, "Yes." I went by bus. She told me she was had been three months pregnant and then had a miscarriage. I cared for her very much and felt terrible about what she'd been through. I wanted to marry her and would have if she wanted to marry me, but she didn't say no or yes. She lived in New Jersey, I was living in New York and it wasn't going to be easy not being together.

A lot of women came to Atlantic City. Some were sad to see a GI without a limb. Some women would make the GI's very happy by showing them a wonderful time. This kindness brought some of these guys a lot of laughs. I even knew of one woman who came to visit a wheelchair-bound GI. She'd push his wheelchair up to a hotel, take him out of the wheelchair and carry him to a room for a good time. Then she'd carry him back to his wheelchair and bring him to the hospital. It was funny and he had a great big smile on his face each time she came to town.

Once in a while we'd have some hospital orderlies run into our room to open the unlocked door of the closet very quickly. We couldn't figure out what was going on. We were told they found a GI with a wheelchair in a closet with a woman. He was hanging by the coat hangers making love to her. He couldn't use a bed, so he'd used the closet. That's why they rushed in to open a closet door trying to catch a GI having fun at any given time. Why? And who was he hurting?

Ever since the fistfight in my neighborhood when I was fifteen, my front teeth had given me a problem. At the hospital I developed an abscess. I met a dentist who was a captain and everyone called him "Cup Cake." He was a hell of a nice dentist. While he was working on my teeth we became friendly. I said, "You look pretty bad this morning, Captain." He said, "Well, I've been seeing this lady and all she wants to do is make love. I've got to get up at 5 o'clock in the morning to take care of you GI's." I said, "Well, why don't you find someone for her?" He turned to me, "Do you want her? I'll fix you up." I said, "No, give me her phone number, maybe I'll call her one day." Sometime later I called. We went out for a couple of drinks, and for a ride in her big Chrysler New Yorker and had fun. My friend Pete asked me to go on a date with his girl Shirley and her girlfriend Rose. I had been with Rose a couple of times and it was always a bad date. I would love to have known what kind of feelings we had for each other. I would like to have slept with her. But instead I went with the lady with the car. She was older and more experienced with men. Yes, I did have a relationship with the lady. It was a nice relationship but she did not want to get involved because she knew I would be discharged and moving away. She said, "I'll be by myself here in Atlantic City." I said, "Well, if you want, you could come to New York to visit me, or if you want me to visit you, I'll drive down to see you." We left it up in the air, not knowing what might happen soon after I was discharged, and I went home some months later.

Some GI's would go to a bar on the boardwalk and get drunk. Many times they didn't have enough money to pay their bar tab so a bartender would take their artificial leg or arm and put it behind the bar until they paid their bill. I do not know how they were able to walk to the hospital with an artificial limb left at the bar.

We had cases of psycho's in the hospital. One we called Benito. This GI was short, heavy set, and missing a right leg above the knee. There was something wrong with him upstairs. Out on the boardwalk there were carriage rides available. An operator would push the carriage up and down the boardwalk. Well, Benito would find some older woman riding in one of the carriages and just hop in with her. What could she do—tell him to get out? He'd just stay put. One day we were told he married a very rich lady he met on one of these rides. I guess he got on the right carriage that time.

I wrote to Mr. and Mrs. Kintz and she invited me to Terre Haute, Indiana, to visit them. I met her husband who was a locomotive engineer, very nice and very quiet. In 1943 his locomotive hit a 10,000-gallon aviation gasoline tanker truck at a crossing. The accident burned his earlobes, nose, and fingers. What amazed me about this gentleman was that he could drink the hottest cup of coffee placed in front of him. I couldn't hold it and he would pick it up and drink it down. I don't know if the fire did this to him or not. I was taken back by him, drinking hot coffee I couldn't touch or to drink it.

On the first night of my stay with them, I was going upstairs on my crutches when I fell from the fourth step backwards. I landed on my stump. I have never seen stars and colors like I did that night. They called the nearest Army hospital a meat wagon and a medic were sent. I was taken to the hospital, given a shot, and told to take it easy. We got back to the house and, for some reason, Peggy (the daughter) was not happy I was there, but her parents were happy. The time for me to leave came and I said good-bye. My doctor did not want me to go because I had an infection. I returned to Atlantic City. The doctor who gave me permission to go to the Kintz's was making his rounds. He came in to look at the stump. He found the infection had gone and my stump looking very good. I told him of my fall, the small amount of blood from the fall had helped to drain the infection out and healed it very well.

Also at the hospital was Sgt. Joe DiMaggio, who had an operation on his foot. I remember him sitting on the balcony, looking out at the ocean. He didn't mingle too much with the rest of us. I guess he had his own friends. Later I understood that he was a very private man and maybe that was the reason he didn't associate with anyone who was staying at the hospital.

One day my buddy Pete said, "The girls are coming from Philadelphia." Rose's parents had an apartment on the boardwalk. Shirley's husband had been a gunner on a B-17 bomber, but was shot down and killed. My buddy and Shirley had great times together. Rose and I had a difficult time. She would get all excited and pass out. There was no sex between us. She wanted to see me again but I told Pete I didn't want to be with Rose. So she ended up with another GI. After that date Rose told Pete what a waste of time he was and she wished he could get Frank for her the next time they came to Atlantic City. It never happened.

Shirley fell in love with Pete. One day she surprised him by asking him if he would impregnate her. He didn't think it was proper because of his faith. Shirley was up front with Pete. Rose was playing around with my feelings.

Time was getting close to the end of my Army career. One day they came around and told us we would soon be discharged and there wasn't much more to be done for us. The Veterans Administration would be taking over our care from the Army. I went around to say good-bye to the people I had become friends with and enjoyed knowing. I told the lady at Fralingers she was wonderful and thanked her for lending us money and then allowing us to pay her at the end of the month. I told her to say hello to the girl who bought me the bracelet. She had gone back home to Norristown, Pennsylvania, to school. I told Cup Cakes' girlfriend I had enjoyed her company. I told Bette I wasn't saying good-bye and that I'd be coming down to see her as soon as I bought a car, or she could come up to visit me. I told her we'd work something out so we could spend more time together.

On February 28, 1946, I was discharged with a Medical Honorable Discharge. I remember Lt. Col. Aloyous Martin lined us up to say, "Don't ever be called handicapped; you are disabled. Handicapped is someone who is not able to take care of himself whereas the disabled are able to." He was trying to make us understand we could go out and function as we were before we

Army Hospital

went into the Army. This was good to hear but not really true, as I found out later.

I returned home, not to New York City where I was drafted, but to my new home in Brooklyn. My parents had bought a home there in 1939 and felt the Brooklyn address was better for me since I would only have to walk up thirty three steps to the first floor of our apartment. The other home had 4 hallways, was 4 flights up and had a total of 132 steps.

I was later told that the FBI had taken all the files for the sections of Williamsberg and Bushwick from a Draft Board in Brooklyn. The reason was that many young men were never called or many were deferred for service. I understand draft boards were operated by people who were in the professional field. The families with many sons who were in the service noted this and called in the FBI. From the FBI's investigation, this draft board was closed and many men who had not been drafted, for whatever reason, were now being sent into the service. About time.

Chapter Fourteen

After Discharge

Soon after discharge in March of 1946, I was employed by the Veterans Administration at 252 7th Avenue, New York City. I stayed three months but when I saw the baloney they were giving I resigned. For instance, I was in the Adjudication Department and behind me were two adjudication officers. They had one 10% award to give out. Each had a client, one was a 19 or 20-year-old with a bullet hole that went through his chest and out his back; the other was a captain in ordinance with flat feet. These two were arguing over which client should get this one 10% award. This went on for two or three days until finally I turned and asked, "Tell me, why are you having so much trouble giving out this award to one or the other? Look, one client was probably born with flat feet, so why give him the award? The other wasn't born with a bullet hole in his chest—he was shot. He's only 19 or 20 now but when he reaches around 35 he's going to have trouble breathing plus other problems." They looked at me as if they were trying to figure what point I was trying to make, gosh plain dumb people. My point wasn't well taken. I just locked my desk, went upstairs and resigned.

I made some friends at this office, including some who had lost arms and/or legs. One was Irving Peltz, a ranger with Darby's 6615 Rangers at Anzio, had lost an arm, a leg and was blind in one eye. He said, "DeAngelo, stay here with us, we need guys like you." I said, "Forget about it, Irving—I'm leaving." The other guy was Finegold who lost an arm. He begged me to stay. I could have had a job making good money for the rest of my life. But then I went upstairs to take some aptitude tests to see what kind of job I should look for. The fifteen tests showed that my mind, hands, dexterity, and eyes all worked very well together. I had a choice between becoming a watchmaker or an aircraft instrument maker. I took the watchmaking course. I guess I cannot get away from watches for some reason.

In June, I bought a new black 1946 Model 76 Oldsmobile with automatic transmission. I had the door panels removed so I could install sailcloth over it and found shipping papers inside. This car was to have been shipped overseas to be sold. There was no country listed. Americans were in need of new cars and this one was to be shipped overseas. Then I believe it was just a few months later when I read that Congresswoman Margaret Chase Smith had requested Congress to sign a bill that all service men who had lost a leg or the use of them was to receive a $1,600 new car at no cost. So here I had a 1946 new car, for $1,800. A few months later I received a new 1947 Pontiac without automatic transmission. I was not able to drive it so I sold it to my cousin Frank, who was so kind to me when I was a boy. He paid $1,600, so I was able to pay off my other car. I was offered $2,500.00 by others for the Pontiac. (Funny, Frank had worked for a taxi company after discharge. He told me that a very well known male singer of the times paid one of the company's drivers to be on call for him day or night and when that cab returned to the garage, Frank would find lipstick and women's underwear along with a lot of notes and cards from his fans trying to meet him. He said the cards had their names, addresses and phone numbers on them.)

Soon after I was discharged I went to Angelo's for a visit with Joe. He told me to come back and meet him at around midnight for dinner. When I arrived they were closing for the night. I said to Joe, "I thought we were supposed to eat." He said we were, but that we were going to go up the street to a small place called Luna's where Jackie Gleason would often stop for a late snack. The owners said that they almost wished Gleason didn't come in because he always required fresh linens, silverware, etc. the moment he sat down, even though they had already been replaced before he came in. They also said that he only ordered bread, Italian cold cuts, and wine. The actress June Lockhart, they said, was a real sweet lady and always welcome. It was a fun place and very lively. In fact, one night a group of men came in all dressed up as females, including makeup and lipstick. I assume they performed as women at a local strip club on Second Ave. They looked like good-looking women. One or two of them fooled me.

Soon I needed to buy a pair of shoes. I went with a friend to Florsheim's men shop for a pair of shoes. I walked in the front door and the salesman noticed I was walking as if it hurt when walking. He asked if I had a nail in my shoes. I said I must have a nail or a tack and I just don't know where it can be. He said, "Come with me, we have an X-ray machine to look at your feet and can tell what is going on within the shoes." I placed my feet under the machine and when he turned it on he looked down, viewing my feet and said out loud, "Look at all the tacks in the right shoe and bones in the left shoe." Acting like this was all new to me, I looked down at my feet and asked, "Now, which tack is hurting me?" At that time the prosthetic foot was made out of wood and both the foot and the toe were two pieces. The two were held together by leather, glue and tacks. I would imagine it took around 35-45 tacks to hold the two pieces together. My friend was smiling all the time, as for me, I was dead serious from the moment he asked if I had a tack in my shoe. The salesman turned off the X-ray machine, walked back to the rear of the store and never came back. I needed to buy a pair of shoes but we left since he would not come out to sell me a pair. (Sometimes I am asked how do I take a shower. I reply, "Very carefully", or do I sleep with it on. Some people and their questions).

About six months after being discharged, I received a letter from the VA requesting I look over an attached list of doctors of psychology. New York City had about 20 to choose from and I picked a female

After Discharge

doctor from Germany. I made an appointment with her. After an hour or two of asking questions about what I liked or did not like, she said she had noticed that I had repeatedly removed my left moccasin shoe and replaced it onto my foot by my foot action and she'd like to know why. I said, "For the very same reason you have been playing with that plastic drink stick in your hands since I've sat here." She then looked at the item in her hand and said, "You need not come to see me again. I will inform the VA that to do so would be a waste of our time."

In August 1946 I took a two-year course at The Joseph Bulova School of Watchmaking. We had class for five hours a day, five days a week with two weeks off a year for vacation. This beautiful school was next to Bulova Watch Company at Woodside, Long Island, New York, and was founded for wounded veterans by our friend Andre Bulova. The VA had enrolled me and in addition to my compensation I received an extra $75 per month. One day while I was working I heard a lot of snickering and laughter from the other guys. I started to smell something burning. I thought it was one of the timing or cleaning machines in front of me. Thinking something was wrong, I looked down and there was Dominic, a friend, on his hands and knees. I don't know how he got down there, but my right shoe was on fire. I asked, "What are you doing Dominic?" He replied, "I'm trying to give you a hot foot; can't you feel that?" There were books of burned matches all around my burning shoe. I said, "No, stupid, you're burning the wrong foot!" The whole class was roaring with laughter. It was funny to see Dominic's red face.

We learned how to repair watches and when we graduated we were given $500 worth of tools for free. I left with tools, ready for work, but still wanted more education. There were two Public Laws that entitled veterans to benefits. One was Public Law 16, for the disabled. The other was 346, for anyone who spent more than ninety days in the service. I was entitled to take both Public Law 16 and 346. I had completed the watch course under Public Law 16, and I went to the VA and asked if under Public Law 346 I could go to an electronics course that was offered by RCA. A VA training officer asked, "What for? You just completed a course at Bulova." I said, "I know, but I feel watchmaking and electronics will combine one day in the manufacture of electronic watches." He looked at me as if to say you dumb SOB, but he said, "Do you see that General Electric clock up on the wall? You see a power cord going into the 115 volt AC socket? That's the only way I can think electricity would run a clock." I said, "You mean to tell me you can't visualize electronic watches?" He replied, "No." Not much of a brain there (so what else is new?) and I wondered where do the VA find these guys?

I should have forced the issue, but I am headstrong and instead told him where to go before walking out. This guy was typical of some of the people working for the VA. They had no foresight, no understanding, nothing. It would have been nice to have two trades to fall back on while seeking employment. It was not easy to find jobs if you were disabled. As a side note, very soon thereafter, electronics burst into TV and radio.

Dominic and I went to a midget racing car event in the Bronx, N.Y. one day and stopped off in the lounge for a drink afterwards. Dominic was a walking paraplegic, injured when he crashed in a B-24 in Colorado in a blinding snowstorm. I always said he was walking paraplegic but he never used a wheelchair. The bartender recognized him from other racing events. He told the old gentleman next to me we were veterans who had been disabled during the war. This gentleman turned to me and said, "Son, I heard you lost a leg." I said, "No, I appreciate your asking me, but I know where it is." We all got a kick out of it and had a few more drinks all around.

Some years later I had to drive to Philadelphia and I asked Pete to ride down with me. By luck, we ran into Shirley. I knew he wanted to see her, but she told him she was getting married and wouldn't be able to continue seeing him. He said he understood and wished her a lot of luck. When we were driving home he said he was kind of sorry he didn't impregnate her, especially since she had begged him. But he also knew it wouldn't be right.

Figure 82. My mother had given me a ruby birthstone ring when I was 15 years old. The stone had fallen out when I was digging a foxhole in France somewhere. I knew it could be anywhere but, by sheer luck, I was able to find the stone. I had it fixed when I got home and then, a few years later at the Bulova School, I lost this stone again. I had no idea where exactly it had fallen out. On a Monday afternoon, I arrived for class just as the previous class was leaving. I asked one of the guys who was leaving if by chance he found a ruby stone. He stopped and looked at me. He put his fingers in his watch pocket and pulled out my ruby. Now why would I ask this particular guy? He had found the ruby days before and was just hanging on to it. It was another one of those almost scary feelings that I have from time to time. Is it a good thing to have such feelings? It's like when I refused to dig a foxhole where my lieutenant had ordered one, and instead dug one behind a tree just hours before an artillery barrage came in on us.

Figure 82. The author's ruby ring given to him on his 15th birthday by his mother. Twice the stone was lost and both times it was found.

One day I received a letter from Murray who had been discharged from the Army as a captain and was married with children. He was going to be in New York City at a Congressional Medal of Honor Reunion for all the Congressional Medal of Honors issued to the 3rd Infantry Division. He invited me come see him. I went to the hotel and Murray introduced me to some of the men who received the CMH. He introduced me to Audie Murphy, who was a nice looking young man, but very quiet. As the meeting was getting ready to start it was noted anybody who was not invited and didn't have the CMH would have to be excused, so I excused myself. Before I did, Murray was telling me that he didn't like his job with the Veterans Administration. I told him that when I was discharged I also took a job with the VA but soon quit. I said, "Why don't you go back into the Army? You have the Congressional Medal of Honor, you'll have it made and you can be whatever you want to be." He said he'd been thinking about rejoining and would let me know what he decided.

About two months later he wrote to tell me he had gone back into the Army, retained his rank of captain, and was enjoying himself. He wrote, "Guess what, DeAngelo? I can't get M-1's for my men. The Army doesn't have any to issue." This was probably 1946 or 1947 and I don't know what happened to all our M-1's. He said his troops were training without rifles, what a joke. I wrote him that if he felt comfortable in the Army then that's where he should be. In my letter I said, "Some GI's spend so many years in the military and after they are discharged they don't think much about it. But then there are others who miss the military. One might not miss it for a while, but eventually they will. Some of us are meant for military duty while others are not." I feel the military was right for Murray and me, but where were the M-1's for Murray's men?

Chapter Fifteen

Back Home

I had promised Larry I would see Jackie so I went to visit her. She told me she was getting engaged that same night. I was embarrassed and stunned in a way. We left the party to talk and I told her what Larry had said about how much he loved her. She looked at me and said, "Frank, I like Larry, but I don't love him. It wasn't the same way with me as it was with him. I liked him very much as a friend but not more than that." I was not invited to her wedding six months later and never did find out what happened to her.

My brother had gone overseas after I was discharged and took part in the occupation. He was working with some heavy equipment trucks and has some glossy 8x10 black and white photographs showing row after row, after row, after row of Sherman tanks, and M-10's all in line. He said they put five gallons of gasoline inside and ignited each one of them. To me that was sinful, because all of those vehicles could have been returned to the US and stored indefinitely. The US stored airplanes in outdoor storage in Arizona, so I don't know why they couldn't have kept the tanks there for later use in Korea. Some smart government person said, "Burn them up and destroy them." I think we should know who gave such an order. In addition to this wasteful destruction, our Navy dumped planes off the decks of aircraft carriers just to get rid of them. Of course, after the war the Navy went to Chance Vought to request to manufacture 250 new Corsairs. What happened to all the old Corsairs at the end of the war? The new Corsairs were sold to the French Naval Air Force some months later. Why?

I was not happy in civilian life. In 1949 it was tough, even with a good trade, to get a decent job with a disability. Employers wouldn't touch us because of insurance company policies. In 1950 President Truman requested Congress to create a law that would allow some disabled veterans to return to the military. They would have to give up their VA compensation, but at least they would have a military job. They could leave the military if and when they wanted and re-file for VA compensation. Wonderful.

This sounded good to me so I drove to Fort Dix, NJ, for my military physical. Unfortunately, they had not heard of the new law and thought it was a joke that a guy with a wooden leg wanted to rejoin the Army. I was there for three days before someone finally contacted Washington and realized that Army disabled persons where to be readmitted.

After my physical, they told me I could come back in the Army as a Private First Class. I said that was ridiculous, since once I was a Buck Sergeant and active staff. I requested they give me Buck Sergeant or Staff Sergeant so I would have enough money to compensate for the loss of my VA compensation and also help pay for the use of my car. They refused. I was disgusted and realized that I should have gone to the top in the first place.

Before leaving Fort Dix, I met some friends from my neighborhood. They had recently been drafted. We talked for a while and soon I left to drive back home. Weeks later I saw these GI's at home on weekend passes. They told me that, soon after the Korean War broke out, the Army was looking for combat veterans and was willing to re-enlist them at a higher level based on their experience. They said, "Most of the Fort Dix GI's didn't have any combat experience, they were rear echelon who had trained others during the war. If you had joined you probably could have gone as high as you wanted to go, maybe even up to captain." I said, "Well, it was their choice; they didn't give me what I wanted." At times I wonder; what if?

Soon a strange thing happened. There was a military surplus

building around the corner in my neighborhood. The owner had bought all military surplus items he could for practically nothing. Then the Army and Navy came in one day and bought the entire inventory at a very good price. He became a wealthy man overnight and he built a brand new brick building. At this place, I purchased a wooden foot locker of photos, U.S. 5th Army 1942-1945.

When World War II ended, nearly everything surplus was sold or junked. Then when the Korean War started, the military found itself short of many items, particularly vehicles like Jeeps and trucks. They went out to the old battlefields and collected as many wrecked vehicles as they could and had them shipped to Japan where they were taken apart, cleaned and repaired, and re-manufactured into new vehicles. They may have had 60,000 destroyed vehicles and were re-manufactured into 30,000 like new vehicles, sometimes a second time to be re-manufactured.

I don't know what happened to Andy. He was a wild kid from New England who wanted me to use the boxing gloves. One thing I do know is that he had a pretty bad temper. I have a temper but it is controlled at times. I think his temper was like opening up a gas valve and lighting a match—that was it. After the war I paid a visit to his family and they told me they received a telegram stating he was killed in Africa. Well, when we arrived in Casablanca on The Empress of Scotland, all combat was below Cassino, so why were they told he was killed in Africa? I feel he must have gotten himself in trouble, or he might have been one of the GI's the Arabs took care of. I have no idea, I think in my mind I visualize seeing him running on top of the troop train. The trains we took from Casablanca to Bizerte. If I'm not mistaken he might have been the type of person who would get on top of the roof of the train, going through lots of tunnels. My gut feeling, and I do have these feelings, is that he somehow was killed accidentally or let's say killed by other means other than being wounded or killed in action. I never did voice these feelings to his parents, I didn't think it was proper, as long as the Government said he was killed in action in Africa. I let it go at that. I know there was no combat in Africa at the time of his death.

After graduating from the Bulova Watchmaking school, I was informed that a school for watchmaking in Baltimore, Maryland was in need of instructors. A former student, who was now in charge of school training, asked me to apply. In need of a job, I accepted. The school was called Morgan School of Watchmaking and it was located in the black part of town. I had 40 black students, paid by the VA, to learn the trade. Many of these students were working in hard construction such as brick laying, etc. and their hands were in bad shape. There was another white instructor with me whose brother was also working at the school. School started at 3:00 p.m. and at 3:30 p.m. I would call out the names to see who was attending. Then at 8:30 p.m. I would again call out names. One night a particular student was present at 3:30 p.m. but not at 8:30 p.m. It seemed that he had cut class. As requested by the VA, I was to report him to the office. I did not report him that day, but decided to do so if the same thing happened the next day. Some individuals wanted to learn, and others were attending just to receive checks to add to their income of the jobs they had.

The next day, at the time of head count, this particular student was attending. I called him aside to ask what had happened the night before. He said he did not cut class and that I was wrong. I told him not to do that again and I went to my desk. He became very upset and spoke out as he stood up. He then said he was an army P-51 fighter pilot and was shot down twice, breaking his legs. I felt like he was trying to belittle me in front of the rest of my students. When he was done, he sat down and I proceeded to pull up my right pants leg to show my artificial wooden leg. I told him that I was sorry to learn of his wounds. The class seemed to be taken back by this. I said that I was there to teach them a better trade than they had now, and that those who were there just to get a VA check should not interfere with those who were truly there to learn.

Later that evening, the other instructor in the class told me that showing up that student was wrong and that I would be beaten up tonight. I told that I would not because some of the students had respect for me, but you and your brother will be the ones beaten. He looked at me and said, "I did not fight with that student, you did." I looked at him and said, "You and your brother do not care or want to help them, and they know it. They also know I am trying to help them." As I was going down the stairs on my way home that night, the students were lined up on both sides. As I walked down between them, I heard them say, "Good night, Mr. DeAngelo". There was no problem of any kind and from that day forward my class went on without any trouble.

I recall an incident late one Friday night as I was going home for the weekend with some other instructor. We were on a ferry boat crossing the Delaware River on our way to Chester, PA. At the top of the ferry was a coffee shop. That night it was closed. As I was coming down the stairs a number of GI's were coming up. I said, Guy's Place was closed for the night. As I was walking to the car these GI's walked up to me and one asked, "How would you like to have a nine inch blade stuck in you?" I turned to him and said, "If you feel you must do that, I can tell you I shall pull it out and stick your knife in your body. Then I will throw you off this ferry, into the river." They walked away and I got into my car. My passenger, sitting inside, said he had never seen or heard of something like what he just heard. I said, "If I had shown them I was afraid I would have been stabbed. But hearing I would do what I said I would do made them think otherwise." I have found at times if you show fear you will be in trouble. It is best to keep a cool head and think on what to say and do. Most guys will back off if you show no fear at times, then maybe not.

Sometimes when it is quiet and I am by myself, I think back on all that happened during those years. Did I really go through that stuff? Did these things happen to me? Did I sleep and dream it all? Is it only in my mind? But I can assure you that everything I have written is true. I have seen it, been in it and remembered it all. I have been able to recall all of this by memory.

I'm glad I've been able to put all my writing together and hope it will be read. That someone will read about a young man who enjoyed the Army and did the best he could possibly do. I'm a little upset about what they call heroes today. I'm referring to the incident that happened when a flyer escaped and it took him 5-6 days to make it back to his lines. They made him a hero when all he did was his job and I think that's a bunch of bull. I feel he didn't accomplish anything, he didn't shoot anybody, and he didn't help anybody else. To me a hero is someone who helps another person in need and who is not worried about what can happen to him. A guy who puts his life on the line for someone he knows or doesn't know, that is a hero in my opinion. It was his job to try to escape—nothing more. But a hero, never.

One night, on May 14, 1948, I was sitting in my friend's new Chevrolet when we turned to the 11 p.m. news. It said that the United Nations had voted to give Israel its country. I said, "Joe, you know this will cause a great deal of problems for all the people in that part of the world from this day on." Once more my gut feelings were correct. Each day we read of more problems in the Middle East and my feeling is that the US needs to get out of the United Nations. Why? Because I believe it will only get worse, plus nothing gets completed. The United Nations was a bad idea for us; it failed when it was previously tried, after World War I, under the name "The League of Nations." Some of its members bite the hand that feeds them—our great country called "America".

Chapter 16

Present

The officer who broke me from a buck sergeant to a private when I was AWOL from the hospital trying to get back to my outfit was wrong. To me, this officer should never have held his rank. Actually, I would say he could only have held a rank below that of a private. When an officer does not return a salute to someone twice, it indicates a character of low quality. Not too long ago, I had a discussion with a colonel and he told me that I had shown more intelligence than I got credit for. I mentioned what the manual says about what a non-commissioner who is a POW should do. "You proved he did not know the law or the instructions of the soldiers' handbook. He just wanted to show that he was an officer and you were a nobody." I was also told that only my Company Commander was the one to break me, not him. I would like to get that part of my record corrected but have been told that my records in St. Louis were burned. It's kind of strange that a year after I was told my records no longer existed, I received a second set of my medals from St. Louis. I had not asked for them. Were my records burned or was someone telling me a fib? To me, my records are still someplace, or why would I get these second medals after a fire…unbelievable.

I think I mentioned about a speck of dirt that was lodged in my face when the sniper tried to kill me at my machine gun position on Anzio. I could see that speck for a long time before it eventually worked itself out. When ever I looked in the mirror I would spot that speck; it wasn't big, it was just always there reminding me of that particular early morning, February 7, 1944.

The Army made a weapon called "The Liberator," a .45 caliber projector called M1942, that was air dropped to the people in France, Holland and Belgium to help in their fight against the Germans. The Liberator was manufactured by a General Motors Division "Guide Lamp" at a cost of $2.10 each with 10 rounds; its cover name was "Flare Projector." This division also manufactured the new M-1 Grease Gun at $20 each. Before the war, this GM division manufactured headlights and taillights for its cars.

I believe very deeply in the Second Amendment right to bear arms. In the early 30's, the French, Dutch, and Belgian governments issued weapon laws that required everyone who had a weapon to register with the city, mayor, or government. Years later, German agents in the aforementioned countries, stole those records of who had weapons. Then when WWII came along the Germans marched into these countries and took the weapons away, leaving those people defenseless. Our Allied planes dropped captured weapons at night so the French, Belgians, and Dutch could keep up their fight. Just think, if 250 million guns were in the hands of American people today, who in his right mind would attack us or fight to overthrow us? Now some of our people want to take away our guns. If this happens we won't have any weapons to defend ourselves. Any country could just come and take over. We would be at the mercy of whatever government came to our shores. I think those who would take away our right to bear arms should be called traitors. Do not remove the Second Amendment; do not change it; do nothing to help these traitors. I have a license to carry a concealed weapon, which I take with me each time I travel. Some people (I call traitors) in this country want us to give up all our weapons, like the countries listed above, during the 1930's. That's all I have to say about that.

Now, regarding spies ... I don't know what's wrong with Washington. If a man is caught as a spy and we have the goods on him, why screw around with him, why? Just find the nicest big tree and hang him. You might think I'm bloodthirsty, but I'm not. I simply love this country and I hate to see someone be disloyal to it.

I really believe spies should be put to death–not this year or next year or three years from now, but now. Let them hang; it should be the way we do business with them.

One of the worse kinds of combat is the type we faced in Vietnam. Our troops were wearing uniforms while the bad guys did not. In the daytime they were farmers yet at night they fought in the same clothing, making it difficult to figure out who was a friend and who was a foe. I don't think we will ever do combat the way we did in WWI and WWII. Instead, small groups will take action as they did in Vietnam—hit and run, go underground, and then again another quick attack. Is it not happening today?

Some years back Lt. Murray and his wife visited us in Florida. He said in all the years he was in the Army in Korea and Vietnam he only met one other person who he thought was like me. I don't know any other details about this other GI, but I do wish I knew more about him.

Figure 83 shows a daily report sheet that had to be filled out each day by the C Company clerk showing the names of men who were wounded, missing, or killed. It shows I was a Sergeant, MOS Number 653 PD, and AWOL. The name of the clerk is Cpl. Norval N. Knouse. I met him recently with his wife at our 3rd Infantry Division Reunion that was held in Savannah, Georgia, on September 22, 1999. Fifty-five years had passed and he said he still remembered the day I had shown him my left shirt or jacket pocket with a rip across it, which he said was torn by a bullet. I do not recall this; 25% tells me it did happen and 75% says I was not the person. But under stress one can easily forget. Maybe one day it will come to me so I cannot say no it was not me, but I feel it could be.

Whenever I filled out a job application, I had to sign over my rights to any new design or method that I came up with for the company. The company then owns the idea (or design) and you are dead in the water. I remember thinking that maybe I should have someone else sign my name, just in case? I never did, it was just a thought.

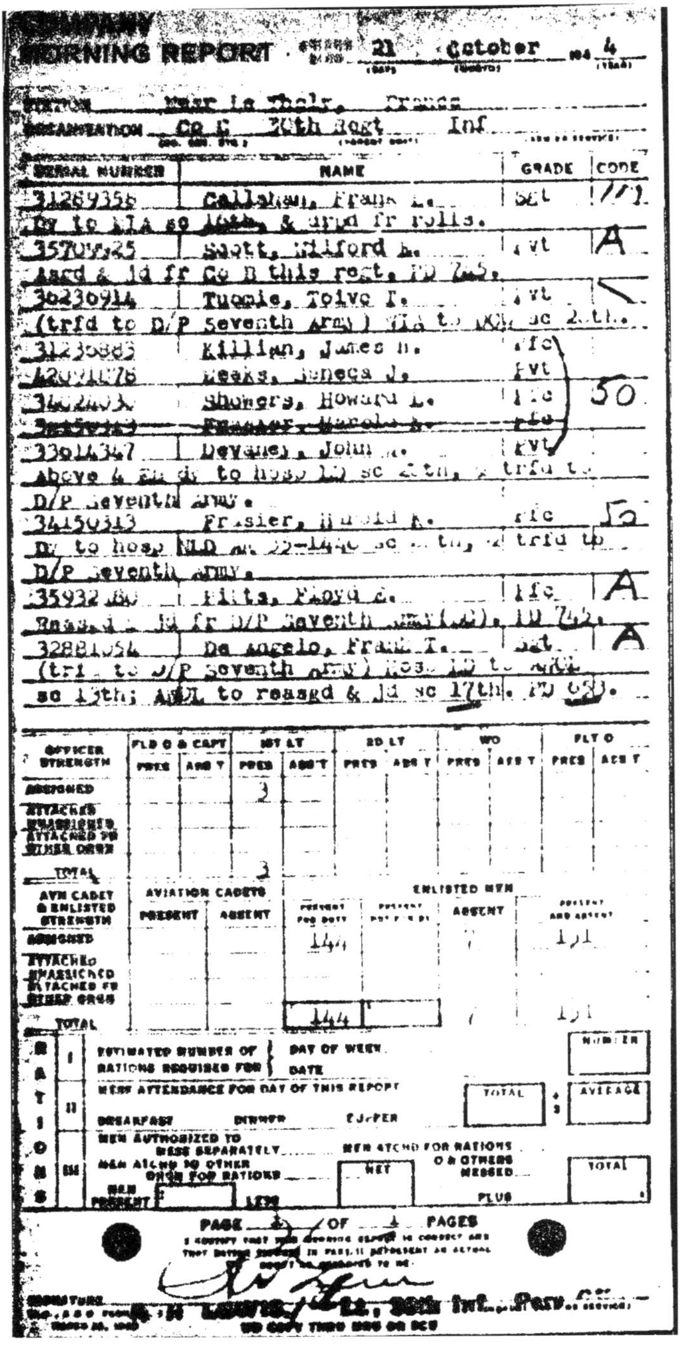

COMPANY MORNING REPORT 21 October 1944

STATION Near Le Tholy, France

ORGANIZATION Co C 30th Regt Inf

SERIAL NUMBER	NAME	GRADE	CODE
31269356	Callahan, Frank L.	Sgt	
Dy to KIA so 16th, & drpd fr rolls.			
35709525	Scott, Wilford L.	Pvt	A
Asgd & jd fr Co B this regt. PD 765.			
36230914	Tuomie, Toivo I.	Pvt	
(trfd to D/P Seventh Army) WIA to LD so 2.th.			
31230883	Killian, James H.	Pfc	50
42091076	Weeks, Seneca J.	Pvt	
3602403	Showers, Howard L.	Pfc	
33014347	Devaney, John	Pvt	
above 4 ... to hosp LD so 2.th, & trfd to D/P Seventh Army.			
34150313	Frasier, Harold	Pfc	50
Dy to hosp NLD ... 22-1440 so ...th, & trfd to D/P Seventh Army.			
35932180	Pitts, Floyd E.	Pfc	A
... jd fr D/P Seventh Army (...), PD 742.			
32881054	De Angelo, Frank T.	Sgt	A
(trfd to D/P Seventh Army) hosp LD to ... so 13th; ... to reasgd & jd so 17th. PD 68.			

OFFICER STRENGTH	1ST LT PRES
ASSIGNED	3
TOTAL	3

AVN CADET & ENLISTED STRENGTH	PRESENT FOR DUTY	ABSENT	PRESENT AND ABSENT
ASSIGNED	144	7	151
TOTAL	144	7	151

PAGE 2 OF 4 PAGES

I CERTIFY THAT THIS MORNING REPORT IS CORRECT AND THAT ENTRIES SHOWN IN PART II REPRESENT AN ACTUAL COUNT OF PERSONNEL TO ME.

SIGNATURE ... LEWIS, 1st Lt, 30th Inf. Pers. O.

Figure 83. A daily report for C Company on October 21, 1944, as a Sgt., filed by Cpl. Knouse.

Many applications also asked if I was a minority. Was I correct if I placed an x in all areas listed? Because of the blood transfusions I had, who knew whose blood was put into my veins? Though I never did that, I don't think I would have been wrong.

Many years before I went into the Army I had a vision I was going to return home in a taxi. It stopped in front of my home, the taxi pulled up next to a fire hydrant, I opened the door and as I stepped out I noticed I was missing my right foot. Was this thought put into my mind years before? It all came to pass on September 20, 1945, on a weekend pass, when getting out of the taxi it all came back as something I had seen before.

Before I went into the Army, I became acquainted with a girl named Marie who lived in the neighborhood. We were just friends and there was nothing serious going on between us but we did go out for ice cream together. After I was discharged from the Army, I was down at a subway station and we saw each other. We didn't speak and something inside told me not to approach her. I found out that my grandmother had mistakenly told her I had been killed. I think when she saw me on the platform she probably thought, "Who is he? He looks like Frank, but he was killed." She had a funny look on her face as if to say, "I can't believe what I'm seeing." We never spoke and even today I don't understand why we didn't say hello.

In some way I have had strange thoughts and yes, feelings I cannot fully explain. Like the slit trench behind the tree where I wanted to dig. Lt. Murray and others thought I had great intuition to be able to feel things before they happen. This happened with my red ruby stone. My asking someone unknown if he found a red ruby stone. For example, I will remember a movie I had seen so many years ago and then, that very same day, I read of it playing on TV that night, or in a few days. This is what I mean. What is it?

I have so often had strange feelings that I cannot fully explain. Maybe it is some kind of intuition or maybe it's deja vu; I don't know. I still remember one hot summer night when some guys I knew were outside our house singing quite nicely in low voices. They weren't bothering anyone, but someone called the police who arrived and broke up the group. The next day I saw the guys and one them was pretty angry. He asked if I had called the police and I told him no, but added that I thought I knew who did. I told him the guy's name, though I had no reason to actually know he did it. A few minutes later, the guy I thought had called the police showed up and admitted that the singing had bothered him and that, yes, he had called the police. So the question was, why did I mention this guy's name? I had no proof he was the one but somehow I just knew it.

Some years later, I happened to stop to see a friend, a 4th Platoon Sergeant named Polenchar, who was a policeman living in Bethlehem, Pennsylvania. He said, "DeAngelo, guess who's in town? The GI who went to London" I said, "You're kidding me?" He said no and so we called him, he came over and the three of us had a great time reminiscing. He said, "I'm glad you picked Paris, DeAngelo. I never came back because I was shipped home." Goes to show you how things turn out. I guess if he's still alive he still talks about me having seniority—I got to go to Paris and he got to go to London and then home. I went on and was wounded and then home.

Figure 84 is a photo taken at the 3rd Infantry Division reunion. When I was looking for the 30th Regiment Register book so I could sign in and see who else was attending, there was a guy next to me writing in a register. I asked the man behind the desk where the 30th Regiment Register book was when the guy next to me said, "Here it is, I'm finished with it. What's your name?" I replied, "DeAngelo." He said, "I was your supply sergeant, Ducy." In the photo, I'm on the left side, striped tie, and dark suit. The gentleman in the middle is McGregor, the radio man, and next to him is Ducy, our supply sergeant. I don't remember who the other two were. I think they belonged to our company somewhere but I don't recall their names or where or when.

Figure 84. 3rd Division reunion of C Company. Left to right: the author, McGregor, and Ducy on his left shoulder. Others unknown.

Years later we had another 3rd Infantry Division reunion. I ran across a GI who told me of another person who was at this reunion. We stayed up talking until two or three in the morning. Every Christmas I would send this other person a Christmas card, but I never received a return. It bugged me. Then I recalled the incident that had taken place on the bank of the Fecht River so long ago. I guess somehow I had completely forgotten about it. His not returning any reply opened the door of my memory of that episode. He was ashamed or he didn't want to be reminded of it. I warned him but he never took my warning seriously.

Figure 85 is a photograph of me, taken January 2, 1954, in Miami at the Bon Art Studio, the same photo firm in Jacksonville who took Figure 8. Believe it or not, this photograph was taken to be put on the jacket of this book I was going to write about my

Figure 85. The author's photo taken in Miami, Florida on January 2, 1954.

Army experience. Like I said, I started writing this in 1954. Two days after writing one or two pages on a yellow pad, I realized I couldn't read my terrible handwriting. So I bought a manual typewriter but that didn't help either since I was only typing with two fingers and was making so many mistakes. We didn't have a typewriter that could remove mistakes then.

One day I was having lunch at Boeing at Kennedy Space Center at pad "A". A few guys were telling stories about what they had hunted. They asked me what kind of hunting I did but before I could say a word, one guy said, "He's from New York City; what would he hunt?" I took off my glasses and looked at them and said I had hunted the most dangerous game in the world. I heard their snickers and one guy asked, "What did you hunt?" I said, "Another soldier with a rifle who was hunting me." All four had no other comments and walked away.

I would say World War II had very good men in it. I guess it's because we grew up during the Depression and knew what it was all about. We didn't have much of anything.

From time to time, I run across articles in military publications or in a newspaper clipping about a landing or a capture. Most veterans will say their outfit was the best, well, out of about 350 of the Congressional Medal of Honors issued during World War II, the 3rd Infantry Division received 37 medals. Now, that's a big percentage. So, if we were not as good as other Divisions, or great, or outstanding, why all these 37 medals? We must have been doing the right thing. We were all nineteen and twenty years old. Other divisions had the same age of GI's like us.

After the war, German Gen. Albert Kesserling stated that our GI's in Africa, Sicily and Italy received quick combat experience while his divisions broke to fall back to lose ground. Our GI's did not. Also, Field Marshall Kesserling was asked what were the best American divisions his troops faced under his command in Italy and Western fronts, he said there were four–two infantry and two armored divisions, the 3rd Infantry Division placed first on his list. Thus a great deal was learned and passed onto others. In other words, he was saying that the GI's in the Mediterranean learned an awful lot awfully fast. They learned the tricks of the trade. Gen. Kissering stated that if it had not been for these GI's, Normandy would and could have been a failure. I don't know if this is true or not. I know one thing, though. We learned a lot very quickly and then were able to pass our experiences onto others. In Africa, the British and French troops said that our GI's were like the Italian troops who did not have the heart to fight.

I hear some veterans bitching about this and that. But if you ask them if they ever fired a weapon at the front, most of them would answer no. They were in the rear echelon or quartermaster, or something.

It's kind of strange that the only time you see the 3rd Infantry Division white and blue patch is when they show "To Hell and Back" with Audie Murphy. It was also painted on both sides of our helmets. I don't know if I mentioned this before but one day I received a letter about how to find my family crest. For the heck of it, I requested it and when it arrived it showed a crest with three white bars and four blue bars placed horizontal, all in the same sequence as those on the 3rd Division emblem. The blue was the same blue but the division's colors were angled. Was it not strange?

Figure 86. I went to a reunion recently at Fort Benning, Georgia, where I got to visit my old regiment and meet GI's of the new 30th Regiment. We were taken to see its museum, had lunch, and some were taken out to fire a lot of new weapons. That night at the regimental dinner, there were soldiers in uniform at our table. I looked at them and said, "You GI's will have to pay me royalties, 15 cents each, every month, ." They looked at me like I was nuts. I said, "Do you see the patch you're wearing? Well, your patch is a copy of my family crest." They looked at me kind of strange until I pulled out a photograph of my family crest. They all laughed and I told them I was kidding; the 3rd Infantry Division patch was only 80 years old, my family crest is 400 years old. We got a big chuckle out of that.

I was talking to someone with the 30th Infantry Regiment Society regarding Japanese-American interned in camps. Recent information shows some Italian-Americans were put in camps on the West Coast by Gen. DeWitt, but were quickly released. When Ed Sullivan was asked what percentage of what nationalities were in the service during WWII he said the biggest percentage were Italian-Americans. If our families had been put in camps, I think we would have seen mass desertion from all branches of the service. There is a book written by Steven Fox called, "Unknown Internment" about

Figure 86. The author's family crest and shield, 400 years old.

Italian-Americans who were interned at those camps on the west coast.

I read of an actor who, with his son, was refused to be picked up by a cab driver in New York City. On September 6, 1945 I was home from the hospital, also trying to hale a cab in New York City with my dad. I too was refused. I was in an Army uniform on crutches with my right foot missing. Some cab drivers will do that. The next cab stop we got in.

About the M-1 Garand–it was a great weapon. The Russians had manufactured some rifles which were captured and then issued to German troops. They were pretty decent but not as good as the M-1. The Germans had captured these Model GEW.41's from the Russians. They redesigned some parts, then it became the GEW.43 model and was used during the latter part of the war. They were not able to go into full production for the Germans.

The Japanese had captured our M-1's. The Japanese tried to make a copy of our M-1. I don't remember if it became operational. I know I did see a photo of the Japanese model that looked like the M-1.

I don't know how good the Johnson rifle was. One thousand of the Johnson rifles were bought and issued to our Marine Corp. I never heard anything bad or good about them. I do know the reason our government went to the M-1 was that it cost $100 per unit, while the Johnson cost $1,000 per unit. I understand a private company designed the Johnson and the Springfield Armory in Massachusetts, which was owned by the government, designed the M-1.

Figure 87 shows a letter from Terry Murphy, the son of Audie Murphy. Some years back when I was living in Miami, I heard an announcement asking anybody who served with Audie Murphy to call the studio as they were going to promote his new movie, "To Hell and Back." I knew a bit about him so I called in. They asked me to come down to the studio and I was put on TV for about five or ten minutes. I told them Audie and I had been in the same outfit and I told them about the incident where I was offered a commission but refused to accept one because I would have to be transferred. "To Hell and Back" is a good movie and I've seen it once or twice. Yes, it did bring back memories–some good, some bad.

Figure 88 shows Murray. At the time of this photograph he was a full colonel in Vietnam. He sent me this photograph to let me know he was alive and enjoying the Army.

Today's date is February 10, 1999. The movies, "Saving Private Ryan," "The Thin Red Line," and Tom Brokaw's book, "The Great

Present

AUDIE MURPHY RESEARCH FOUNDATION
A NON-PROFIT PUBLIC BENEFIT CORPORATION

President
  Terry M. Murphy
Vice President
  Chris J. Glazier
Executive Director
  Larryann C. Willis, Esq.

18008 Saratoga Way, Suite 516
Santa Clarita, CA 91351

Phone: (805) 252-0780
Toll Free Phone/Fax: (888) 314-AMRF
Email: Audiemurphy@altuir.net

September 27, 1997

Frank T. DeAngelo
1090 N. Romana Ave.
Indialantic, FL 32903

Dear Mr. DeAngelo:

    I want to thank you for your financial contribution. I also appreciate your recollections of having served with the 3rd Division.

    I got a kick out of your story about getting roped into plugging TO HELL AND BACK. TV fame is a fleeting thing, isn't it?

    Thanks again

Sincerely,

Terry Murphy

Figure 87. The above from Audie Murphy's son to the author.

Figure 88. Colonel Murray in Vietnam.

Generation" are popular. When I started writing this book in 1954, I was probably premature and not quite ready for it. But now I have written it so I won't forget all of it. I think it's time for me to remember a lot of things, just sit down and put it all together. I hope it makes good reading for somebody who wants to understand what it was like to be in combat and to enjoy the fellowship of men and to be there for my men. It would be interesting to go through it again if it was possible. I have never regretted my wounds, which I do not think about.

There was never a yellow streak running down my back. Each morning when I look in the mirror, a lot of thoughts come to mind. I came across recently *Figure 89*. The SS Leopoldville, a troop ship, sank on December 24, 1944, as they were going from England to France for the Battle of the Bulge. This group of GI's were from the 66th Infantry Division, the Division I took basic training with at Camp Blanding, Florida. The 264th and 262nd Regiments of the 66th Division were on this ship crossing the Channel when a German

Figure 89. The ship SS Leopoldville, sunk on December 24, 1944.

submarine sank it. Over 800 GI's drowned. This was confidential for many years. Eventually a book called *"The S.S. Leopoldville Disaster"* was written by Allan Andrade . My concern? Where was the 263rd Regiment, the one I was attached to when I joined the 66th Division at Camp Blanding? Was the 263rd used as a replacement to be sent overseas to Africa to fill in for casualties in Africa, Sicily, and Italy? Nothing has been mentioned of the 263rd; what happened to them? Was it disbanded because its men were used as replacements, or what? It would be nice to know. Later I learned the 263rd Regiment had been shipped by another ship to France and landed safe and sound. The cold water in that area off England did not help much for those GI's and I sure hope they didn't have the Kopak life preservers that were only good for 24 hours, like we had crossing the Atlantic Ocean in 1943. I recall seeing a film on TV of 1943 showing captured Germans from North Africa on board ships wearing Cork life preservers. They were going to camps in the USA. GI's were wearing the type called Kopak. I wonder why?

I'm always surprised at how I run into people who are related to or knew guys I served with. One day at a drugstore, I heard a young lady say her last name was Carter. I asked if she knew a Jake Carter. She said he was her uncle. Carter was in K Company and was killed on Anzio. Another time I came across the name of someone living nearby called Dannic. I called and found he was the cousin of the Dannic I knew who had been killed on Anzio. I told him what I knew about the details of his death.

We had a little GI, a redhead, by the name of Pfc. Jerome Katz. He was a quiet GI and I felt he needed someone like Rothstein had needed, so we spent time together. One day Katz went out to help a wounded GI and was killed by a sniper. Once I ran across the very same name and called to ask if he was a family member of the one killed. The answer was no.

I think it was in 1978 that The Anzio Beach Head Society first reunion was held in Tampa for all veterans who had served on the

Anzio Beach Head in Italy, 1944. It didn't matter if you were Army, Navy, Air Corp, or Coast Guard, if you were on Anzio you could join the society. There were about 200-300 and each member was asked to stand up and tell what outfit they had belonged to. When it was my turn, I stood up and told my name, address and what outfit I had been with. Later, while sitting in the bar I noticed three men looking at me. They asked me if I was sure I was at the Anzio Beach Head. I said yes, and the men wanted to know if was it possible it had been my father and not me. I asked why they thought that and was told I did not look old enough to have been there! "In fact," I said, "I was the first GI to march into Rome because I spoke Italian". I was placed 150-200 yards in front of the two scouts in order for my company to spend the night at the Tiber River. I don't know whether they believed me. It was funny that they looked much older than I.

A lot of things were said about Gen. Patton. I believe his idea that being on the offensive was always better than being on the defensive was on target. History has shown that more casualties occur on the defensive. He believed in, push, push, push, and in not giving the enemy any opportunity to dig in and develop a defensive position where you have to fight to capture it. The incident where he slapped the GI was embarrassing to him and to others, but you would have to be in his shoes to understand. He was temperamental. He was our only general who was paid $1 per year. He was wealthy. I understand at one time his family owned Catalina Island. I truly believe he was the best general we had. I think he liked his men, believed in them, and they believed in him. Of course a lot of his men called him "Old Blood and Guts." But the situation is this: do you sit and wait for them to chop you up, or do you go after them and chop them up?

Montgomery was a pain and both he and Patton hated each other. Bradley was Eisenhower's friend, a good officer. I don't think Bradley and Patton got along too well. Eisenhower was our Supreme Commander of the Military during WWII. If he had been a division commander, I don't know if he would have been good at it. He was good in his position, but to be like Patton, I think not. The Germans hated to face Patton. They said they thought they knew what he was going to do, but that he rarely did what was expected.

It's a tradition, when a new President is elected, the outgoing President and wife always had tea with the incoming President and his wife. When Eisenhower became President, they refused to meet the Trumans. Why? Remember, Truman was once Eisenhower's boss.

I'm happy the Boeing Company acknowledged me by making me "Man of the Month" and later "Man of the Year 1967." NASA gave each of us a book of names of those who were instrumental in helping NASA in their "Manned Flight Awareness" project. These names were placed at the Library of Congress and the National Archives in 1968. A plaque with our names also was placed on the moon.

Before the very first Apollo/Saturn space vehicle launch on November 9, 1967, it was found that blue vinyl tape was needed before the flight. No one had this tape. A supervisor named Jim Long was told that if anyone had this tape it would be DeAngelo. Long approached me and asked if I had any of it. I gave him a carton of 24 rolls. He said if none could be found the launch would be called off. On November 9, 1967 Apollo 4 was launched after having been taped. I was told it was needed on the vehicle to be seen and photographed by cameras through its first flight from Pad "A".

Figure 90. This photo was taken for the "Manned Flight Awareness" in 1968 at Cocoa Beach, Florida. The author with wife Hazel, two first Astronauts Wally Schirra and D. A. Slayton with Admiral Middleton, January 23, 1968.

I knew I had talent but my lack of a college degree kept me from using a lot of it in the workplace. One day I got an idea to invent an electronic magnetic compass. Later, I founded a company and our very first product was the world's very first magnetic digital compass. It was known by its trade name, "Worldguide." It is still in service today on airplanes, armored vehicles, and on high-speed patrol

GREETINGS FROM THE PRESIDENT

Figure 90. This photo was taken for the "Manned Flight Awareness" in January 23, 1968 at the Kennedy Space Center. The author and wife Hazel with two of the first astronauts Wally Schirra and D.A. Slayton and Admiral Middleton.

boats in the Far East. Worldguide compass was the first of its kind to be applied to the new GPS (Global Positioning System) and was interfaced with Magnavox electronics. *Figure 91*.

In our town we have a very good engineering school. One day I was asked if I would stop by and give a speech to some students

Figure 91. The world's first "Worldguide Magnetic Digital Compass", invented by the author.

who had received their degrees and would be looking for employment. I was happy to pass on what I learned. I asked how many had written a résumé, all hands went up. I told them to omit from their résumés sports like baseball, football, hockey, and basketball. I told them to only put down golf. A few students asked me why golf and not the others. I explained that if you put golf, one day your boss will ask you to meet with an out-of-town buyer over a round of golf and that golf is a great way to climb up the ladder. Not only do you impress your boss, you will get information that no one else will have. I told them that many deals have been completed on the golf course with a drink.

At Boeing, my general manager was Tex Johnson. He was the first pilot to test flight the new Boeing 707 jet. Without orders, on two occasions, he did a slow barrel roll over the concerned crowd of people looking up . Mr. Allen, Chairman of Boeing, was not happy and Johnson soon found himself general manager at Kennedy Space

Center. In 1973, there were a lot of cutbacks and Johnson left and purchased Clark Hardware Store in Melbourne, Florida. I went in there one day and I was surprised to see my old boss. We had a great time reminiscing.

A funny thing happened at a reunion in July 1999 at Fort Benning, Georgia. I went to the desk to register and was told that some of my former C Company guys were at the bar. I walked into the bar but didn't see anyone I recognized. I returned to the registration desk and one of the GI's told me that Col. Murray was in the bar. I went back, still wearing my sunglasses, and walked up to Murray who was talking to someone. I was close to him and said, "I'm looking for a guy in here by the name of Murray or something like that." He turned around and looked at me and I could tell he was thinking who the hell was this guy. I said, "Hi, how are you doing Chuck?" He looked blankly at me. Finally, I said, "DeAngelo!" He started to jump up and down, grabbed hold of me, and I think if I was a woman he would have kissed me. His wife, Ann, came running over and hugged me. He said he hadn't recognized me and I told him I hadn't recognized him either. We had a lot of fun and talked for a long time. I saw him again in September 1999 at the reunion in Savannah. It was kind of him to request that I go to Paris to receive a battlefield commission. *Figure 92* is his letter dated October 20, 1985.

Figure 93, showing a large solid silver punch bowl that was purchased recently by some members of the 30th Regiment. The old one was either misplaced or taken by unknown persons as it was on its way to Fort Benning from Germany to be placed in the 30th Regiment room. I have asked about this missing bowl and no one seems to know how, where or when it disappeared. I hope that one day it turns up and can be placed next to the new one. Let's hope it didn't meet the same fate as a lot of the silver pieces that came up missing from some of the great hotels and restaurants of New York in the 1930s. I read that, piece by piece, soup spoons, forks, and knives were stolen and melted down into molds to make silver dollars,

Present

CONGRESSIONAL MEDAL OF HONOR SOCIETY
UNITED STATES OF AMERICA
CHARTERED BY THE CONGRESS

NATIONAL OFFICE AND ARCHIVES

INTREPID SEA · AIR · SPACE MUSEUM
INTREPID SQUARE
WEST 46TH STREET AND 12TH AVENUE
NEW YORK, NEW YORK 10036
(212) 582-5355
October 20, 1985

Mr. Frank T. DeAngelo
1090 N. Ramona Avenue
Indialantic, Florida 32903

Dear Frank:

Exactly forty-one years ago today, you and I met for the first time, at an observation post overlooking the town of Le Tholy, France. By this time, you were an old combat veteran; I was fresh from the States. Our unit was 3d Platoon, Company C, 30th Infantry Regiment, 3d Infantry Division. There was never a better platoon or a better company.

Except for brief stays in hospitals and rest centers, the two of us were almost constantly together from that time until you were evacuated almost five months later, as I progressed from platoon leader to company executive officer and then company commander. We fought through the Voges Mountains and reached the Rhine River at Strasburg before the end of November. We then moved south toward Colmar, living and fighting in freezing weather and snow, capturing Neuf Brisach - the old fortress we called the Waffle City - and again reaching the Rhine in February. It was for action during this period, on December 16 near Kaysersberg, France, that I was awarded the Medal of Honor. It was also during this period that we met with serious problems near the bridge at Maison Rouge on the Ill River, when we thought everything was lost. But we survived.

Next, after a period of rest and retraining near Nancy, France, it was time to think about breaking out of France and into Germany itself. During the early morning hours of March 15, we broke through the main German defenses forward of the Siegfried Line, near Epping-Urbach. As I know you will recall, the going was tough and we suffered a number of casualties, more than I want to remember. We did the job, however, as always. It was the next night, in the process of trying to cross a minefield which could not be avoided, with six men from the 1st Platoon ahead of us, that I stepped over an unseen mine or trip wire and you hit it. As always, we were together. When you were evacuated, part of me went with you.

Afterwards, we busted through the Siegfried Line, crossed the Rhine River and fought across Germany until we reached Austria as the war ended. You might have been with me until then if I had ordered you to accept a commission rather than to permit you to turn it down. I know that you would not have refused an order.

In friendship and with warmest personal regards.

Chuck
Charles P. Murray
Colonel, US Army (Ret.)

Figure 92. Murray letter to the author dated October 20, 1985.

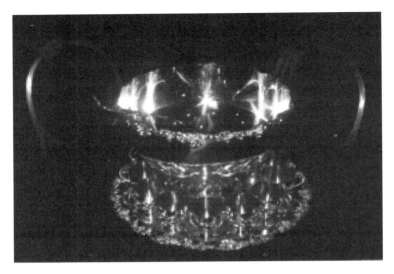

Figure 93. The new 30th Regiment punch bowl, replacing the lost one at Fort Benning, GA., July 16, 1999.

Figure 94. The author at Fort Benning, GA at the museum at the 3rd Division monument. July 16, 1999

Present

Figure 95. The author at Fort Benning, Georgia museum on July 16, 1999; found his 66th Division in the background which he had trained at Camp Blanding, Florida, May-August 1943.

GREETINGS FROM THE PRESIDENT

Figure 96. Members of C Company with their wives at Fort Stewart, Georgia on September 17, 1999 3rd Division reunion. Kane, Knouse, McDonough, Oglesby alone, and the author.

Figure 97. McDonough, Murray, DeAngelo, and the leg of Kane.

half dollars, quarters and dimes.

Figure 94. At the 3rd Division Reunion at Fort Benning, GA. I am standing by the 3rd Infantry Division monument at Fort Benning, GA, on July 16, 1999. *Figure 95* is also at the museum with the 66th Division Panther in the background.

At this reunion Hayden Kane told me the name of one of the men who came into the minefield for me. I need to ask him again who he was so his name can be placed in the book. No such luck. *Figure 96* shows Kane, Knouse, McDonough, Oglesby, DeAngelo.

Figure 97 shows McDonough, Murray, DeAngelo and the leg of Kane.

```
RE Remarks. Company Morning Reports, Company C, 30th Infantry,
De Angelo, Frank T., Serial Number 32881054.

21 October 1944.  Near Le Tholy, France.
Sergeant.  (transferred to Detachment of Patients Seventh Army)
Hospital Line of Duty to AWOL, 13th; AWOL to reassigned and
joined, 17th.  Primary Duty 653.

23 October 1944.  Near Bruyeres, France.
Sergeant.  Reduced to grade of private, 20th.

8 December 1944.  Achenheim, France.
Included in roster of 26 enlisted men, Company C, 30th Regiment,
appointed Privates first class, 8 December 1944.

17 December 1944.  Near Kaysersberg, France.
Private first class.  Duty to hospital Line of Duty, 16th, and
transferred to Detachment of Patients 7th Army per paragraph 2
Circular 69 ETOUSA.

19 January 1945.  Ribeauville, France.
Private first class.  Reassigned and joined from Detachment of
Patients 23rd Station Hospital, 17th, Verbal Order of Commanding
General, (Line of Duty, Non Battle Casualty).  MOS 653

16 March 1945.  Volmunster, France.
Private first class.  Duty to Severely Wounded in Action, evacuated
to hospital, 15th, and transferred to Detachment of Patients, 7th
Army per paragraph 2 Circular 69 ETOUSA.
```

Figure 98. The authors list of duties.

Figure 98 shows a list of my duties.

Figure 99 is the 3rd Infantry Division Travel Guide showing where our tour began and ended.

I have four grandchildren. We have Garrett, Ashley, Carter and Dawson. Carter always looks at my stump. When I remove my

Figure 99. The 3rd Division Travel Guide.

artificial leg to rest my stump, he always comes up and puts his arms around me as if he wants me to know he loves me in spite of my being wounded. One day he said to me, "Pop Pop Frank, tell me what happened." I told him what happened and he asked, "Where is it?" I said, "It's far away, Carter." He replied, "Well, can you and I go look for it?" I said, "Yes, we can, when you grow up. You and I will go there and look for my leg." He walked away happy. I lost half of my foot in the minefield; the other half was removed in a field hospital. Later another section was removed to fit an artificial leg at Atlantic City. There were three places I had left parts of my body; it

ies Sept. 15, 1992

Kurt Jeck, retired electrician

Visitation for Kurt Fred Jeck, 72, of Bradley, will be from 6 to 8 p.m. today at the Bradley chapel of the Schreffler Funeral Homes.

Committal services will be at 10 a.m. Wednesday at the chapel at Mound Grove Gardens in Kankakee. The Rev. Guy Warke will officiate.

Mr. Jeck died Sunday (Sept. 13, 1992) at the Riverside Medical Center emergency room after a sudden illness.

Mr. Jeck

He was born Jan. 30, 1919 in Berlin, Germany, the son of Fred and Louise Jeck.

Survivors include his wife, the former Catherine Miller, whom he married Jan. 20, 1950 in Kankakee; one stepson and stepdaughter-in-law, Leland and Janet Metz of Kankakee; one stepdaughter, Pamela Metz of Denver, Colo.; three grandchildren; two brothers, Harry of Tucson, Ariz., and Fritz of Bradley; and two sisters, Ursula Hill and Marie Boudreau, both of Florida.

A daughter, Cheryl, is deceased.

Mr. Jeck was a member of Our Savior Lutheran Church.

He was a veteran of United States Army service during World War II.

An electrician, Mr. Jeck was employed for 19 years at Armour Pharmaceutical Co. and retired in 1981. Previously he was employed for 25 years at Kroehler Mfg. Co. until plant 3 closed.

Figure 100. First Sgt. Kurt Jeck.

was kind of sweet for the little guy to ask to help me look for it.

The 3rd Infantry Division suffered the most casualties: 24,334, the 45th: 18,521, the 36th: 16,828, and the 34th: 14,815.

Recently, I had a friend's wife check her files to see if she could help me find First Sgt. Kurt Jeck (*Figure 100*) who was very kind to me in basic training at Camp Blanding with the 66th Division in May-August of 1943. She called to tell me that she did find him and gave me all the information she was able to find on her computer. He died on September 13, 1991, after a sudden illness. I called his hometown newspaper in Kankakee, Illinois, and requested his obituary be mailed to me. I called the only Jeck listed in the phone directory and left my message to please call me. After 10 calls, there was nothing. Sgt. Jeck was so kind to me that I must tell what a great person he was . I shall never forget him. Years later I tried to contact Calvin in his hometown of Rosalie, West Virginia. But I was unable to find either him or the town.

I also tried to contact Robert Hall. Sadly, he passed away in 1991. His wife told me that he spoke of the GI's in room 224 many times and had always wished he knew how to contact us. I am also sorry I did not contact him as well.

I guess that's about it. I hope it's not boring to read, but for a street kid, it was kind of exciting. It was something that had to be done, there were times when it was very hard for us not to break down, especially when we lost friends. Yes, we were always afraid. We didn't know what was going to happen, it just panned out that I was very fortunate to come home. Many others did not. I think about it, not everyday, but I do think about it. I'm happy to say I met great friends in the Army and the hospitals were great. I don't remember seeing or hearing of anyone mistreating a GI with wounds. Then it was all forgotten. Eighteen, nineteen and twenty-year-olds going through hell. We became old men in a very short time. I am proud of my part during WWII, like many others.

>Thank you very much,
>*Frank T. DeAngelo*

AUTHORS COMMENTS

For some time I have tried to find a publisher to help me with my memoirs. I turned down offers from at least 5 and also turned down and had to fire three editors. Why? Because they were rewriting their memoirs, not mine. Some publishers wanted me to add more to my combat actions, to remove the drinking and the friendship of women, in which I have not included words in detail of what took place. I know that most military people, when on a weekend pass, seek the company of women. These men are away from home and family and yes, they are lonely.

I have written as it happened, adding nothing that was untrue. What took place did, in fact, take place from page one to page 302.

To purchase *Greetings From The President*, contact :
Frank T. DeAngelo
P.O. Box 867
Destin, FL 32540
Toll free, 1-888-533-9295
By check or money order, plus postage.

For credit card orders, contact:
Blue Note Books
400 W. Cocoa Beach Cswy., Suite 3
Cocoa Beach, FL 32931
Phone: 321-799-2583
Fax: 321-799-1942
website: bluenotebooks.com